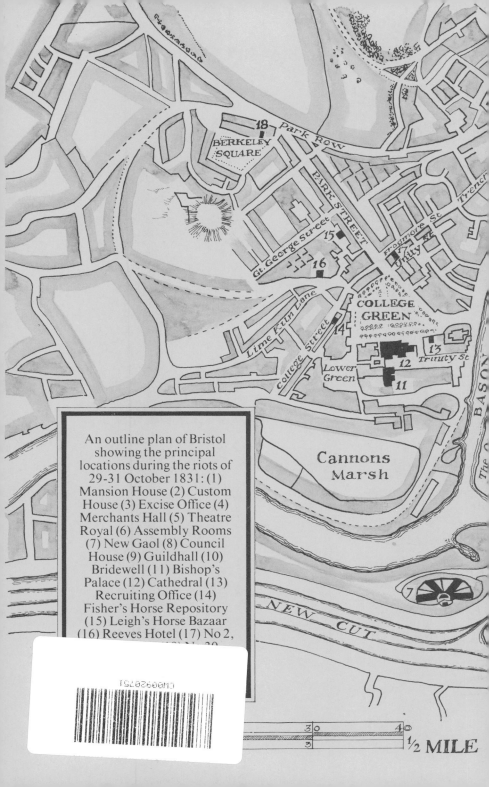

An outline plan of Bristol showing the principal locations during the riots of 29-31 October 1831: (1) Mansion House (2) Custom House (3) Excise Office (4) Merchants Hall (5) Theatre Royal (6) Assembly Rooms (7) New Gaol (8) Council House (9) Guildhall (10) Bridewell (11) Bishop's Palace (12) Cathedral (13) Recruiting Office (14) Fisher's Horse Repository (15) Leigh's Horse Bazaar (16) Reeves Hotel (17) No 2,

CITY UNDER FIRE

CITY UNDER FIRE

The Bristol Riots and Aftermath

by

GEOFFREY AMEY

LUTTERWORTH PRESS
GUILDFORD AND LONDON

First published 1979

For Jean

ISBN 0 7188 2445 8

*Printed in Great Britain by
Butler & Tanner Ltd, Frome and London*

Contents

AUTHOR'S NOTE AND ACKNOWLEDGEMENTS 9

INTRODUCTION 11

1. THE LAW MAN COMETH 17
2. STICKS AND STONES 36
3. FAREWELL TO ARMS 49
4. SPREAD OF FLAME 58
5. BLAZING FALLS THE NIGHT 67
6. COMINGS AND GOINGS 76
7. THE HORROR OF QUEEN SQUARE 86
8. ROUTING THE RIOTERS 96
9. THE GREAT ROUND-UP 104
10. COLONEL ON THE CARPET 114
11. 'YOU WILL BE TAKEN HENCE . . .' 121
12. LAUNCHED INTO ETERNITY 132
13. TO BE OR NOT TO BE? 139
14. 'THE INJUSTICE I HAVE BEEN DONE' 149
15. THE CASE OF THE CAUTIOUS CAPTAIN 157
16. FINAL VERDICT 168
17. THE AFTER YEARS 178

Appendix. THE TRANSPORTED CONVICTS 182

PRINCIPAL SOURCES OF INFORMATION 213

INDEX 217

List of Illustrations

(between pages 64 and 65)

1. Sir Charles Wetherell, Recorder of Bristol.
2. Poster reporting the sailors' meeting.
3. A call to the citizenry.
4. Two posters issued after the riots.
5. Conflagration at Gloucestershire County Prison, Lawford's Gate.
6. View of the widespread fires.
7. A similar dramatic impression from Pile Hill.
8. The fires at their height.

(between pages 128 and 129)

9. Queen Square became the main centre of revelry and destruction.
10. *Above:* Ruins of the Excise Office.
    Below: Ruins opposite the Assembly Rooms.
11. *Above:* Ruins of the Mansion House, Custom House and other buildings.
    Below: Ruins of the Bishop's Palace.
12. *Above:* The west side of Queen Square.
    Below: The north side of the Square similarly destroyed.
13. Poster calling upon inhabitants to identify prisoners.
14. Sir Nicolas Conyngham Tindal.
15. A petition to the King.
16 A caricature of Lt-Col Thomas Brereton.

7

Line Drawings: *page*

Condemned to hang: Christopher Davis   135

Condemned to hang: William Clarke, Thomas Gregory,
Richard Vines and Joseph Kayes   137

Acknowledgement for Illustrations

All illustrations are reproduced by kind permission of the Avon County Library (Bristol Reference Library) with the exception of that of Sir Charles Wetherell (courtesy, National Portrait Gallery) and those of the five rioters condemned to be hanged (*The Bristol Mercury*).

Author's Note and Acknowledgements

THE ISSUES, actions and reactions concerned with the Bristol Riots are surely open to various interpretations and, after nearly 150 years, the picture has inevitably become blurred. One is confronted by a many-sided mirror of bias, contradiction and discrepancy and in a few instances, where the reflected evidence is particularly conflicting, I have considered it reasonable and fairer to compromise with an amalgam. Even so, nothing in this book has been knowingly 'manufactured' by me.

It has not been my aim to draw categoric conclusions nor, moreover, to attempt any profound political or sociological analysis. Rather have I endeavoured to present a descriptive and balanced reconstruction of an astonishing episode in Bristol's long and glorious history—a happening without parallel in this country—and in doing so, despite certain personal preferences, to remain impartial. The dramatic event rated countless columns in newspapers throughout Britain and overseas, as well as begetting a host of broadsheets, booklets and pamphlets. Resultant civil and military trials also received widespread press coverage, but it has been possible for me to include only very brief versions of those proceedings.

In addition to distilling from the mass of published information, I have tapped lesser-known sources and managed to locate some hitherto unpublished material. Surprisingly this is, I believe, the first full-length factual book devoted exclusively to the subject since immediately after the riots. The account could not have been completed without generous help, although I claim sole credit for its shortcomings.

I am sincerely indebted to Mrs Hester Marsden-Smedley, Mr Anthony Pretor-Pinney and Mr Michael Pinney—direct descendants of Charles Pinney, the Mayor of Bristol during the riots—for their encouragement and for allowing me to quote from correspondence contained in the Pinney Papers at the University of Bristol Library, where Mr Norman Higham (Librarian) and Mr George Maby (Archives Department) facilitated my researches. For some of the details regarding Lt-Col Thomas Brereton, military commander during the disturbances, I am similarly indebted to Mr John M. Brereton and Mr Patrick Montague-Smith—both distant relatives of his.

My warm thanks also to Mr Geoffrey Langley (Avon County Reference Librarian) and his staff at the Central Library, Bristol; to Mr Andrew Hart, who has himself delved into the economic, political and social aspects of the riots; to Mr Herbert Payne, of Clifton; to Mrs Mary McRae (Principal Archivist, Archives Office of Tasmania, Hobart) and Mr D. J. Cross (Senior Archivist, Archives Authority of New South Wales, Sydney) for their willing co-operation in supplying records of the riot-convicts transported 'Down Under'; to the Controller, Her Majesty's Stationery Office, for permission to quote from Crown copyright documents at the Public Record Office, London; to the respective staffs at the PRO and at the British Library Newspaper Library, Colindale; and to Longman Group Ltd for permission to use extracts from *A West-India Fortune* by Richard Pares.

Indeed, I am most grateful to everyone who has assisted me in the course of preparing this book—not least to two staunch friends of mine, Roy Boswell and Peter Branch, for their support when it most mattered. The gold award goes to my wife, Jean, who has suffered my variable disposition and irregular working hours with her most enviable brand of serenity. I am quite convinced that even the Bristol Riots would have failed utterly to disturb such equanimity. To her, then, my loving admiration.

GEOFFREY AMEY

February 1979

Introduction

THE REJECTION of the Reform Bill by the House of Lords in the early morning of Saturday, 8 October 1831, precipitated an overflow of popular protest. Demonstrations and riots occurred in various parts of the country and prominent anti-reformers were attacked and abused.

The cauldron of political and social unrest had been simmering for years, bubbling over periodically into violent industrial clashes, and was frequently the passionate subject of large-scale meetings and petitions as well as the cause of considerable horse dealing. In Britain, as was happening elsewhere in Europe, age-old systems showed signs of crumbling.

In the immediate wake of Waterloo had come a depression in trade with its inevitable unemployment, a massive national debt, falling revenue and poor harvests. Social discontent and economic distress reached a peak and soon, alongside calls for more jobs and cheaper food, could be heard demands for universal suffrage and legislative changes as antidotes to the nation's ailments. Working-class opinion found expression in public orators like Henry Hunt and encouragement through radical journals, of which William Cobbett's *Political Register* was probably the most influential.

Nothing generated more bitterness than the 'Peterloo Massacre' at Manchester on 16 August 1819, when cavalry with sabres drawn were ordered by panicky magistrates to charge into the midst of 60,000 people attending a comparatively peaceful and, moreover, lawful rally for parliamentary reform; in the resultant dispersal and slaughter, about a dozen died and some 400 were injured. All classes of society were outraged but, despite much opposition, the Government succeeded in passing the 'Six Acts' which, in effect, sought to shackle the movement for radical reform by banning big public meetings and restricting the pro-radical press.

Such repressive measures, but more likely a noticeable improvement in material prosperity, tended to soften the spearhead of radicalism during the 1820s, although it was never more than marginally below the surface. A number of important reforms was effected including the repeal in 1824 of a twenty-five-year-old Act outlawing trade unions (because of strikes, however, another modified Act came into being the following year), a substantial revision of the criminal laws, the Catholic Emancipation Act in 1829 and, in the same year, the establishment of a properly-organized police force in London.

Towards the end of the decade when prosperity appeared again to be waning, there was a marked resurgence of interest in democratic advancement and the steady emergence of political unions—modelled on the powerful Birmingham Political Union with its middle-class leadership—subsequently began to add weight to the renewed calls for parliamentary reform.

If an aroma of revolution could be sniffed in the English air, then national nostrils were further activated by news filtering through from Paris in July 1830 that an almost bloodless insurrection had overthrown the reactionary government and brought about the fall of the Bourbon monarchy. The event apparently sparked-off disturbances in other European centres, notably in Brussels, and was said to have heartened those Liberals in Britain who desired change without extremism.

The uprising in Paris took place just before a General Election in England where the Whigs, firmly pledged to a reform bill, defeated the Tories who had held office almost continuously for sixty years. The new government proved no less severe than their predecessors had been in crushing popular protest movements, however. In agricultural riots, which spread across mainly southern and eastern counties during the winter of 1830–31, ricks were fired and threshing-machines smashed by farm labourers demonstrating for higher wages and against mechanization; of more than 1,900 duly brought to trial, 19 were hanged, 481 transported and nearly 650 gaoled.

In addition to burning ricks, there was by this time a widening and fiercely-burning insistence upon major changes in the political, social and economic structures of the country. As

G. M. Trevelyan put it: 'From squire to postilion, from cotton-lord to mill-hand, everyone was talking of the need for Reform, though with great varieties of meaning and emphasis.'

In 1831, the overwhelming majority of the adult male population in Britain had no vote in a palpably inequitable electoral system virtually controlled by the powerful landowning aristocracy. A number of sparsely-populated county constituencies returned many more MPs than did teeming industrial areas; some tiny towns and villages boasted one or two Members apiece, whereas important centres like Birmingham, Manchester and Sheffield had no direct parliamentary representation whatever.

The wide-ranging Reform Bill sought to establish a much fairer distribution of seats, to abolish 'rotten boroughs', to cut out corrupt election practices and to extend the franchise. There was strong organized support from the middle classes (especially among wealthy manufacturers), who, in the event, were to gain the most from such legislation. Lower orders in the social spectrum also anticipated the reforms would bring immediate benefits to their own living standards and working conditions. As it turned out, they were mostly to be sadly disillusioned.

The build-up and far-reaching effects of the Bill (it was finally given the Royal Assent in June 1832) are of paramount significance in the political history of this country, but the purpose here is briefly to set the scene for the riots which flared at Bristol and continued unchecked for almost three days. Although unquestionably the worst, they were by no means the only serious disturbances to follow the Bill's defeat in the Lords.

On that very day, for instance, demonstrators at Derby stormed the city gaol to release prisoners and subsequently committed other outrages during which 'several lives' were lost. At Nottingham on 10 October, a mob marched upon Colwick Hall—home of John Musters, a well-known opponent of Reform—vandalized furniture and valuable paintings, but failed in an attempt to burn the place down.

That evening, Nottingham Castle (a mansion, then deserted and almost unfurnished, belonging to the Duke of Newcastle) was set ablaze and reduced to a smouldering hulk. The duke, a hated symbol of anti-reform, allowed the gutted building to remain as a 'standing disgrace to the inhabitants of Nottingham' and it stayed roofless for forty years. At nearby Beeston, a silk mill was attacked by a large mob and burned to the ground (three men were hanged for the crime, despite a strong petition for clemency).

Clamorous meetings and affrays occurred elsewhere. In London, the newly-formed police were hard-pressed to disperse crowds and often engaged in running battles with determined groups of agitators; Apsley House, home of the Duke of Wellington, became a target and many windows shattered; the Marquis of Londonderry, while riding on horseback to the House of Lords, sustained a severe head wound when assailed by stones and had to be rescued by a unit of cavalry. A carriage, in which Lord Tankerville was travelling with his daughter and son-in-law, was bombarded with missiles at Darlington and the party fortunate to escape. Anti-reforming bishops, whose 'block' vote had helped to throw out the Bill, were subjected to unsavoury oaths and threats. Numerous other incidents were reported during this alarming period of spreading disquiet and disorder, but none was remotely to approach the magnitude of events at Bristol which, it is interesting to ponder, did not erupt until three weeks after the rejection of the Bill and, moreover, may well have 'kindled' disturbances, albeit very much smaller, which broke out at Worcester and Coventry a few days later.

Bristol was then suffering from a decline in trade and has been described by Michael Brock in *The Great Reform Act* as a 'turbulent port containing all the ingredients for a riot'. The self-elected corporation, regarded as weak and certainly unpopular, was Tory-dominated although the Mayor, who had 'chaired' a public meeting the previous year approving the July revolution in Paris, was currently a Whig and a moderate reformer.

Although the Bristol Riots cannot be viewed entirely in isolation inasmuch as they formed part of the political agitation and turmoil then sweeping the country, there is little doubt that they were also exacerbated by local grievances and a dissatisfaction harboured over many years at the manner in which affairs were being handled by the city's governing body.

Assertions at the time that the rioters were properly

organized and the disturbances fermented by infiltrating insurgents from outside the city would appear to have no basis whatever, while stories that the rioting was intentionally allowed to escalate because of political machinations might be safely ascribed to party propagandists. It seems clear the rioting was perpetrated by a largely uncontrolled mob (with the acquiescence of countless onlookers), progressively strengthened and tempted to further outrages by the virtual absence of lawful counter-measures.

What happened at Bristol highlighted shortcomings in the municipal administration, emphasized the urgent need of an effective constabulary of police and, furthermore, tragically underlined the serious hazards that can arise when the military is called upon to support a civil authority.

The dramatic episode also illustrated, perhaps, just how precarious could be the balance between the preservation and the breakdown of law and order in a vulnerable urban area in early nineteenth-century England—before the general introduction of a professional police force and, of course, without the sophisticated means of communication we take for granted today. The possibility of such a breakdown must surely have been a genuine fear in a city which could become 'marooned' in an age when its fastest links with the outside world were dictated by the speed of a horse.

That fear became reality at Bristol where an unrestrained mob went on the rampage. . . .

Chapter One

THE LAW MAN COMETH

A SQUADRON OF 14th Light Dragoons, in jackets of blue with orange facings and silver lace, descended from Clifton into Bristol and, following a semi-circular route which avoided central streets, took up position inside the cattle market. Almost simultaneously on that overcast Saturday morning of 29 October 1831 a troop of 3rd Dragoon Guards, their coats of scarlet with yellow velvet facings and gold braid, trotted in from the opposite direction to halt at the New Gaol about three-quarters of a mile away.

Those regular cavalry detachments, drafted in to support a jittery magistracy, had been camped outside the city for three days. Responsibility for their disposition, as accordingly required by the civil authorities, now devolved on Lieutenant-Colonel Thomas Brereton (Inspecting Field Officer, Bristol Recruiting District). He viewed this unexpected temporary command from the hierarchy at the Horse Guards in London not only as ill-defined, but also one he would have happily foregone.

The colonel, a tallish man of forty-nine with sad eyes and normally of gentle demeanour, had known brighter days. As an enthusiastic young officer in his mid-twenties, he participated in the capture of the French possessions of Martinique and Guadeloupe in the Caribbean and subsequently—in 1815 when only thirty-three and a lieutenant-colonel in the Royal African Corps—was appointed Lieutenant-Governor of Senegal and Goree (West Africa), colonies also gained by the British during the Napoleonic Wars. Afterwards, from 1818 until 1823 (latterly with the 49th Regiment of Foot), he served in the Cape of Good Hope, experiencing a taste of frontier action in the Kaffir Wars and, for a while, being in command of the Cape Town garrison.

Such moments of glory and status had faded with the years, however, and from July 1823, when he succeeded Lt-Col John Daniell (by exchange), Brereton merged increasingly into the colourless routine of the relatively undemanding post at Bristol and might even have been regarded as something of a military back-number. Since he first left home in King's County [now Offaly], Ireland, at the age of sixteen to enlist as an ensign in the 8th West India Regiment in 1798, Brereton's army career (predominantly overseas) had been periodically dogged to some extent by indifferent health and he now suffered from hepatitis. Neither had he recovered from the shock of his second wife's death[1] in January 1829, after less than six years of marriage, but he derived considerable consoling joy from their two little daughters.

The amiable mild-mannered colonel, albeit sometimes liverish and now perhaps further disturbed by misgivings about his new role, probably wished for nothing more than a continuing quiet life before retirement. Indeed, prior to this, he was reportedly 'in treaty for the sale of his commission'.

Equally anxious to avert trouble was Charles Pinney, a prosperous thirty-eight-year-old West India merchant, who arose early that dismal morning to only his forty-third day as Mayor of Bristol. Without then entirely realizing it, he had inherited a civic time-bomb. The fuse was rapidly getting shorter.

Pinney, whose well-known reformist views had hitherto appealed to the citizenry, now resided in official comfort at the Mansion House, situated at the north-eastern corner of Queen Square bounded by stylish homes and private businesses as well as public places like the Custom House and the Excise Office.

---

[1] On 1 January 1818, while in England and after a spell on half-pay, Brereton had married Mrs Margaret Anne Whitmore—the widow of Major W. Whitmore and daughter of the late John A. Olton, a West Indies planter of Barbados. She went with him to the Cape, but died suddenly of a fever on 8 September the same year, aged twenty-nine. Brereton's second wife (they were wed at Marylebone, London, in 1823) was Olivia Elizabeth Ross, the nineteen-year-old elder daughter of a prominent Cape merchant, Captain Hamilton Ross, formerly of the 81st Regiment. This marriage was also to end tragically, the young Mrs Brereton succumbing to an attack of influenza on 14 January 1829.

A tree-lined perimeter road separated the buildings from an inner expanse of grass which, surrounded by post-and-rail timber fencing, was intersected by pathways radiating from a central point dominated by a bronze equestrian statue of William of Orange. An occasional warehouse obtruded above the roof-lines, while not far away ran stretches of an inland dock system and its attendant bustle. The heights of elegance and fashion may have been attracted progressively to the heights of Clifton but Queen Square, then still a reputable middle-class precinct, remained steady and respectable. Before that day had departed, however, the comparative peace would be wildly shattered.

Mayor Pinney, doubtless apprehensive about what the immediate future held in store, left home before half-past seven. He was conveyed by carriage, which rattled along echoing narrow thoroughfares in unwelcoming fuzzy light, to the Council House—situated at the junction of Corn Street and Broad Street—and there spent a few minutes in earnest conversation with Daniel Burges, a person in his mid-fifties who, besides being the Mayor's clerk, was City Solicitor.

The two men emerged and crossed to the adjacent Exchange, embedded in front of which were (and are) several capstan-shaped metal tables with flat circular tops—the 'Nails'—where merchants used to conclude cash transactions by paying literally on the nail! Entering the eighteenth-century building (designed by John Wood, of Bath fame), Pinney noted with mixed feelings that each of about 300 men, drawn up in divisions between the stone columns, was carrying a heavy stave.

The Mayor was promptly greeted by Under-Sheriff William Ody Hare, a forty-six-year-old lawyer, whose unenviable task it had been to recruit that multifarious band of constables. No paid effective full-time police force then existed in the city, which had an unreliable top muster of just over a hundred parish constables and about the same number of night-watchmen, and it became customary when the occasion demanded (for Bristol was no stranger to civil disturbances) to rely on public-spirited citizens, preferably from the 'respectable' classes, to complement the strength by acting as 'specials'.

19

Because of a positive disinclination by inhabitants to co-operate this time, however, the magistrates had authorized Hare to 'buy' the deficit. So the force included 119 'hired' men among whom, almost certainly, were some pretty unlikely characters. Moreover, too small a percentage of the whole had sufficient knowledge—let alone any practical experience—of just what peacekeeping duties entailed, nor the necessary self-discipline to see them through. By now, of course, it was much too late to rectify that.

After being addressed somewhat equivocally by the Mayor, who urged them to act with moderation and firmness, the posse dispersed along a route leading to beyond the southern extremity of the city boundary. His Worship returned to the Mansion House to change into ceremonial attire for the formal opening later that morning of the autumn assizes. Pinney was of small stature, his light frame being unhelped by a stoop.

Civilian and military contingents waited at the alert; a massive crowd gathered; anticipation mounted. Events quite unparalleled in the city's long and glorious history were about to erupt. Already on his way was the provocative link, the widely-adjudged villain of the impending drama—Sir Charles Wetherell, the sixty-one-year-old Recorder of Bristol.

The people had also filled the streets some three months earlier, but then in a mood of jubilation, not condemnation. In common with every town and village in the realm, they celebrated the coronation of William IV who, at sixty-four, brought to the throne a degree of frugality which contrasted sharply with the gaudy opulence favoured by his self-indulgent predecessor and elder brother, George IV. The crowning of the affable 'Sailor King' temporarily diverted the spotlight from the deep-rooted issue engrossing and dividing the country—Reform.

No place appears to have been more alive to the burning question than Bristol, from where several petitions supporting the Bill went to Parliament, the most recent bearing no fewer than 17,000 signatures. So when Sir Charles Wetherell told the House of Commons that 'Reform fever has a good deal abated in Bristol' and then repeatedly expressed his view of the city's 'indifference', the local people reacted angrily.

By virtue of his judicial office, Wetherell was (by charter) also the city's senior alderman and it seems likely his political diagnosis stemmed from shaky information relayed by his brother aldermen, most of whom not only lived outside Bristol but were also said rarely to visit the wards they represented and, therefore, to be out of touch with the pulse of public opinion.

Sir Charles, a brilliant lawyer and debater who had twice been Attorney-General, was an ultra-Tory and currently one of two MPs returned by Boroughbridge, Yorkshire, which had a tiny electorate of forty-eight (nearly all 'influenced' in voting by their landlord, the Duke of Newcastle) and due to be abolished when the Reform Bill became law. Despite warnings of the probable consequences because of his unpopularity, Wetherell declared that he would hold the Bristol assizes as scheduled and, furthermore, intended to make the traditional public entry into the city.

Apart from the controversial utterances of 'the very learned and eccentric knight' (as *The Times* once described him) another factor, perhaps even more significant, undoubtedly inflamed subsequent developments. Such an inward-looking organization as Bristol Corporation, immersed in self-interest and having too little regard for municipal improvement or the well-being of the vast majority, inevitably aroused considerable mistrust and aversion. Such local governments were common in England but, as one critic commented, 'in no part of this country has the exclusive system more strongly developed itself than in the city of Bristol'.

As Mayor and Chief Magistrate, Charles Pinney occupied a place of substantial authority but, in practice, the senior aldermen surely wielded the most power. Although the pious Mr Pinney may have had reservations about becoming Mayor (one suspects even some reluctance), such status was good for business and, above all else, he was a successful merchant. Indeed, as time would soon graphically demonstrate, he looked far better suited to his counting house than to the Council House. He was now in partnership with his former clerk, Robert Edward Case, the firm operating healthily as sugar-factors and shippers.

The Pinney enterprises, detailed by Richard Pares in *A West-*

21

India Fortune, were founded by Azariah Pinney (1661–1720) – exiled in 1685 for ten years to the diminutive Caribbean island of Nevis for his part in the Monmouth Rebellion. He stayed in that remote spot much longer than the imposed decade—in fact, for most of his remaining thirty-five years—establishing sugar plantations and laying the basis for accumulative riches. The estate was handed down through the family and in 1763 inherited by John Pretor, a great-great-nephew of Azariah, who (complying with a condition of the bequest by his cousin, John Frederick Pinney) promptly assumed the arms and surname of Pinney by Royal licence. The newly-styled John Pinney was but twenty-four when he first arrived in Nevis at the end of 1764, spending nearly all the next nineteen years there developing the property and expanding trade.

John Pinney returned to England in 1784 and from the moment 'he set up his merchant house in Bristol', wrote Pares, 'this was the heart of the family's life, and the foundation of a fortune at least five times as large as that which he brought home from Nevis'. He quickly flourished in the city—the importing base of his West Indian sugar interests—and, after living for some years in Park Street, moved in 1793 to Great George Street nearby and into a fine detached house [now the 'Georgian House', open to the public] carefully designed and built to his own specifications. There the family dwelt in comfort and counted among their friends Wordsworth and Coleridge, said to have first met through the Pinneys.

The youngest of John Pinney's seven children [the first five were born in Nevis] was Charles, who arrived on 23 April 1793, by which time his father was almost fifty-four, his mother (Jane) over forty and their eldest child, John Frederick, already twenty. Pares declared: 'Charles was small and weakly, but he managed to grow up and become the family's man of business. Probably he could not have made a fortune like his father, but he was cunning and alert enough to keep one already made, and even to get most of it safe out of the West Indies at a time when that was not an easy thing to do.... He was not a very attractive creature—a cold-hearted, evangelical Pecksniff. His piety seems to have been real enough, for he took some trouble to promote the education of negro children in Nevis though he consistently opposed the abolition of slavery.'

Despite setbacks during the latter 1830s, the firm went on trading with the West Indies; Charles Pinney's enthusiasm begane to wane, however, and the death of Case in 1844 finally accelerated his resolve to cut his losses, get out of the Caribbean and to live as a rentier.

In 1831, though, such thoughts were doubtless far from his mind. In addition to his commercial and civic responsibilities, Pinney had just entered into the personal commitment. On 8 March that year at Walcot Church, Bath, he married Miss Frances ('Fanny') Mary Still, youngest daughter of the late James Charles Still, of East Knoyle, Wiltshire, who was to bear him two sons.

In at least one important respect, Pinney personified an odd sock in the corporation's top drawer for, whereas nearly all the most prominent members were hidebound Tories, he was a Whig (and the only magistrate not created an alderman) and, when installed as Mayor, regarded by the populace as 'one of themselves; he was a professed Reformer'. He seems soon to have wavered politically, however, and consequently was held suspect by elements in both parties. In short, he was considered by some to be a trimmer.

Currently the city languished in an economic trough—the result of declining overseas trade which Bristol, once enjoying wealth and the highest status as a port, had found increasingly hard to swallow since the turn of the century. A proportion of that former affluence had been derived from slave trafficking but, when changing circumstances (caused not least by the American War of Independence) began to erode several aspects of Bristol's commerce, the irresponsibility of successive corporations was apparent in their failure to improve port facilities in a financially viable manner or effectively to stimulate local industries. Now the impending abolition of slavery loomed to threaten even further Bristol's plantation trade in the West Indies.

Although the famous Floating Harbour was constructed between 1804 and 1809 [a lock at Cumberland Basin impounding three miles of the River Avon, which meandered through the city, and tidal water diverted via the New Cut—an artificial channel two miles long—to rejoin the river upstream], advantages to be gained from that costly engineering project were more than offset by the imposition of exhorbitant harbour dues and levies. The dock company and the corporation thus neglected to maintain Bristol's prestige as the country's second premier port and vitally-needed trade went instead to Liverpool (where charges were half as much), to Hull and to other fast-developing seaboard centres. This protracted waning of business had gnawed away at civic pride and also into the wage packet, not least among the unskilled workers.

For the most part, the corporation acted without recourse to outside opinion; their deliberations were virtually secret and they did not even publish a balance sheet of what were, theoretically at least, public funds. They controlled the pattern of commerce, comprised the local judiciary and exacted a wide range of taxes and emoluments. Indeed, the corporation had been guilty for decades of mismanagement and selfish extravagance.

It is not hard to appreciate, therefore, why much of the community viewed with deep distrust a local administration which favoured comparatively few. The progress of the Reform Bill was closely watched by all factions (for varying reasons, of course) because the introduction of such national legislation was envisaged also as a forerunner to the early reconstitution of municipal corporations. Ironically, in the light of future events, Bristol was to benefit little (the working classes nothing) from parliamentary reform alone; the city already returned two Members—both Whigs, James Evan Baillie (Mayor Pinney's brother-in-law) and Edward Protheroe—whereas industrial expansions like Manchester, Leeds, Birmingham and Sheffield had no direct representation at all at Westminster.

Although it would be superfluous here to go into detail about the Bill's constitutional journey through Parliament, the briefest outline of the position prior to Sir Charles Wetherell's ill-fated ride into Bristol is relevant. The first reading in the Commons was a formality, but the second provoked fierce debate before the Bill was carried on 23 March 1831 by the dramatic margin of a single vote (302–301). During the subsequent committee stage, however, the Government was defeated on two points, whereupon Prime Minister Earl Grey resigned and called for a General Election. By finally consenting to dissolve Parliament, William IV thus protected the Bill—to the undisguised delight of the people. The Whigs were later returned to power on a surge of renewed support for Reform with a handsome majority of 136. A slightly revised Bill then passed through all the requisite phases in the Commons but, on 8 October, it was rejected by the House of Lords.

Animated protest meetings in Bristol roundly denounced Wetherell; neither was it overlooked that among those who helped to throw out the Bill were the Bishop of Bristol (the Rt Rev Robert Gray) and the Bishop of Bath and Wells (the Rt Rev George Henry Law). All signs pointed to a hot reception should Wetherell set foot in the city and, when it became obvious that he determined to go ahead with the assizes as usual, the magistrates pictured the prospect with growing apprehension. If the Recorder would not stay away, then he had to be protected.

Efforts to raise an adequate civil force met with a discouraging response. Various avenues explored included a clumsy attempt to recruit sailors as bodyguards. The Mayor received a requisition, signed by a number of West Indiamen skippers and local pilots, seeking permission to hold a meeting, the ostensible purpose being their wish 'in times of danger and difficulty, to express our loyalty, together with that of our fellow-seamen of this port, to our friend, our father and our fellow-sailor, King William'. His Worship not only consented, but also agreed to its taking place aboard his own ships—the 390-ton *Earl of Liverpool*, renowned for fast Atlantic crossings, and the *Charles*, a smaller vessel of 282 tons, which was berthed side-by-side.

The meeting on 18 October was presided over by Christopher Claxton, a retired Royal Navy lieutenant and formerly one of Pinney's merchantman captains. The 'loyalty' motion was carried without dissent, of course, but when Claxton introduced a resolution calling upon the sailors to 'pledge themselves to assist the magistrates in putting down rioting', there were spirited interruptions from a 'large body' of reformers who had hastened to the quayside and now swarmed around and over the ships. Claxton went on asserting that 'idle and dissolute' people in the city wanted to exploit 'the present

25

excitement in the public mind', but added that he was among those who believed that if the seamen resolved to support the magistracy it would inspire others to follow.

Vehement exchanges ensued on the main deck of the three-masted *Earl of Liverpool* between Captain Claxton, backed by some skippers, and the interlopers who claimed it was quite improper for him to put forward such a recommendation. Claxton retorted that as it was a private meeting the objectors were themselves out of order; amid clamour, he then declared the business closed and directed them to leave 'my ship'.

The dissenting citizens, accompanied by sympathetic seamen, withdrew to the dockside to continue the discussion. John Wesley Hall, a forty-year-old radical, whose forenames reminded one that a far greater orator of the eighteenth century had enjoyed close ties with Bristol, was elected to the 'chair'. He condemned the duplicity involved in trying to induce unsuspecting sailors to protect Wetherell, contended that it would be illegal if the authorities so employed them and, in any case, quite unnecessary. Other speakers also foresaw little or no danger of any serious disturbance and, furthermore, described Claxton's prediction of a riot as 'monstrous'. If there were disorders, conjectured one gentleman, they would be sown by opponents in 'an endeavour to throw odium on the reformers and their cause'. This declaration was loudly approved: 'That the Sailors of this Port, on the present occasion, earnestly express their decided and loyal attachment to His Majesty and his Government, but will not allow themselves to be made a cat's paw of by the Corporation or their paid Agents.'

It is asking too much to believe the Mayor and magistrates had no idea of the 'recruitment' reason behind the sailors' meeting, although Claxton said it was openly organized with the best intentions and the resolutions 'seen and approved by many' beforehand. That those who infiltrated the ships were not tipped-off to something strange being in the wind is equally difficult to accept; even so John Gover Powell, a well-known progressive, maintained they were not an official body but merely peaceable citizens who, having heard of the event by pure accident, 'went down to witness the proceedings'. Anyway, the 'secret' was soon common knowledge:

Second Edition
of the
MERCURY
An Account of the
MEETING
Held this Day
On Board The
Earl of Liverpool
For the alleged purpose of Engaging the Sailors of this
Port in a Pledge to support the Magistracy in preventing
Rioting; or, in other words, to put down Popular Opinion
on the Public Entrance of
SIR CHARLES
WETHERELL
Is Just Published and may be had at the Office
9, Narrow Wine-Street
Tuesday, Oct 18, 1831

Only the previous day, Claxton had written 'from a sense
of duty' to Home Secretary Lord Melbourne telling him of an
'inflammatory speech' by Powell at a recent pro-Reform Bill
rally attended by an estimated 3,000 people. In a postscript,
he warned: 'I think it right further to inform your Lordship
that there is reason to apprehend mischief on the 29th inst.,
the day our Recorder (Sir C. Wetherell) will arrive to
administer the laws.' The Honourable George Lamb, Under-
Secretary of State, replied by return post that 'Lord Melbourne
has no doubt that the Magistrates will take proper measures
for preserving tranquility [sic]'.[1]

The magistrates were trying to do just that and, on 19
October, sent a three-man deputation to urge the Recorder to
postpone his visit until passions had cooled or at least to dispense
with the customary processional entry. Under-Sheriff Hare and
City Solicitor Burges travelled together to London where they
joined William Fripp, a forty-six-year-old alderman, already
there on private business. Wetherell remained adamant that
the assizes should proceed in full accordance with the law and
precedent.

[1] Pinney Papers.

27

Writing from London on 20 October, Fripp told Mayor Pinney that Wetherell nevertheless 'thought all proper precautions should be taken to protect the sheriffs and himself—and to maintain the peace of the city and that this could not be accomplished by ordinary means; therefore, the aid of the military should be required and that he should be *escorted* by them. Upon this we differed, thinking it would be more prudent to have them within call and not to seek their interference but in case of absolute necessity; we then submitted to him the propriety of our application to the Secretary of State in which he concurred ... from what Lord Melbourne said, I am satisfied we shall have troops if we shall to-morrow still see the necessity. I need hardly add that secrecy upon this point is most essential; if it should be known we have applied for this aid, it may induce the people to organize themselves in a dangerous way....'[1]

Not only was Wetherell present at a second meeting between the deputation and Lord Melbourne, but Bristol's two MPs were also called in; James Evan Baillie, who was fifty, had represented the city only since August the previous year; although he first entered the Commons in 1813 (then as Member for Tralee); thirty-three-year-old Edward Davis Protheroe, who hailed from a prominent Bristol family, was formerly Member for Evesham and had been MP for Bristol exactly six months. The latter had close ties with the local political union.

The corporation's delegates emphasized the growing ill-feeling and, consequently, fears of disorder in the city. Melbourne, it seems, had no doubts: to adjourn or in any way restrict the assizes would be pandering to popular agitation, but he assented to the magistrates' request for military assistance provided it was used only as a last resort. He was said to have looked surprised when Hare, enquiring how many soldiers would be sent, remarked: 'The reason is that the extent of the riots to which a Bristol mob may go is, I fear, not sufficiently appreciated.' Indeed, Hare's comment was prophetic for, in the event, the force dispatched was lamentably small.

The problem of recruiting even a minimum civil peacekeeping force proved formidable. While most inhabitants had no intention whatever of impeding the lawful progress of the unloved Recorder neither were they prepared, in the role of

[1] Pinney Papers.

special constables, to jeopardize their own skins safeguarding him. One local printer suggested lightly that Sir Charles might best be protected from demonstrators by hurling him into the river! There were swingeing verbal attacks against Wetherell, of course, and some exhortations to 'true reformers' to voice their disgust when he arrived. On the other hand, appeals for responsible behaviour came even from several of the most radical sources which stressed that any violent disturbance would only injure the cause of Reform. Although they cannot possibly have expected the advent of the military to remain completely secret, the magistrates doubtless hoped to delay and limit such knowledge and must have been shaken, therefore, to learn of the distribution of handbills which stated:

BRISTOL POLITICAL UNION

The council of the Union have heard with feelings of surprise that the Corporation have requested and obtained the assistance of armed troops for the purpose of conducting Sir Charles Wetherell, in his judicial capacity, into this city. It is the opinion of this council that if the magistracy of the city feel themselves incompetent to preserve the public peace without being supported by the military, they should resign their offices and suffer the civic authorities to be elected by a majority of the votes for their fellow citizens. The council think that a man clothed in the robes of magistracy ought never to be a politician, as such a magistrate cannot be expected to possess the public confidence, without which he will always be found incompetent to preserve the public peace. They would therefore recommend to the Corporation the immediate resignation of Sir Charles Wetherell as Recorder, such being the means best calculated to prevent riot and perhaps bloodshed. At the same time, the council earnestly recommend members of the Union, and reformers in general, at all times of popular excitement, to use their most strenuous endeavours for the preservation of the public peace, as it is only by such a course they will be able to obtain the rights they seek.

By order of the council,

October 25, 1831   J. P. Ven, Secretary.

Here, then, was an organization directly challenging the corporation by publicly questioning their ability to govern—a sentiment shared by countless inhabitants—but the recently-formed union still represented something of an unknown

29

quantity. Although suspected of being under the immediate control of the powerful Birmingham Political Union (with whom they liaised) and also of subversive activities, the Bristol Union in fact was seemingly almost self-reliant and of pretty reasonable outlook. The principal officers comprised men of professional status and, according to Susan Thomas in her booklet on the riots, 'membership appears to have been tightly controlled and while an initial attempt to restrict admission to householders failed, there is no indication that the Union recruited from social groups below that of the artisan'.

Mainspring of the union was the vice-president, thirty-five-year-old William Herapath, the Bristol-born son of a maltster and by no means an unstable rabble-rouser. A founder-member and a Fellow of the Chemical Society of London, he had been appointed professor of chemistry and toxicology at the Bristol Medical School when it opened in 1828. After the Reform crisis, Herapath's success professionally and in public office led to a cooling of his radicalism. He gained a widespread reputation for chemical analyses, being called as an expert witness at a number of murder trials including that in 1856 of the notorious poisoner, William Palmer.

By 26 October, two troops of 14th Light Dragoons pitched camp at Clifton and a troop of 3rd Dragoon Guards had reached Keynsham. A former editor of *The Bristol Mercury*, Thomas John Manchee, subsequently referred critically in a pamphlet to supposed sabre-rattling by the military in the city's streets 'from the 24th or 25th of October, incessantly down to the period of the riots'. He argued that any such intended intimidation was doomed to failure, because 'to parade from fifty to a hundred soldiers ... in the midst of a population of a hundred thousand was calculated only to irritate the feeling of the whole and to excite the insolence of those who were inclined to outrage'.

Manchee's dates do not tally with those cited by Major-General Lord Fitzroy James Henry Somerset (Military Secretary at the Horse Guards), who informed Melbourne 'the orders to the 14th and 3rd were given on the 21st and 22nd and the former were put in march from Gloucester on the 24th and arrived at Clifton on the 26th, and the latter moved from Trowbridge on the 25th and arrived at Keynsham either that or the following day'.[1] Fitzroy Somerset, then forty-three, was the seventh and youngest son of the fifth Duke of Beaufort and had lost his right arm at Waterloo. Noted for his urbanity, tact and impartiality, he proved an excellent desk man—a forte only too tragically confirmed some twenty-three years later when, as Lord Raglan, he became Commander-in-Chief in the Crimea.

A hint of the unrest simmering in Bristol occurred on 24 October, when Bishop Law consecrated the Church of St Paul at Bedminster. He was greeted outside the building by a noisy group with 'marked disapprobation' and, after the service, treated to some earthy epithets and pelted with mud and a few stones as his carriage bore him swiftly away. It was said the bishop, in whose ears echoed shouts of 'Reform—we will have Reform', wept when he left. The instigators of a provocatively-worded placard, which had sparked off the rowdyism, were disowned by all parties. It read:

Reformers—read, mark, learn and inwardly digest. The Right Rev Father in God, the Bishop of Bath and Wells, will consecrate the new church in Coronation-road on Monday, the 24th Oct. Receive him with every demonstration of respect that becomes his exalted rank and late vote in the House of Lords. Refrain, therefore, from hooting, pelting, groaning, hissing, or any other annoyance that may be offensive to the man who has so recently declared himself against the voice of the people.—A CHURCHMAN.

Hopes persisted that nothing more sinister or violent than this unseemly incident was in the offing. The magistrates directed copies of the following be posted throughout the city:

Council House, Bristol,
27th October, 1831.
It being apprehended, from information received through various channels, that some indiscreet persons may be inclined to promote feelings of irritation and excitement on the arrival of the Recorder in the city, the Mayor and Aldermen most earnestly hope that all classes of their fellow citizens, however they may differ on political subjects, will see the propriety of cordially co-operating to maintain peace and good order; and that they will abstain from manifesting any declaration of their opinion on so solemn and important occasion

[1] PRO HO 40/28.

as the delivery of His Majesty's Gaol, in cases affecting the lives of the persons to be tried for offences against the laws of their country. The Magistrates confidently trust that they may rely on the good sense and discretion of the inhabitants not to depart from that orderly conduct which has hitherto prevailed in the city; but should any disposition be shown, tending to create disturbance, they feel it will become their imperative duty to use all lawful means for the apprehending and bringing to punishment all persons who may be found committing any breach of the peace or other illegal act.

By order of the Mayor and Aldermen,

LUDLOW, Town-Clerk.

Ebenezer Ludlow, MA, who had been Town Clerk for twelve years, was a lawyer of no mean repute. A product of Oriel College, Oxford, he became a barrister (Gray's Inn) in 1805, at the age of twenty-eight, and a serjeant-at-law in 1827. Like his civic colleagues, he now waited somewhat apprehensively for the much-heralded appearance of the man described by one local priest as 'our comical Recorder'.

The city's press could be relied upon to keep the political pot bubbling with extensive reports and richly-spiced comment of unabashed bias. Bristol then boasted no fewer than five newspapers—all weeklies—each costing sevenpence, which put them beyond the purchasing power of most people. Nevertheless, although actual sales were relatively small, it was estimated a single copy might reach up to twenty readers.

Most radical of the quintet were *The Bristol Mercury*, directed for the past two years by William Henry Somerton, and *The Bristol Liberal* with Philip Rose as editor. At the opposite end of the spectrum stood *Felix Farley's Bristol Journal*, implacably Tory and anti-Reform to the last well-turned phrase, controlled by John Mathew Gutch (whose schoolfellows at Christ's Hospital during the 1780s included Coleridge and Lamb) and James Martin. Somewhere between those extremes came *The Bristol Gazette* and *The Bristol Mirror*, which appear generally to have been comparatively moderate in outlook. Somerton, a doughty champion of Reform, published this a few days before the Recorder was due:

If the cause of public peace and order were left entirely in the hands of The Reformers of Bristol, I am sure they would need no admonition on the subject of preserving them to inviolate ... Sir Charles Wetherell, the Senior Alderman and Recorder of Bristol, is expected to arrive on Saturday to take his seat in the Court as Judge of Assize. It is perfectly true that this man has distinguished himself in the House of Commons as the bitterest and the most vexatious, as well as the most ridiculous, opponent of the opinions and wishes of the King— the representatives of the people and the nation at large—and, as demerit will not fail of its due, he is, at this moment, enjoying his reward in the contempt, not say the hatred, of the wise and good of every class. And this is sufficient revenge. As a man and an Englishman, his person is entitled to the protection of the law—still more in his *official capacity* to which, it must be remembered, he was chosen by the authorities of the city—he ought to be exempted not only from interruption, but from insult on account of his misconduct in another place.

According to their lights, each newspaper reported and reflected at length upon the tense situation. There was complete agreement on one point, however. They expressed a confident belief that everything would be—and should be—tranquil on Saturday, 29 October.

So Bristol waited. Undercurrents of taut expectancy there might have been, but life went on as usual. Quaysides bustled; clerks, squatting on high stools, pored over bulky ledgers in ill-lit offices; the markets jostled; street vendors yelled their wares; wealthy merchants tattled and bargained in oak-panelled coffee rooms; the sweating miners of Kingswood hewed coal in the dark depths. The Theatre Royal in King Street had just re-opened after major renovation and patrons enjoyed a performance of *The Rivals* while, later that week, opera-lovers experienced the ebullience of *The Barber of Seville*. Madame Tussaud and her sons announced an extended run of their exhibition of waxen figures at the Assembly Rooms in Princes Street [now Prince Street].

Funds were being sought to finance the building of a suspension bridge across the Avon Gorge—to the design of a twenty-five-year-old engineer called Isambard Kingdom Brunel; the Rev Dr Lant Carpenter lectured at the Bristol Institution on astronomy, his talk being illustrated by 'models and numerous representations of the celestial phenomena'; some residences of a 'highly desirable' character at Clifton were up for sale; Messrs Hart, surgical and mechanical dentists, invited the attention

of 'Nobility, Gentry, Etc., of Bristol, Clifton, and their vicini-
ties' to consider an offer of 'Indestructible Silicious Mineral
Teeth'; a gentleman, hiding hopefully behind the initials
'L.L.', also made an offer—of himself— to form 'a matrimonial
alliance with a lady of congenial sentiments to his own, who
is possessed of moderate property'. Upon such important trifles
does the world go round. Night fell.

On Saturday morning, the military began to move into the
city. Despite the uneven clip-clop of hooves and jingling har-
nesses the combined cavalry detachments, ninety-three strong,
entered 'with the least possible display'. Lt-Col Thomas Brereton, who had consulted with the civil authorities several times
that week, rode to the cattle market where he stationed himself
with the 14th Light Dragoons and checked final details with
John William Gage who, at thirty, ranked the regiment's
senior captain. The colonel had also verified personally that
the 3rd Dragoon Guards were just approaching the New Gaol
and headed by Captain William Henry Warrington—only six
weeks younger than Gage, but with nearly seven years less service. [Later that day, the troops were transferred to livery-
stable quarters—Leigh's Bazaar and Fisher's Repository, a
short distance from each other—close to College Green and
about 200 yards from the Army Recruiting Office, which would
serve as a central alarm post.]

Brereton had impressed upon both troop commanders at previous meetings the vital importance of restraint and he now
repeated that no action was to be undertaken unless explicitly
ordered. Although stuck at the rank of lieutenant-colonel for
sixteen years, all Brereton's promotions (albeit for overseas
duties) had been obtained without purchase—an effort which
suggested a character of some resource and diligence to duty.
Such qualities were soon to be probed and, regrettably, with
tragic consequences.

The army units were thus positioned in the wings, a far from
satisfactory civilian force had been scraped together and, in an
attempt further to minimize trouble, the magistrates arranged
for the Recorder to arrive two hours before the pre-announced
time of noon. That alteration soon became widely known, however, and by ten o'clock thousands of people lined the route.
A large number assembled outside the *Blue Bowl Inn* at Totter-

down, an aptly-named place on a switchback of hills to the south of the city, where Wetherell was scheduled to change from his own carriage to Sheriff George Bengough's coach for the ceremonial ride to the city's Guildhall. Eyes strained to catch a first glimpse of the controversial figure. He was late.

At half-past ten, a carriage, drawn by four lively greys, hove quickly into sight from the direction of Bath and pulled up in a flurry of dirt. Out stepped Sir Charles Wetherell. He had hardly put a foot to the ground before the jeering and hissing began and, without wasting a second, climbed into the sheriff's coach. So, closely guarded, the Recorder embarked upon his processional entry into Bristol.

From all sides rose a torrent of abuse. Then someone threw a clod of earth. It was followed by a stone, and another...

Chapter Two

STICKS AND STONES

IT BECAME frighteningly apparent that Wetherell's presence in Bristol prickled with potential danger. To proceed so ostentatiously, his carriage surrounded by marching constables and with a mounted bodyguard hugging each side, it seemed little short of foolhardy. It was no secret that cavalry units were at the alert within the city. The seeds of impending disaster germinated. Indeed, the whole affair had been already pronounced by some citizens as a dreadful mistake.

The outcry of the populace—they lined the streets, hung out from upper windows or clung precariously to other vantage points—reached a crescendo. Horses struggled in taut trappings, coach-drivers hauled on the reins and yet, surprisingly, the cavalcade retained a semblance of order.

Wetherell must have felt extremely vulnerable whenever a missile thudded against the vehicle, but he was not without considerable courage and probably reacted with lofty disdain, convinced of his correctness in adhering meticulously to the time-honoured processional approach to the Guildhall. Sir Charles wasn't going to permit what he regarded as a rowdy collection of contemptible oafs to interfere with tradition or, moreover, the due process of law. After all (and who could gainsay it?), he was but exercising his judicial rights.

Having crossed Hill's Bridge [now Bath Bridge, outside Temple Meads railway station], where the stone-throwing increased, the procession passed through Bath Parade and entered the half-mile-long Temple Street with its tightly-packed buildings, a number of which tilted towards the congested thoroughfare. A mass of people pressed forward and the constables, though harshly jostled and cursed, showed admir-

36

able restraint. The 'hired' men, in particular, were harangued for selling-out to the corporation and also for protecting the most unpopular man of the moment.

The clamorous crowd included 'persons, evidently without stated employment, which the densely populated purlieus of wretchedness and vice in St Philip's and in the neighbourhood of Lawford's Gate had sent forth on the occasion. Not a few among them were women of abandoned character and these, by their violent language, seemed well fitted to urge them on to desperation.' Leaning from widows overlooking the seething street, 'the lower order of females were particularly vociferous in the expression of their feelings, frequently charging the men with cowardice and want of spirit'.

As the procession moved across Bristol Bridge and into the High Street, one constable—'a respectable tradesman'—fell victim to a brickbat and sustained 'a dangerous contusion in the head'. The leading coach eventually reached the Guildhall in Broad Street where Mayor Charles Pinney, accompanied by city and county dignitaries, waited formally to greet the Recorder, but it was obvious that even a truncated outdoor ceremony would have to be forgotten. Wetherell, hissed and booed, squeezed from his carriage and hurried into the court-room but not before a stone, intended for him, struck Under-Sheriff Hare on the head.

No sooner had the Recorder taken his place on the bench than the hall was 'thrown open to the populace and, in a few minutes, the area was completely choked up'. The invading crowd kept up a constant babble and Ebinezer Ludlow, bellowing to make himself heard, said he believed no-one present intended to insult the commission of the King. However, he added, if Reform was the reason for the hullabaloo, then it had nothing whatever to do with the current proceedings. The din grew and Wetherell looked displeased at the Town Clerk's reference to such a thorny political matter.

Sir Charles then announced that if there was further interruption those responsible would be committed for contempt. 'The only effect of this notice', commented an observer, 'was to raise, if possible, a louder clamour than that which it was intended to suppress.' Constables managed to eject several culprits, but they were quite unable to restore complete order.

37

So, against a background of barracking, the formal prelimi-
naries were muddled through and, according to custom, court
was adjourned until the following Monday. The interrupters
gave three cheers for the King and fought their way outside.

That raucous exhibition was but a mild foretaste of what lay
in store. Although most of the aggression and noise came from
comparatively few, the vast majority in the growing crowd
appeared perfectly happy to let it continue. Such unspoken con-
sent, as it were, surely mirrored widespread contempt not only
for Wetherell but also for the corporation.

The procession re-formed for the drive to the Mansion
House, traditionally the venue of the official banquet in honour
of the Recorder. Pinney and Wetherell shared a coach,
although even the Mayor's presence did nothing to diminish
an almost continuous chorus of groans and general disapprobation. Doubtless to the pleasant amazement of Sir Charles, a knot
of spectators outside the Commercial Rooms, Corn Street, actually raised a cheer *for* him. Bumped and berated, the constables
stuck unexpectedly well to their primary task of safeguarding
the Recorder.

People raced along short cuts and were already in position
outside the Mansion House to 'welcome' the magistrates,
sheriffs and other notables. When the first carriage, containing
Sheriffs George Bengough and Joseph Lax, drew up at the front
door, those following were obliged to stop. This presented a
stationary target of the Mayor's coach to stone-throwers and
the crash of glass signified some accuracy. Emerging nimbly,
Pinney and the Recorder scurried into the house unharmed.
It is probable they now assumed the worst was over and that,
having had their fun, the demonstrators would melt away. No
such thing happened. Sections of the crowd went on catcalling
and, while most agitation was being caused by no more than
about seventy-five men and boys, others in Queen Square derived pleasure from egging them on.

Inside the Mansion House, a galaxy of gentlemen sipped
wine and chatted uneasily about the morning's events; outside,
clustered a formidable phalanx of constables. So far, nothing
more serious than abuse and a few stones had been hurled. At
this juncture, the whole business should have been settled. With
a modest degree of organized determination, the constables

could have dispersed the small core of the mischief-makers and, with the show at an end, it seems likely the rest of the large crowd would have drifted off. It was not to be.

The rowdies, realizing their actions were going unpunished and, furthermore, being encouraged by onlookers, became bolder. The opposing constables, dispirited by the lack of public support and proper leadership, grew apprehensive and frustrated; they had endured insults and threats, they were hungry and their tempers fraying. The sands of moderation began to shift.

Stones aimed at windows of the Mansion House shattered a number of panes, but several inevitably hit nearby constables. Unfortunately, a group of them over-reacted (viciously, some witnesses declared) and, devoid of effective direction, rushed headlong into the crowd, hauled out a couple of suspects and beat them up. This reckless procedure was more or less repeated half-a-dozen times, resulting, on occasions, in the wrongful arrest and ill-treatment of innocuous bystanders. It was clear that such tactics, which further alienated the 'specials' in the eyes of the populace, would only exacerbate the situation.

The active mob's total swelled to about 200. There were cries of 'To the Back' [Welsh Back, alongside the Floating Harbour, east of Queen Square] where stood piles of faggot sticks and, thus primitively armed, an avenging horde returned in an attempt to rescue prisoners. It was now after one o'clock and the constables, hastily re-organized to some extent, met the attack with resolution. With heavy staves, they proved more than a match for the rabble, who were disarmed and chased from the immediate vicinity of the Mansion House. Running skirmishes occurred in Queen Square and adjacent streets, the area being strewn with hastily-discarded sticks and a number of groaning injured.

Versions of just what happened naturally differed: some spectators maintained the special constables, whom they dubbed 'bludgeon men', panicked and acted with needless severity, while others considered the mob got no more than their just deserts. Many people were quick to emphasize that none of it would have taken place but for what they viewed as the Recorder's arrogant rashness in publicly entering the city at such a tinderbox time, plus the puerile efforts of the Bristol

CITY UNDER FIRE

authorities. It is reasonable to suppose that a sizeable percentage of those condemning the magistrates had refused to assist
them in the first place.

Apart from sporadic minor mêlées, the afternoon passed relatively peacefully and some special constables, possibly because
no further trouble was expected but more likely due to dis-
enchantment and rumbling stomachs, left the scene. Others
were officially released, but told to report back that evening.
The time lapse proved fatal. At about four o'clock, the mob
started to re-assemble in strength and again pelted the Mansion
House with stones. Frightened constables retreated into the
building, which now echoed to frequent sounds of smashing
glass and lacerated woodwork. An attempt to storm the house
was repelled, but Mayor Pinney and his colleagues, still comparatively safe in the upstairs rooms, were only too aware of
the worsening position. Meanwhile, the military detachments
had moved to quarters near College Green.

One chief constable, John Cossens, who described the mob
as 'very riotous', personally advised the Mayor to call in the
troops. Wetherell, extraordinarily calm in the circumstances,
broke in to say there were insufficient grounds to warrant it.
With hands thrust deeply into pockets and 'his breeches partly
down', the Recorder discussed the matter with the Town Clerk
who believed it time to summon the soldiers.

Some inside the Mansion House still thought a charge by constables, supported by loyal citizens, would soon rout the mob.
Fewer than a hundred constables remained, but it seems fair
to assume (because of their remaining) they included a pretty
high proportion of experienced men. Just where other public-
spirited inhabitants were to be found near the scene posed a
problem for, as an eye-witness said, 'there were thousands of
persons present, but there appeared no disposition in them to
repress the mob, although they would have had no difficulty
in doing so'.

Charles Pinney now displayed much pluck. Accompanied by
several aldermen and corporation officials, he went outside to
address the crowd. His unexpected appearance surprised the
agitators, who fell into a sullen silence, and he urged everyone
to disperse quietly. Pinney was accorded three cheers, which
probably astonished him, after warning the people of the

'impropriety of your conduct' and assuring them the magistrates had no wish to introduce stringent measures unless compelled. Recovering from the shock of the Mayor's sudden emergence, the mob became loud in their disapproval and stones were slung at the civic representatives. One alderman had his hat knocked off, more windows were broken and the Mayor and his companions smartly withdrew.

The building was further assailed but the pressured constables, again engaged in hand-to-hand fighting, prevented all but two or three offenders from entering. The whole situation was rapidly deteriorating, however. When the closely-guarded Mayor re-appeared outside the Mansion House just before five o'clock, the mob gave him a hostile reception. At this moment, his courage cannot be doubted. Standing upon a chair in the forecourt, he read the Riot Act. Just how many heard him above the noise is anybody's guess. Certainly he went unheeded by the mob, who continued throwing stones—Daniel Burges got one on the head and another in the stomach—and, for the second time in little more than half-an-hour, His Worship was forced quickly to retire. Urgent dispatches now went to the military for immediate assistance.

There was no holding the mob who, launching an all-out attack on the Mansion House, burst in through the windows and doors. A journalist wrote graphically:

In an instant, the windows and sashes were smashed to atoms; the shutters were beaten to pieces; the doors forced; and every article of furniture on the ground floor broken up. Tables, chairs, sideboards, mirrors, chimney-glasses—in fact, every thing that could be found was demolished. The iron palisades, together with the curb-stones in which they were set, were thrown down as if they had been mere reeds stuck in a mud bank, and furnished many a desperate villain with a formidable iron bar; young trees were torn up by the roots and converted into weapons of destruction; walls were thrown down to provide bricks with which to assail the upper windows; and straw and combustibles were procured, with which to fire the whole premises.

In the words of the Mayor's official report later, 'the constables being unable to maintain possession of the hall, in consequence of the brickbats, stones and pieces of timber with which it was raked, the mob effected an entrance, destroyed all the furniture in the rooms on the ground floor and, it appears, had provided and placed a quantity of straw in one of the rooms'.

The constables, some badly mauled, stopped intruders from getting upstairs but, even without the possible additional hazard of arson, the lives of everyone 'trapped' in the house were at risk. The large crowd in the Square made no move to intervene. The kitchen staff of the Mansion House fled—'meats were turning upon the spits and, on the range, the saucepans and kettles were boiling without a soul to tend them'. Inside the surrounded building, the Mayor, sheriffs, aldermen and the apparently phlegmatic Wetherell helped to barricade upper windows and some doors with beds, sideboards and tables.

When a contingent of cavalry—led by Lt-Col Brereton—trotted into Queen Square, the mob withdrew from the Mansion House and, like a dog deprived of a bone, hung about awaiting developments. 'We had supposed,' commented *The Bristol Mercury*, 'judging from the conduct of the mob in the morning that the appearance of two troops of horse would have been a signal for a general rout. We were, however, deceived. They had now aquired a considerable accession of force and it was obvious that they had been joined by some of the most determined and desperate characters. Instead of retreating the thousands who were present, clustering like bees on the adjoining walls and elevations, cheered the troops with the greatest enthusiasm.'

With mounted soldiers patrolling the Square, Brereton reported to the Mayor. That and subsequent meetings were to become focal points of controversy. Unquestionably, the colonel was told to clear the area, but it seems he received no precise instructions as to how the magistrates wished that to be done. Brereton opted for a policy of pacification—a decision which later brought upon his head severe censure and even some imputations of cowardice. He ordered the troops in no circumstances to open fire and, moreover, not to draw sabres. Chants of 'King William and Reform' rent the air.

Convinced that the mere presence of the military was an adequate deterrent, Brereton rode quietly into the crowd and tried gently to persuade them to go home. Not surprisingly, this was interpreted by some as a sign of weakness. He persisted in his sweet talk, however, and much would be made by critics that he was seen laughing with the crowd and supposedly shaking hands with rioters. While the colonel doubtless saw no reason for making enemies unnecessarily, it is likely some with whom he shook hands were onlookers known personally to him. It was also said many people reached up to grasp his hand as it hung at his side.

As things turned out, Brereton was wrong in believing a kid-glove approach would succeed. Even so, one can appreciate his probable thinking at that stage. By the time troops got to the Mansion House, the mob were on their way out; admittedly, considerable damage littered the ground floor and there was plenty of noise but to Brereton, fresh upon the scene, the overall picture in the evening gloom may not have appeared dire. Had not the soldiers been cheered by the throng?

Brereton now perceived no justification for force and, in assessing the situation, a significant factor almost certainly crossed his mind. To charge a defenceless crowd was to take on a heavy responsibility; to slash with sabres or to employ fire-arms without the written assent or physical attendance of a magistrate could (in his view), if proved unwarranted, lead to an indictment for murder. He had not been given such unequivocal orders.

However, the chances are that Brereton's reckoning was based on a genuine assumption the crowd would quietly co-operate. The colonel was kindly and humane by nature if, perhaps, somewhat naïve.

Sitting astride his charger, Brereton spoke to the populace in Queen Square like a benevolent schoolmaster admonishing a class of naughty pupils. The dragoons did not fare so comfortably; their harassed horses bumped into people and revenge came in the form of bricks and sticks. There was growing impatience in the ranks to deal firmly with trouble-makers, but they were under strict instructions to do nothing provocative. From time to time, Brereton went into the Mansion House to report. Still confident of dispersing the crowd (in fact, some had already left the Square), he stated they were mostly good-humoured and insisted that his mollifying tactics would win the day. Magistrates, watching events from upper windows as best as they could in the feeble glow cast by street gaslights, did not share his optimism, however.

A unit of the 14th Light Dragoons encountered particularly stiff resistance from one alley, the narrowness of which prevented the entry of more than a single horse at a time. They withdrew under a barrage of stones and chunks of iron and Captain Gage, taking matters into his own hands, rode to the Mansion House to seek permission to use carbines.

According to him, the Mayor hesitated but appeared just about to agree when Brereton came in and strongly advised against it. What he said afterwards to Gage for apparently attempting to by-pass his authority is not recorded.

Desultory skirmishing continued throughout the evening and the dragoons, at the cost of a few injuries, induced part of the crowd to move on. Nevertheless, many did not go very far and the troops were quite unable to dislodge rioters who had scrambled aboard barges alongside The Quay. A special constable offered to lead twenty-five men—if supported by military arms—to flush them out. The Mayor was uncertain, at least one alderman thought innocent people would be killed and Brereton also opposed such stern action. 'If you take my advice', commented the colonel, 'you'll let them alone. It's getting very late and, if you don't disturb them, they will go home to bed.' So the plan was shelved.

At about half-past ten that night, two wounded troopers were carried into the drawing-room of the Mansion House just before Brereton arrived with his latest appraisal. He was angrily rebuked by the Town Clerk who, indicating the injured dragoons lying on sofas, demanded: 'Does that look as if the crowd are good-humoured?' The colonel, visibly taken aback, was then asked: 'Have you any instructions from the Horse Guards or from the Home Secretary which prevent your carrying out the directions of the magistrates?' Brereton replied none whatever, adding that he was there to execute the orders of the civil authorities. 'Well then,' retorted the Town Clerk in the presence of the Mayor and several aldermen, 'your orders are to clear the streets and get the city quiet as soon as possible.'

Again, it seems, no-one referred specifically to firearms, although it was claimed later that such direction was manifestly implied. Without hint of protest, Brereton marched stiffly from the room to prepare the troops who, for the ensuing charge, drew sabres but were commanded to use only the 'flats' of blades.

In a mad rush to get out of the way, people careered about Queen Square like disturbed ants. Some were badly hurt, a few taken prisoner and, within a short time, the immediate area became virtually empty. The mob had severed gas pipes, thereby putting out a number of lamps, and persistent rioters went on stoning soldiers from the cover of dark passages. Shortly after eleven o'clock, however, things were tolerably quiet.

Several hours earlier Sir Charles Wetherell, despite his reluctance, was persuaded by the magistrates to see the wisdom of leaving the city. They had already cancelled the special church service scheduled for the following morning (a customary part of the Recorder's itinerary) and quickly concluded the assizes would also have to be postponed. With Sir Charles gone (it was doubtless reasoned), there might be a better chance of placating the mob.

Climbing on to the Mansion House roof and then descending into a stable at the rear (no mean feat for a man in his sixties), Wetherell escaped 'in disguise'. According to Latimer's *Annals of Bristol*, the Recorder 'changed clothes with a postillion and succeeded so easily in passing through the crowd and reaching a house in Kingsdown that he is said to have taken a stroll through the streets at a later hour in the evening to ascertain the state of the city. Finding the disturbance showed no sign of abatement, he ordered a chaise and left for Newport which he reached early on the following morning.'

Charles Gardiner, captain of a merchantman and a special constable that night, helped Wetherell to get away. He said they arrived at his own house at about half-past six and that Sir Charles vacated Bristol before ten o'clock. It was argued his departure should have been announced to appease the mob, but it seems likely that events were too far gone by then to have had much effect.

At about the time the Recorder quitted the Mansion House, there entered a forty-two-year-old army officer of some distinction—Major Digby Mackworth, aide-de-camp to the Commander-in-Chief, General Lord Rowland Hill. He had been staying with friends at Clifton [his own family home was at Glen

Usk, Monmouthshire] and, hearing that 'something of a riot' was expected in Bristol, decided to remain a few days 'in conformity with what I knew would be Lord Hill's wishes . . . and render any little service in my power to the civil authorities'.

The major, clad in civilian clothes, went to Queen Square shortly before seven o'clock. He got into the Mansion House without difficulty, saw wreckage scattered about the ground floor and noted the 'rooms and staircase were filled with special constables'. After discussion with the Mayor and magistrates, Mackworth decided that there was 'a total want of organization among the civil force' and the constables themselves causing 'serious obstruction' by cramming into the house. His offer to form the men into divisions met with approval and, with the help of dragoons, the scheme effected to station groups of constables around the building.

Mackworth declared that 'in less than five minutes by a trifling, but combined, operation, the whole vicinity of the Mansion House was cleared; and thus it remained till the following morning, except that now and then the constables and dragoons were annoyed by stones thrown from the by-streets, barges and a few from the tops of houses. Notwithstanding this, nine prisoners captured by the civil force were safely conveyed to the goal. Three privates of the 14th were wounded by stones, one severely so, and a subaltern much hurt by his horse falling under him.'

There were other versions, however. For instance Thomas Sheppard, a corn merchant, who lived three doors from the Mansion House, claimed credit for suggesting to the Mayor (at about nine o'clock) the importance of re-organizing the constables, whereupon Pinney spoke to Major Mackworth who agreed to marshal them in four sections. Sheppard himself commanded one unit of twenty-five men—posted at the junction of Charlotte Street and Little King Street [behind the Mansion House]. It seems not to have been quite the success story Mackworth indicated. According to Sheppard, he and the constables had been there no longer than five minutes when a party of dragoons galloped past, their sergeant exclaiming: 'We're not going to stay here and be murdered.' The constables were then stoned by rioters and, Sheppard recalled, 'I had scarcely time to look round before there were only three or four left with me.'

46

By late evening, only a few officials remained inside the Mansion House. Most had gone to their homes outside the city limits, some not to return until after the crises. Much earlier, the Mayor wisely arranged for his wife to stay at a Clifton hotel.

Among those who did not leave for some hours was Major Mackworth whose military record, especially in his younger days, had been outstanding. He joined the 7th Fusiliers as a lieutenant in 1807 when he was eighteen and, during the Penisular War, carried the regimental colours at Talavera and subsequently took part in the famous charge at Albuera. Four years later, he was again in the forefront at the battle of Waterloo and had his horse shot from beneath him during an attack led by Lord Hill. He afterwards served in India with the 13th Light Dragoons and was now one of Hill's most trusted officers.

Mackworth came from a highly-respected family and can have done his social status no harm when, in 1816, he married Maria Alexandrine Ignatie Julia de Richepance, only daughter of General and Baroness de Richepance and a niece of the Duc de Damas Crux. Sadly, she was soon to die but not before giving birth to his son and heir. Mackworth re-married in 1823, his second wife being Sophia Noel Mann, daughter of James Mann and a granddaughter of Sir Horace Mann.

Unquestionably Mackworth was a brave soldier, an officer and a gentleman [he became the hero—'Arthur Vaughan'— of Stanley J. Weyman's novel, *Chippinge*, featuring the Bristol riots]. He was also self-assured, exhibiting perhaps a tinge of military arrogance. Be that as it may, the major stayed at the Mansion House until around two o'clock on the Sunday morning, when 'I really thought the worst of the riot was over'. His was not an isolated view.

Towards midnight some rioters, thwarted by the military in Queen Square, had attacked the Council House in Corn Street. Lt-Col Brereton sent a detachment of 14th Light Dragoons to the scene and, once there, Captain Gage unhesitatingly ordered them to charge. Amid flying hooves and cleaving sabres, the mob scattered.

The zealous Gage explained later that 'the body of rioters were very considerable when I arrived and the attack was very violent'. Thomas Garrard, the forty-four-year-old Chamberlain of Bristol, had no doubts that the mob would have forced an entry and wrecked the place; he was inside with a civil force of thirty-five men, armed with cudgels, but believed they could not have held out much longer. Stones and broken glass showered in upon them. The military, it seems, rode up in the nick of time.

The cavalrymen chased rioters into some of the slender passages off Wine Street. Although unable to follow, the dragoons patrolled the area and were repeatedly assailed. Captain Gage reported: 'The mob in one alley were headed by a man in light-coloured dress who always advanced into the street several paces before he threw a missile of iron or stone. The third or fourth time he did it, I drew a pistol and levelled it at him but it snapped. A soldier immediately on my left fired and the man fell. After that, the mob left that alley and we were no more pelted.'

When satisfied that things were under control, Gage left a small unit with Lt James Dawson to guard the Council House and himself led the rest of the detachment back via Queen Square to quarters.

The shot man, a gaping wound in his chest, survived no more than a few minutes. He was named as Stephen Bush, said to be in his twenties and, it was claimed, an innocent bystander. Another person died later: Daniel James was reportedly walking home from work when slashed by a sabre while in the High Street and sustained a terrible head injury from which he succumbed at the infirmary.

Relating the first incident, *The Bristol Gazette* said that 'at the top of the Pithay where a soldier was struck, he immediately turned round and shot a man dead on the spot. As is often the case, it happened that the innocent suffered for the guilty; this man had just come up from the Pithay on hearing the disturbance and met the fate meant for another.'

As one o'clock chimed in the darkness of Sunday, the city fell almost silent. The drama had barely begun, however.

Chapter Three

FAREWELL TO ARMS

SUNDAY DAWNED GREY. The air was flecked with drizzle and traces of light mist lingered about the trees in Queen Square where a few dragoon guards formed a picket outside the barricaded Mansion House. It had been peaceful from just after midnight, since when the military guard was changed several times. Scattered wreckage and scarred masonry bore testimony to the earlier acrimonious clashes.

The Mayor got no sleep and little, if anything, to eat. The same went for those who stayed all night with him in the drawing-room on the first floor. Jagged glass and splintered sash-wood lay on the carpet; beds and other furniture leant protectively against windows. A mere handful of constables, forcing open tired eyes, lounged on the main staircase. For most other worried residents nearby, slumber, if any that night, was fitful.

It had been a strained period but, as the hours passed undisturbed, growing confidence gradually replaced apprehension. Pinney's colleagues throughout that protracted vigil included Aldermen Gabriel Goldney and James George and the Mayor's clerk, Daniel Burges. Shortly before six o'clock Goldney, a senior magistrate of sixty-five, considering the danger over, proposed he and Burges share a carriage to Clifton where both of them lived. Alderman George, it seems, departed soon afterwards. On their way home, Goldney and Burges met Alderman Abraham Hilhouse heading for Queen Square and assured him all was well.

What of the Mayor's thoughts? In a letter to his widowed sister, Mrs Mary Ames, who resided at 4 Cavendish Place, Bath, he wrote:

My dear Sister—I write a few hasty lines to say thank God we are all safe; fortunately I had the precaution to send off Fanny and her

49

mother early to Clifton. At one time we were in great peril, the mob
had completely knocked down every door and window and made a
wreck of the lower part of the Mansion House—the Constables could
not resist—and a truss of straw carried by some desperate villains into
the dining room covered with turpentine to set the house on fire when
the military arrived—two of the soldiers were brought in seriously
bruised and I fear many of the Constables. I have forebore ordering
the troops to fire—but men could not stand being knocked off their
horses and in one place I fear a man has been shot. The troops are
now bivouacing in the Square and Sir Charles has escaped over the
roof and gone to London and the Assizes are of course necessary put
off—I hope we shall not have a recurrence tomorrow—I was obliged
in the end to read the riot act, one Constable knocked down by my
side and two of the Aldermen struck, one stone lodged in my hat,
but we are now taking much precaution that there can be no danger—
write to my Sister and my Brother, for exagerated [sic] accts will reach
them; I have been as you may suppose with the Magistrates up all
night.

Your affectionate,
5 oclock   Chas Pinney.[1]
Sunday morn, Mansion Ho

For purposes of present assessment, the value of the letter lies
in its spontaneity. This was no rehearsed statement for official
or public consumption, but simply a private family note—an
instant reaction to recent events. Particularly illuminating, perhaps, is Pinney's comment that he 'forebore ordering the troops
to fire' which differs from what some other people—and, to an
extent, the Mayor himself—later intimated.

When Major Mackworth returned to the Square at about
seven o'clock, he saw a 'tolerably quiet' gathering of about fifty
inhabitants in front of the Mansion House and, entering the
building, estimated there were 'certainly less than ten' persons
inside. As he and the Mayor talked, they could hear an
occasional rattle of what sounded like stones striking the
exterior; this soon became more frequent and, above it, rose
excited voices. Peeking through curtains, Pinney and Mackworth saw that the crowd had greatly increased and, to their
horror, realized the soldiers had vanished.

People flung themselves furiously at the building; the main

[1] Pinney Papers.

50

door was smashed, shielding timbers wrenched from windows and there were triumphant shouts as an entry was forced.

Mackworth persuaded the Mayor, whom he described as 'the most cool of the party', that there was no alternative but to run for it. The endangered group left through a landing window between the first and second floors and scrambled on to a roof, from which they dropped into a courtyard. After scaling a wall with the aid of a ladder, they entered the next-door house and, having ascended the stairs, climbed through a window and into the angled protection of a double roof. Crouching to avoid detection, they cautiously made their elevated way to the Custom House where, clambering through yet another window, they descended inside to ground level and eventually got clear via a back street. Accompanied by Mackworth and others, the Mayor walked unmolested to College Green.

Why did the troops leave their post? Brereton apparently explained that he regarded their presence as provocative and also that men and horses needed rest and refreshment. From probably the most honourable of intentions, he had misread the signs and opened the way to further violence by withdrawing the soldiers.

Throughout the tragic course of events (as it will be seen), Brereton appears to have adhered to a notion that if he used armed force, without irrefutable evidence of authority, he would be left to face any unpleasant consequences alone. An understandable fear, perhaps. Nevertheless, it was patently his duty to maintain order to his utmost ability with the means at his disposal although, in fairness, he was not solely to blame for the current and subsequent lack of liaison. The magistrates, it seems, could have shown more foresight and urgency in issuing watertight instructions to the military and, moreover, demanding their prompt and precise implementation—and, not surprisingly, they later claimed to have done just that. What they clearly did not do, however, was to sustain a properly-organized civil force.

At the Mansion House, the mob ran amok. Men and boys destroyed or stole furniture and fittings and, as before, the vandals were very greatly outnumbered by the growing crowd of onlookers. The wine cellars, stocked with 300 dozen bottles of choice vintages, were raided. A highly-colourful newspaper

51

report purported to describe the effect on the plunderers: 'They became madly infuriate and regardless alike of what mischief they committed or what risk they incurred. The scene at this moment was of the most depraved description: all ages, of both sexes, were to be seen greedily swallowing the intoxicating liquors, while upon the ground the bodies of scores were to be found dead with drunkenness. The streets, too, remote from this scene of action became noisy with the turbulence of wretches who were to be seen staggering about in all directions.'

Mayor Pinney meanwhile was engaged in a thankless self-imposed task of calling upon inhabitants near College Green for immediate help in view of the crisis facing the city. Most were apathetic, however, while some became vehement about the magistrates in general and Sir Charles Wetherell in particular. Brereton, who had been told tartly to get his men back to Queen Square, trotted past with a unit of 3rd Dragoon Guards. Abandoning his fruitless recruiting mission the Mayor, with Abraham Hilhouse and others, followed the soldiers.

The cavalry's arrival at the Mansion House had little effect on the rioters and an increasing gallery, except to clear the interior and to attract some cheering and shouts for 'Reform'. Alderman Hilhouse read the Riot Act three times, in vain exhorted the people to leave the Square and then, at the Mayor's behest, directed Brereton to disperse the crowd. There was dispute at a later date as to whether he actually ordered him to open fire if necessary. Brereton intimated that he was refused permission to use firearms (a somewhat strange allegation in view of his pacific outlook), while the alderman was to deny being asked the question. Be that as it may, the colonel resorted again to his role of placid persuader. The Mayor and his colleagues left for the Guildhall.

Any hopes Brereton had of a swift and peaceful solution were dashed by the appearance of a unit of blue-coated 14th Light Dragoons headed by Captain Gage. The fairly reasonable mood of the crowd evaporated and there arose instead angry shouts, hisses and whistles, while some incensed people tried to pull the soldiers from their horses. It was known by now that these troops had crushed the previous night's trouble at the Council House where a man died. The dragoons endured violent threats and some stoning from the mob, but Brereton gave no orders for retaliatory action. To add to the hostile confusion, people began yelling: 'Reds for ever—down with the Bloody Blues.'

Brereton then did something positive—and unexpected. He rode over to Captain Gage and, to the latter's astonishment, instructed him to withdraw his men from the Square and return forthwith to quarters. Gage was later to maintain that the colonel said the presence of the 14th was the sole cause of that particular disturbance.

Despite his indignant disbelief at what he must have felt an insult to his troop and a reflection upon his own handling of the earlier affray at the Council House, Gage had no real alternative but to obey. Realizing they had gained a surprising advantage, some of the mob pursued the hapless departing detachment whom they pelted with stones and iron.

Gage twice turned his men about and, each time, the rioters sought temporary refuge in doorways and passages. The assault continued, but there was a mad rush for cover when the captain commanded three dragoons to draw pistols. As the soldiers pulled away the mob emerged from hiding and, now assuming the display of arms to be a bluff, went on with their bombardment. With his patience exhausted and pride affronted, Gage ordered the trio of dragoons to open fire. One rioter fell dead (it was reported) and two others were wounded.

Thus covered at the rear, the cavalry slowly moved away. It seems they could easily have routed the mob at that stage, but Gage had his orders (which he probably exceeded anyway) and it was a sad and humiliated troop which eventually reached quarters. There, the following gang of attackers vowed to destroy the livery stables and the soldiers as well.

That dangerous and somewhat bizarre cat-and-mouse game had been played along Broad Quay, over the drawbridge, across St Augustine's Parade and into College Green—in full view of some startled churchgoers strolling sedately to morning services. Also in the vicinity walked the Town Clerk, not going to worship but on his way to the Guildhall. A stray bullet, which narrowly missed him, buried itself in the metal-studded timber door of St Augustine's Church. It wasn't Ebenezer Ludlow's day. He then got into conversation with a group of people who lamented the 'murder' committed by the troops and also regretted that Wetherell had been allowed into the city. When the Town Clerk suggested the Recorder was as entitled to his opinions as they were, he was warned: 'You'd better take care of yourself, you're as bad as he is; we saw you at the Guildhall backing him up.'

At the nearby cathedral, the sixty-seven-year-old Bishop of Bristol was soon to preach. Although advised to postpone the service because of the ugly developments outside, he resolutely maintained it was his duty to deliver the sermon.

News of the affray soon reached Brereton, who reacted by making an extraordinary proposal. He announced to the crowd in Queen Square that the 14th Light Dragoons would be sent from Bristol and promised no further shooting if people co-operated by going home in peace. At this, the colonel was loudly acclaimed and reportedly doffed his hat and declared: 'I'm for Reform, my boys, as well as you.' A token party of dragoon guards remained outside the Mansion House, while Brereton rode quietly from the Square. He kept to his unbelievably naïve bargain. The mob, of course, did not.

Meanwhile, in blissful ignorance of this proposition, the Mayor and his civic colleagues conferred at the Guildhall. While they knew only too well many citizens lacked faith in the corporation and also that appeals for active assistance were unlikely to cut much ice in some spheres, the magistrates must have been quite unprepared for the magnitude of public in-difference. Even so, they took steps designed to obtain help by ordering copies of the following posters to be distributed and affixed to strategic sites in the city:

Mansion House
Bristol Oct 30, 1831

It is with feelings of the deepest regret that the MAGISTRATES deem it their duty to call for the immediate aid and co-operation of their Fellow Citizens, to allay the great state of excitement now disturbing the Peace of the Inhabitants. The Delivery of the Gaol has been aban-doned and SIR CHARLES WETHERELL, the Recorder, left the City for London last night.

CHA^S PINNEY
Mayor

Council House, Oct 30th, 1831
Sir Charles Wetherell left Bristol at 12 o'clock last night. The Riot
Act has been read three times. All persons found tumultuously assem-
bling are guilty of Capital Felony.

By Order of The Mayor

One unfortunate billposter, John Byrne, was harassed by
rioters who ripped down some notices and rubbed them into
his face and then, to cap it all, emptied paste from his kettle
which they unceremoniously jammed on to his head. At the
same time, rival billposters were sticking up copies of this placard without hindrance:

Bristol General Union: The Council of the Union know that Sir
Charles Wetherell has left the city and that the Assizes are postponed.
They earnestly entreat that every man will immediately return to his
own home. Outrages only injure the cause of reform.

By Order of the Council
Sunday, 30th October, 1831   W. HERAPATH, Vice-President

The corporation's official printers, John Mills and Son (also
the proprietors of *The Bristol Gazette*), produced copies of this
handbill:

The Magistrates most earnestly entreat the assistance of their fellow-citizens to restore the peace of the city by assembling immediately
at the Guildhall.

Sunday Morning,
Half-past 10 o'clock   Guildhall

The magistrates now suffered an alarming setback. Lt-Col
Brereton arrived, with Captain Warrington in tow, and requested permission to send the squadron of 14th Light Dragoons away from Bristol. The soldiers had upset inhabitants by
firing at the mob, he said; in any case, they were very tired
and needed rest. In the plainest language, the Town Clerk
stated that the magistrates would not authorize it; neither
would they even share responsibility for such action. Brereton
insisted it was imperative the troops went and the nonplussed
Mayor and aldermen appear partially to have agreed,
under protest, provided the dragoons were kept within easy
call.

55

Asked if the men and horses might be rested on a rota basis or fresh mounts found, Brereton replied it was impossible. Anyway, he feared for the safety of all the troops if the 14th stayed—because of the mob's increasing hostility. To say the least, it was a surprising statement. The military were there for the precise purpose of keeping the peace, and, with the 14th gone, only thirty-three cavalrymen [the detachment strength of the 3rd Dragoon Guards] would be left in Bristol. Just how much more vulnerable and ineffective would they then be? But the colonel had given his word—to the rabble!

Were the trained troops really all that weary? Could they not have dealt decisively at that juncture with an undisciplined mob? Was there, perhaps, something more sinister going on behind the scenes? *Felix Farley's Bristol Journal* intimated that the Government had pulled some tell-tale strings to manipulate Brereton 'who, we have reason to believe, had received certain instructions which were unknown to the Magistrates. The consequence was that when the Magistrates ordered him to clear the Square with his men on Saturday night, his private instructions appeared immediately to come into collision with the orders of the Magistracy, as to whether such a degree of emergency existed at that moment as would justify him in obeying the orders of the civil power. Now, the citizens of Bristol demand to know, what were those instructions—and what the extent of the responsibility which the Magistracy were to incur?'

Despite those allegations of political puppetry and other dark insinuations, the affair of the 14th Light Dragoons appears at the time to have added up to no more (and it was enough) than a fatal misjudgment by Brereton.

On leaving the flabbergasted magistrates, he had gone straightway to Fisher's Horse Repository to tell Captain Gage to take the squadron from Bristol. The whole lot would be murdered by the mob if they tarried, he forecast somewhat dramatically. The incredulous captain attempted to discuss the matter. 'For God's sake, Gage, will you get out of town,' snapped Brereton, who, when asked where the troops were supposed to go, answered impatiently: 'Anywhere you please, only go now.' Also according to Gage, someone (he thought an ostler) casually mentioned Keynsham, whereupon the colonel remarked: 'Yes, that will do; now, Captain Gage, move your men off at a trot.'

Present at that bristly encounter (as he had been at the Guildhall earlier) was Major-General Thomas Pearson, a battle-scarred veteran of distinction—latterly of the 23rd Foot—who had seen plenty of action, particularly during the Napoleonic Wars. He lived at Clifton and his view supporting the proposed exit of the 14th almost certainly influenced Brereton's decision.

Bombarded and booed by the waiting mob, the squadron trotted from the stables. A horse stumbled and its rider, who fell to the ground, was rescued just in time. Then the 14th withdrew quickly and, wisely skirting the city centre, reached Keynsham without further incident.

Chapter Four

SPREAD OF FLAME

NOW THAT BRISTOL stood bereft of almost any organized deterrent, the strength and violence of the mob increased. Fears mounted as groups, some the worst for drink, moved through the streets. Although the great majority of active rioters appear to have been from the lower working classes, it is possible that a number of better-off inhabitants hitched themselves to the lawless and seemingly leaderless bandwagon. Many hundreds more people trailed along to watch.

Prisoners taken the previous night were locked-up at the Bridewell, towards which a crowd noisily advanced. The buildings sandwiched a narrow thoroughfare—the governor's house on one side and most of the prison proper on the other—and were connected at each end by a stone archway, which could be closed by heavy double-gates. During the day Bridewell Lane, which bisected the 'House of Correction', was a public right-of-way. Armed with iron bars, sticks, pickaxes and sledgehammers, stolen *en route*, rioters arrived at approximately half-past one on Sunday afternoon. It was raining.

Thomas Evans, the governor, was dining with his wife when he heard the commotion. He saw about half-a-dozen men pass the window and then realized a crowd was assembling within the precincts. Evans acted swiftly. Grabbing three swords, he handed one to taskmaster Boyse and another to William Stone, a turnkey; together the trio managed to clear the area inside the gates which they pushed shut. In the process, Evans received a gash on his head from a brick. There was uproar outside as the mob battered away and, despite sterling efforts by the prisoner officers to resist the pressure, the gate-bars snapped. Rioters poured in.

Evans and his staff retreated into the house, the front windows of which were soon smashed. With a blunderbuss, the governor halted the assailants for a while and tried reasoning with them. He was wasting his breath, as well as risking his life, and sledgehammers were raised against him. Instructing a gaoler to hand over the keys, Evans urged the mob to take only those prisoners brought in Saturday night and then to depart peaceably. The rioters would have none of it, however.

Amid the confusion, Evans's wife and servant girl, the taskmaster and Stone and his family escaped with the help of neighbours through a skylight in the governor's house and into a cooperage next door. Evans remained, but was unable to do more than watch from an upstairs window as the mob released all the prisoners. Flames issued from the chapel and other buildings, all of which were burned down (either then or later that day) with the exception of a few cells arched in stone. Two entrance gates were lifted from their hinges and hurled into the nearby River Frome. In due course, Evans was compelled to flee his own house, which was damaged and looted before being put to the torch.

Smoke and flame from the Bridewell rose into the damp atmosphere for hours. Not a restraining soldier or constable was to be seen. James Prowse, a surgeon, who joined the numerous onlookers, believed an armed civil force of 'twenty at most' could have overcome the mob who, when he was there, totalled 'perhaps sixty or seventy men and boys and women and girls'.

Exhilarated by their success, many rioters left the Bridewell and, accompanied by a large crowd, proceeded to the city gaol—the 'New Goal' as it was known—which stood solidly opposite the New Cut (an artificial channel for the Avon and an integral feature of the non-tidal dock system). The Rev Dr Lant Carpenter, a Unitarian minister, reckoned the mob to be some 'five or six hundred' strong as they marched down Clare Street on that 'wet and murky October afternoon' heading for the prison. 'All I noticed', he was later to comment, 'were the dregs of the city and a large part were under twenty years of age.'

At the Guildhall, the magistrates received news of the attack on the Bridewell but, without an effective constabulary and doubtless greatly stunned by Brereton's decision to send away

two-thirds of the cavalry, they came to no worthwhile conclusion. While they pondered, William Humphries (governor
of the New Goal) arrived to seek assistance. He was informed,
evidently, that 'you are to use your own discretion as to the
prison but, mind, the magistracy gives you no direction'. At least,
that is one version of what was said.

Undaunted by such apparent timidity, Humphries proved
to be quite persuasive. Supported by Aldermen Abraham Hilhouse and John Savage and about thirty other citizens, including several constables, he returned to the gaol. An astonishing
sight confronted them. The whole area was covered by a massive crowd, a thousand or more of whom milled around upon
a narrow strip of land situated between the prison and the
plunging New Cut. There was also a vast amount of noise.

As the governor and his group hove into view, they were
attacked with sticks and stones. A number was hurt, among
them attorney S. G. Little, who tottered away after being struck
in the back by a hammer. The would-be peace restorers
scampered for their lives, some taking temporary refuge in a
nearby hotel.

Rioters banged a hole in the gaol entrance gates, which were
flung open by two or three who had wriggled through the
jagged woodwork to pull back the weighty retaining bolts.
More than 300 people streamed inside and, having forced a
terrified turnkey to unlock the inner doors of iron, soon began
creating havoc. To the undisguised delight of the crowd, the
gaol caravan (a kind of 'black maria' for conveying prisoners
to and from court) was trundled outside the walls and upended
into the river's chasm.

All the 170 male and female prisoners were liberated, some
who divested themselves of convict clothes to avoid detection
looking equally conspicuous as they ran or walked to unexpected freedom 'almost in a state of nudity'. A few others
chose to join the mob in destruction. Recalling the scene
Samuel Selfe, an ironmonger, said that between 150 and 200
people, including 'a great many women and boys', were actively engaged in plunder and he saw a lot of beds and cooking
utensils carried away. Although there were 'many thousands'
of onlookers, he added, no resistance was offered.

A cry that 'the soldiers are coming' sent some rioters scurrying, but most remained unperturbed. A detachment of 3rd Dragoon Guards arrived at a jingling trot. Heading the 20 cavalrymen was Cornet Charles Kelson, a young man of only sixteen months' service, who had been told by his troop commander, Captain Warrington, to report to Brereton at College Green. Instructing the unit to proceed to the New Gaol, the colonel appeared unwilling to issue positive orders (because he could not find a magistrate, Kelson stated later) but stressed on no account was force to be used.

Kelson, who came across 'an immense mob', led his men to the front gateway from where he watched 'a great number of people inside the gaol knocking things to pieces'. After a few minutes, Kelson put the soldiers 'threes about' and took them back to College Green. According to the cornet, Brereton asked him if it was true the troops had shot four men at the prison and seemed much relieved when Kelson replied that they did 'nothing of the sort'.

During the brief inspection of the gaol, the dragoon guards were said to have waved their hats in friendly acknowledgement to cheers from the crowd. Whatever the truth about that, one thing is indisputable: the mob continued to pillage at will.

The chapel, treadmill and the governor's house were set on fire and other buildings wrecked. William Stratton, the taskmaster, had a good view. Although powerless to check the mob, he stayed discreetly within the walls and, peering through a spy-glass from an upper window, saw prisoners freed, wholesale destruction and the futile momentary appearance of the military. He calculated the crowd on the outside to be upwards of 10,000 and that, at one time, about 400 rioters were inside the gaol.

Before he departed, the surveying taskmaster probably noticed William Herapath and other council members of Bristol Political Union mingling with the mob and, in vain, exhorting them to stop. Rioters sat in a circle in the prison-yard brazenly discussing potential targets. Proposals included the Bishop's Palace, banks, shipping, the Mansion House, the Council House and, on a more personal level, the home of anti-reformer Thomas Daniel, who, besides being the city's most influential alderman and a wealthy merchant, was chairman of the powerful West India Company. He had a country house at Henbury, but it was his residence in Berkeley Square, Bristol, the mob had in mind. In the event, several toll houses— situated not far from the gaol—were the next places to be burned down.

Meanwhile the bemused magistrates, shocked by the miserably small attendance of citizens at the Guildhall that morning, had agreed to hold another public meeting at three o'clock. To that end, constables went to their respective parishes to drum-up support. The magistrates' pleas for help had also been made known to church congregations.

The Mayor, still in ceremonial clothes donned early the previous day, had not slept for some thirty hours and was prevailed upon by colleagues to rest. The fatigued Pinney finally consented to go to the *White Lion Inn*, Broad Street, where landlord Isaac Niblett had a room reserved. His Worship had barely time to shave, let alone sleep, before learning the Bridewell was under attack and he returned at once to the Guildhall. There was a rather better muster of citizens at that building during the afternoon, although at no time, it seems, were more than 200 gathered together.

Matters were not improved by the re-appearance of Lt-Col Brereton, who reported that the 14th Light Dragoons had left Bristol for Keynsham. He was told bluntly to bring them back or, at least, nearer the city, but he again explained that to do so would imperil their lives. The Town Clerk erupted: 'Good God, is this a soldier's reason? I didn't expect such an answer from an officer in the King's service.' Brereton countered crisply: 'Soldiers lives are not to be sacrificed unnecessarily more than any other.' The Town Clerk was angry: 'But they were sent down here by the Horse Guards and the Secretary of State to protect the city of Bristol and we have a right to demand that attention.' The colonel replied that while quite prepared to risk his own life if it would do any good, he wasn't jeopardizing those of men under his command.

This acerbic exchange filtered through to citizens chattering in the hall below and, for any doubters among them, confirmed that two-thirds of the military force had indeed been sent away. Not unnaturally, a number refused to act without adequate army backing unless an overwhelmingly strong civilian posse was properly organized instead.

The magistrates and Brereton proved quite incapable even now of co-operating to produce an effective plan. Micawber-like, they seemed to be waiting for something to turn up. The Mayor had earlier signed urgent requisitions to yeomanry corps in the neighbourhood and to regular army units farther afield calling for help, but there was no guarantee that any fresh troops would arrive on that Sunday. In any case, the crisis plainly demanded some immediate action.

Various abortive schemes were mooted. Samuel Waring, a prominent merchant and devout Quaker, even suggested burning an effigy of Sir Charles Wetherell to soothe the rioters! For a time there was some support for the proposal that a hundred resolute men, armed only with staves, could lick the mob, many of whom it was contended, were hopelessly drunk or but small boys. It came to nought.

According to several accounts, the meeting was both muddled and worthless; some people, disgusted at getting no reasonable response to their recommendations, left the Guild-hall for home. Commented Henry Bulgin, a well-known local bookseller: 'The magistrates gave no distinct or positive order. All was confusion. I heard much dissatisfaction expressed by those present at the conduct of the magistrates; there was every wish to assist them and many who attended were con-stables who had their staves.'

At about half-past four that afternoon, the magistrates did reach one decision—to adjourn to the Council House, which contained the city muniments and, perhaps more to the point, afforded better protection in case of attack by rioters. An ac-countant, Benjamin Holder Green, said that when the Mayor asked citizens, in effect, 'Well, gentlemen, shall we stay here or go to the Council House?' there was 'as complete a panic as I ever saw'. In Green's opinion, 'they broke out in terror, that the place itself would be besieged by the mob'. To be fair, his was the most sensational description of what happened; even so, it is unlikely there was merely a leisurely stroll from one building to the other.

Half-an-hour after transferring 'headquarters', the magis-trates were visited by William Herepath. He told them of the mob's threatened programme and, as a result, warnings went out to the banks (though just what their officials could have done without assistance will never be known). Herapath also outlined his plan for marooning rioters at the New Gaol by simply turning round the swing bridges, thus confining them to a sliver of land surrounded by water. The idea did not find favour, however, Alderman George Hilhouse fearing other rioters would gain revenge by setting fire to his own ships and the docks.

Asked if the union would help quell the disturbances, a faintly surprised Herapath replied that they had strongly disapproved of the military being summoned at all but, in the light of recent developments, believed he could get a worthwhile force to rally behind him. The thought of union members winning glory under their own leader did not commend itself very highly to the magistrates, however. They further hesitated and Herapath retired.

During the late afternoon and evening, groups of rioters converged on Gloucestershire County Prison at Lawford's Gate—more than a mile from the New Gaol. Again, they released all prisoners and set buildings alight. About 400 yards away Mrs John Mack, wife of the landlord of the *Hibernia Tavern*, West Street, stood at the back door watching the flames. While her husband visited friends in Ireland, she was being helped by her brother, William Field. A dozen young tearaways returning from the burning prison stopped outside the inn (which also served as a post-office) and, sensing trouble, Mrs Mack and Field locked the doors.

Within a few minutes, nearly a hundred people were jostling and yelling in front of the house. Some demanded whisky and, when refused, became extremely hostile. Armed with iron bars, several men burst inside and knocked both Field and his sister to the floor. The couple put up a tremendous struggle and, wresting a cudgel from one assailant, Field even drove the ringleaders back into the street.

For a time Field checked the mob with an unloaded gun but, when they realized it was empty, he again suffered a beating and Mrs Mack, struck on the head, staggered away to protect her youngsters, who were in bed. She could only find her month-old baby, however. Field and Mrs Mack eventually fled to a neighbour's house where, to their intense relief, the missing children were being cared for. The inn was ransacked: hardly

1. Sir Charles Wetherell, Recorder of Bristol

BRISTOL
SAILORS' MEETING.

AT A

Meeting of the Seamen,

HELD THIS DAY, ON BOARD THE

EARL OF LIVERPOOL,
CAPT. CLAXTON,

Who was the Self-Elected CHAIRMAN, and who brought the only Resolution to be proposed in his pocket, on reading of which some of the by-standers remonstrated with him on the impropriety of such proceedings, when Mr. Claxton thought proper to dissolve the Meeting; and, on further remonstrance, informed them, that the Ship where the Meeting was held belonged to him, and imperatively *ordered* every person to leave the deck. On the persons *who composed the Meeting*, reaching the Shore, a Temporary Hustings was immediately *erected, and* John Wesley Hall, Esq. *unanimously called to the Chair, when the following Resolution, moved* by Mr. J. G. POWELL, *and seconded by* Mr. WEBB, *was unanimously carried,*

That the Sailors of this Port on the present occasion earnestly express their decided and loyal attachment to His Majesty and His Government, but will not allow themselves to be made a cat's paw of by the Corporation, or their paid Agents.

J. W. HALL, Chairman.

Mr. J. W. HALL having vacated the Chair, it was immediately taken by Mr. J. G. POWELL, Jun. when a Vote of Thanks to the Chairman was carried with three times three Cheers.

Full Particulars of the Meeting will appear in the *BRISTOL LIBERAL* of Saturday next.

OCTOBER 18, 1831.

Philip Rose, Printer, Broadmead, Bristol

2. Poster reporting the sailors' meeting

Mansion House

BRISTOL, Oct. 30, 1831.

IT is with feelings of the deepest regret that the MAGISTRATES deem it their duty to call for the immediate aid and co-operation of their Fellow Citizens, to allay the great state of excitement, now disturbing the Peace of the Inhabitants.

The Delivery of the Gaol has been abandoned, and SIR CHARLES WETHERELL, the Recorder, left the City for London last night.

CHA^s*. PINNEY,*
Mayor.

(Mills and Son, Printers.)

3. A call to the citizenry

Council House
1st NOVEMBER, 1831.

THE MAGISTRATES
Give Notice that they have appointed the
EXCHANGE,
As a Receptacle for
Property saved from the FIRE,
and have directed the *Exchange Keeper* to take it.

N.B. All Persons after this Notice detaining Goods for which they cannot account, will be Guilty of Felony.

MILLS AND SON, PRINTERS, NICHOLAS STREET, BRISTOL.

The Inhabitants
OF
TEMPLE WARD,
are earnestly requested to remain within doors after SIX O'CLOCK this evening, as VIGOROUS MEASURES will be resorted to PRESERVE THE PEACE.
TEMPLE CHURCH,

WILLIAM GWYER.

October 31st 1831.

4. Two posters issued after the riots

5. Conflagration at Gloucestershire County Prison, Lawford's Gate

6. View of the widespread fires

7. A similar dramatic impression from Pile Hill

8. The fires at their height

a fixture remained intact, contents had been smashed or stolen, gas pipes severed and curtains charred.

Mrs Mack was able to identify three of the offenders, for they had been customers on previous occasions. That trio (Joseph Mills, William Spokes and Henry Hurd) were subsequently convicted at Gloucester Assizes of riotous assembly and also of breaking into the premises and causing damage estimated at £100. They were transported for life. Mr Justice Taunton referred glowingly to the bravery of Field and Mrs Mack, rewarding them with £10 apiece. Prosecuting counsel observed that with a hundred men of Field's calibre the Bristol riots would soon have been put down, to which the judge rejoined: 'Aye, twenty like him would have done it.'

Fire now swept three prisons and four toll houses. A small band of rioters, carrying metal bars and bludgeons, went to the lock-up shop for debtors in Tailors' Court, Broad Street, demanding the release of the inmates; Richard Ponting, a sheriffs' serjeant, had to comply, but at least he was unharmed and the tiny gaol undamaged. Other rioters revisited the Bridewell where they stoked up existing fires, started fresh outbreaks and committed more destruction.

Staying at Clifton during the riots was Isambard Kingdom Brunel, then the comparatively unknown son of a famous father and destined to emerge as arguably the finest engineer of the nineteenth century—immortally associated with Bristol. During that hectic Sunday young Brunel, engaged sometime that week-end as a special constable, went to the Mansion House, which he found almost deserted. The building had been broken into again and plundered. In his biography of the engineer, the late L. T. C. Rolt told how Brunel dashed inside and assisted by two friends, Alderman Hillhouse [*sic*] and a Mr Roch, managed to salvage pictures and plate which they then carried over the roof and into the Custom House. [The 'Mr Roch' was more than likely Nicholas Roch, a member of Bristol Common Council.]

Possibly a reporter of *The Bristol Gazette* unwittingly referred to Brunel when he wrote: 'The valuable paintings at the Mansion House would have been inevitably either torn to pieces or burned, but for the presence of mind of some gentleman; he suggested the impossibility of carrying them off in their present state and therefore proposed that they should be carefully disengaged from all the framework and folded in a roll; this was done and, in this shape, they passed for a bundle of old sailcloth.'

The seemingly ubiquitous Major Digby Mackworth marched into the Council House that Sunday evening. He found 'about 200 inhabitants were assembled and Alderman Savage employed in keeping their stormy debates in some kind of order. All were crying out "We are willing to act, but have no one to direct us" and all seemed ready to take the direction, but everyone differed from his neighbour and nothing was resolved on, as is usually the case in large deliberating bodies where all are speakers and no hearers. Some said, let us go home and each defend our own house; and others, more wisely, agreed to cause a *posse comitatus* to assemble under the new Act, but very few seemed willing to serve.'

The major said he offered to organize a posse himself if citizens would meet in College Green at six o'clock next morning. Response was only lukewarm, however. 'I here cannot but acknowledge with shame', Mackworth confessed, 'that disgust at the party spirit I had witnessed among the inhabitants of Bristol so overcame a sense of duty that I retired to rest, resolved to do nothing till the following morning.'

While the major went to rest and some of the arguing citizens left the Council House for their homes, rioters prepared to attack the Bishop's Palace—within a modest sledgehammer throw of the army alert post.

Chapter Five

BLAZING FALLS THE NIGHT

BY SUNDAY EVENING, rioters roamed the centre of Bristol virtually unopposed. Every public building became a potential target (perhaps on no more than a drunken whim), dissenting passers-by were in danger of being assaulted, shops the possible objects of plunder and liquor-houses the scenes of theft and threat. While many alarmed citizens shuttered windows and bolted doors, large numbers ventured from their homes to watch the spreading lawlessness. It was said the flickering reflection of fires could be seen from nearly fifty miles away.

William Jones was butler to the Bishop of Bristol. His master had been in residence for several weeks at the episcopal palace—situated next to the cathedral on the southern side of College Green—but was now out visiting a daughter convalescing at Almondsbury, some six miles from the city. At around eight o'clock, Jones heard the mob hammering loudly on the double gates of iron which sealed off the entrance to the cloisters and to the palace itself.

About a hundred men and boys soon stormed into the courtyard and a number began attacking the palace door with sledgehammers and crowbars. From the hallway, the butler looked on helplessly as splinters flew inwards from the heavy timber panels and then saw a rioter crawling through the serrated aperature before he escaped via a rear window and a high wall into Trinity Street. Showing considerable courage, Jones went back to the front of the palace; people were inside the building, a large group thronged the yard and for a time, unrecognized in the darkness, he mingled with them.

A small detachment of 3rd Dragoon Guards, headed by

Lt-Col Brereton and Cornet Kelson, arrived—yet apparently did nothing positive. According to Jones, his request for a few soldiers to dismount to help him clear the palace was flatly rejected by the colonel. Some constables, supported by a handful of other public-spirited citizens, nevertheless succeeded in thinning-out the mob and even made several arrests. Re-entering the palace, the butler found much damaged furniture and shattered porcelain and glass; he also discovered beds in four rooms alight, slashed mattresses having been filled with burning coals. These, he extinguished.

All was now fairly quiet, the mere presence of the military perhaps representing some kind of deterrent. Twenty minutes later, however, Jones heard shouts that the mob were returning in force. The reason suddenly became obvious. The soldiers had withdrawn, leaving the cathedral, palace and chapter-house completely unguarded. Jones was cornered in the kitchen by rioters but, after a brief struggle, he rushed upstairs, scrambled through a window and got away. Again, he ran round to the front door although, this time, nothing could be done to check the intruders. Even the constables, forcibly relieved of their captives, had melted away.

At the palace during the second attack was the Rev Robert Gray (Rector of Sunderland), namesake-nephew of the Bishop. In a letter to Lord Melbourne, he said that when the military retired 'I could see a considerable body of rioters re-assembling in the adjoining square. The constables, apparently dismayed by this procedure, for the most part quitted the palace and I was left in it with three or four of them and two of the manservants. The mob now returned in strength and, without difficulty, re-entered the premises ... and within a short space of twenty minutes the palace, with its valuable furniture, books, etc., was in flames.' The clergyman, who wrote on his uncle's behalf, continued : 'The City of Bristol is at present entirely in the possession of an organized banditti, of the very vilest and yet of a most dastardly description, prepared to disperse on the least show of resistance and re-assembling again with a readiness and vigilance which mark a designed and preconcerted plan of lawless depredation and for the dissolution of society.... Unless the most instant and vigorous exertions be made to concentrate a powerful military force in Bristol, the unbridled fury of the bands now commanding the city may be carried to any extent.'[1]

The Bishop's Palace was soon ablaze. Yellow flames leapt through windows and burst from the roof, while thick smoke and a myriad of sparks rose high into the sullen sky. Rioters broke into the chapter-house from which they threw documents and books to their cronies who, in turn, tossed the priceless records into the burning palace. Another fire, started nearby, was also fed with irreplaceable scrolls and papers. Cries of 'The King' and 'No Bishops' echoed against the crackling background. Hundreds of onlookers kept their distance.

Nevertheless, a few gallant souls did what they could. John Walker Newcomb, a local printer, and two others saved some valuable parchments from the chapter-house, despite being attacked. An attempt to break into the cathedral was thwarted by sixty-one-year-old William Phillips, the sub-sacrist, who bravely barred the way, and also the timely intervention of several other gentlemen (among them Benjamin Ralph, James Norton and solicitor James Livett), who, by 'entreaties and expostulations', somehow persuaded the vandals to 'desist from throwing brands into the church'. Within the cathedral precincts stood the house of Edward Hodges, doctor of music; it remained intact because his former clerk, Thomas Henry Crook, and brother John Crook held off rioters, and fireman John Lewis risked death to prevent flames extending from the palace.

Much of the bishop's property was stolen or wantonly destroyed and, even as the palace flared, the wine cellars were plundered and bottles offered for sale at a penny or twopence each. A library of about 6,000 volumes vanished, the books being burned, ripped apart, appropriated or dumped into the dark waters of the harbour. Destruction was committed quite overtly, the perpetrators lustily boasting to the crowd and among themselves; for their part, most spectators did nothing to hinder and even stepped back politely to make room for departing rioters loaded down with loot. By morning, the bishop's splendid residence had been reduced to a smouldering ruin.

Back a few hours in time to the magistrates who, throughout that Sunday afternoon and evening, had received reports of

[1]PRO HO 40/28.

fresh outrages. They continued to talk inconclusively and, not without justification, felt aggrieved at being let down so badly by the military and the vast majority of inhabitants. The aldermen and senior officers of the corporation were not themselves anxious unaided to confront the mob, who had already at least the tacit approval of hundreds of bystanders. High-priority requisitions for military aid had been whisked from the city by express messengers. James Bush, for instance, sped away in a chaise to cover the fifteen miles to Dodington Park to alert the commander of the local yeomanry cavalry troop and thence to Tetbury on a similar mission. Dispatches also included one to the Gloucester depot of the 14th Light Dragoons, whose comrades Brereton had banished to Keynsham, and another to Bath.

In an appeal to the commanding officer of troops at Cardiff, the Mayor stated that Bristol was in the 'greatest state of riot and tumult; the mob has proceeded to an extreme, the public buildings demolished, the gaols burnt and the prisoners released'. The officer in question was a forty-two-year-old battle 'veteran', Lt-Col James Frederick Love, who still bore scars of serious wounds earned at Waterloo. [On receipt early Monday morning of Pinney's urgent plea, Love moved with praiseworthy alacrity and, during the evening of the same day, was personally to lead a sizeable contingent of the 11th Regiment of Foot into Bristol.]

On that disastrous Sunday afternoon, while the mob played havoc with the prisons, Lt-Col Thomas Brereton also wrote a letter: his was addressed to Major-General Lord Fitzroy Somerset, at the Horse Guards, to be forwarded to Lord Hill.[1] In it, Brereton concurred with the magistrates' calls for additional troops: 'Allow me to say, in the present state of the city, a strong military force does appear to be highly necessary.' He seems not to have regarded this observation as incongruous in view of his reference earlier in the letter to the dismissed squadron of dragoons.

Brereton related to his superiors that 'the mob promised so earnestly to disperse to their home if the 14th were withdrawn, whom they were otherwise determined to massacre with the aid of the Kingswood men, that I suggested with the opinion

[1] PRO HO 40/28.

70

of General Pearson and some other officers that it would be prudent to remove the 14th to Brislington or Keynsham, to which the magistrates agreed, and I ordered them from hence accordingly'.

Was Brereton being deliberately misleading by giving the impression the magistrates had freely approved of his decision or, suspecting perhaps he might have erred, attempting to shift some burden from his own weary shoulders? Brereton further informed Fitzroy Somerset the mood of the mob had been 'so strongly excited' by infiltrating union representatives from Birmingham that 'I very much apprehend this night will not pass quietly—we have now only one troop of the 3rd Dragoon Guards and they have been under arms so many hours they cannot be considered in a very efficient state'. Such were the colonel's sentiments that afternoon.

Different eyes saw different things or, rather, the same things differently. While the magistrates blamed the army commander who, in turn, held them to blame for ineffectual direction, the few citizens prepared to act decisively tended to blame both. Some viewed the whole matter as one of paramount danger, while others reiterated that a small well-organized group of civilians could easily overcome the rioters. There was plenty of chatter, a plethora of proposals—but no worthwhile action.

As the London-bound mail-coach rumbled out of the city at 5.20, fires lit up the evening gloom and the guard reported that youths chased and stoned the vehicle. Next morning one of the passengers, a Mr Grenfell, wrote from 31 Upper Harley Street, to tell Lord Melbourne that the mob appeared 'neither formidable in numbers or organization' and was confident 'fifty of our London Police' would quickly have dealt with them.

On Sunday evening, the hallway and stairs of the Council House were filled with people impatiently awaiting an official lead. Some departed in disgust; others arrived in hope. The magistrates had agreed to acquaint the Home Secretary not only with the city's plight but also with the role being played (or underplayed) by the military. Apparently it was deemed politic to allow Brereton to see the text before dispatch and, at about six o'clock, two aldermen took the letter to the Army Recruiting Office.

Almost simultaneously, it seems, the Mayor (accompanied by several citizens) also arrived, his purpose being to advise Brereton of a story that the mob intended firing shipping and parts of quaysides. That could have been catastrophic, for such a blaze, fanned by even a slight breeze, might engulf whole sections of the city centre. There is no record of exactly what Brereton then said about the letter (which Daniel Burges, escorted by Sgt Samuel Dineage of the recruiting staff, delivered to the post-office), but he promptly ordered a sentinel to ascertain the mob's whereabouts. It was established rioters were not poised to attack ships, there being more likelihood of a move against the Bishop's Palace.

The Mayor and his party returned to the Council House. At around eight o'clock, Alderman Thomas Camplin entered with news that the Mansion House was burning and the Bishop's Palace destined for a similar fate. Camplin, a gentleman in his fifties and brother-in-law of Bishop Gray, had not long since risen from a sick-bed at his Stapleton home [just outside the city] and, during the riots, seems to have shown rather more initiative than did most of his aldermanic colleagues.

Camplin came out of the magistrates' room and, from the head of the stairs, outlined the latest situation to the assembled citizens. It was generally felt an effort be made to save the palace but, when Camplin called out 'Who will follow me?', the response was limited. Nevertheless about fifty men, including special constables, volunteered and the cry went up for the Mayor to go with them. Charles Pinney's appearance prompted loud cheering and, thus encouraged, the party set off but, on looking back, several saw His Worship retreating upstairs—an incident which gave rise to a widespread story that he had skulked to safety. It was later said he returned only for his hat and to get the Town Clerk to accompany him.

Shortly afterwards Pinney and Ludlow, with other inhabitants, also left the Council House for the palace. In the darkness Pinney went unnoticed by most people and, although that protected him from probable assault by rioters, his 'absence' helped to strengthen an allegation of cowardice on his part. Meanwhile the Camplin brigade had marched down Clare Street and across the drawbridge, but it was evident when they reached College Green their number had somewhat diminished.

The arrival at the Bishop's Palace of the groups, led respectively by Camplin and the Mayor, coincided with the point at which the mob's first attack on the building (described earlier) was being foiled. Believing the danger over, it was said the Mayor and the Town Clerk retired to Brereton's rooms at the adjacent recruiting office, from a bow window of which they watched events. Some rioters were seen running away while, nearby, a unit of dragoon guards appeared to have encircled a batch of prisoners. For the moment, relative order prevailed.

Lt-Col Brereton was there; so was Cornet Kelson, but his own troop commander, Captain Warrington, was then absent from quarters without leave. That unfortunate officer, had he but known, was digging the grave of his military career. Perplexed by circumstances—not least, perhaps, by the colonel's reluctance to employ harsher measures and by the lack of precise directions from the magistrates—Warrington had set off on foot in the rain for Clifton. He rapped on the door of Prospect Cottage, Somerset Place, the home of Major-General Pearson.

Warrington, no stranger to riot operations, had shown zeal less than a year previously in Hampshire during agricultural disturbances; he was used to having a magistrate present when his troop went into action, however. Now he wanted Pearson's advice on whether or not such procedure was required by law. Warrington really ought to have known, for relevant guidance formed part of Army Regulations. [Broadly, it was advisable to be accompanied by a magistrate but by no means essential. Indeed, it became incumbent upon every civilian and soldier to do everything possible to suppress any breach of the peace. Obviously there were borderline cases but, by no stretch of the imagination, could the current crisis be deemed one of them.]

Whatever the general said must have been succinct, for within five minutes of entering the cottage Warrington was walking back through steady drizzle towards Bristol. He had told Kelson of his proposed mission and left instructions for a messenger immediately to be sent for him if the troop were called out. Trooper Martin Dooley did just that, but it appears he went first to the wrong address and when eventually he located Prospect Cottage his captain had departed. Warrington undoubtedly courted serious repercussions by being away at such a crucial time and, on reflection, possibly asked himself if he would not have done better sending his junior officer or even an NCO, with a suitable note, to see General Pearson. Maybe he wondered if the journey was really necessary at all. Or was there more to it than that?

Captain Warrington reached his quarters at the Reeves Hotel [in College Place] at nine o'clock. He did not seek his troop, however, and when Kelson returned an hour later he found the captain partly undressed and apparently preparing to retire to bed!

At the Bishop's Palace meanwhile the Mayor, Alderman Camplin and the Town Clerk, in common with many others, had suffered a severe shock. When it looked as if peace might be restored, the soldiers left and there echoed frantic shouts of 'The mob's coming back' and 'Run for it'. Pinney and Ludlow smartly vacated the recruiting office and, in the dark confusion outside, became separated. Camplin was pelted with stones by rioters and forced to shelter in a nearby house, where he remained until half-past two the following morning.

Charles Pinney stumbled around for a time, undecided on the best route back to the Council House; by now, streets were swarming with shadowy hurrying figures and it was impossible to distinguish with certainty between the innocent and the trouble-makers. Fiery shimmers made patterns in the mizzle-laden sky, the most spectacular glare rising from Queen Square where the Mayor's official residence was ablaze. To that was now added the Bishop's Palace, which burst into flame with startling suddenness.

Unrest around the Mansion House had intensified during the day and, when the light faded, the growing mob overran the building. Dragoon guards did little, if anything, to stem the rioters, who again entered the wine cellars and drank, destroyed or sold the remaining bottles. When the military picket were summoned to the Bishop's Palace, more of the populace invaded the Mansion House—to smash and filch and, with a final flourish, to set the place alight. Soon afterwards, all soldiers left the area.

So the entire troop of 3rd Dragoon Guards, the only military force in Bristol, went back to quarters—less than 200 yards from the palace inferno. Of course, the resources of that tiny contingent were drastically overstretched anyway but, with the hesitant approach to the situation by both Brereton and the magistrates, their task became nigh-on impossible.

Rioters began to extend operations and rumours abounded. John Gardiner, the Bristol postmaster, received a tip-off that the mob intended demolishing the post-office. He deftly bundled up all letters destined for or via London, ordered a chaise and drove to Bath, where he handed them to the guard of a mail-coach departing for the nation's capital. In a message to Sir Francis Freeling, Secretary of the General Post Office, the enterprising Mr Gardiner hoped his action 'will meet your approbation'. Mail from Bristol to other parts of the country, he assured Freeling, also 'got off very well'. As it happened, the post-office was not attacked.

Having escaped from the recruiting office, the Mayor paused in College Green. He felt tired, hungry and shaken. In such a demoralized state, therefore, it was a relief to see a friendly face in the person of Henry Daniel, a local surgeon. The doctor warned Pinney against chancing a return to the Council House and advised, alternatively, they both went to Daniel's own home at Clifton. The Mayor declined, saying it was necessary for him to stay in the city, and thought it likely Sheriff Joseph Lax would allow him temporary accommodation. The two men went to the sheriff's house in Park Street, a thoroughfare rising steeply from College Green, only to be told by a servant that Lax and his family had left town.

After further attempts to find suitable lodging, the Mayor and Dr Daniel walked to 30 Berkeley Square, the home of Daniel Fripp—brother of Alderman William Fripp. It was getting on for eleven o'clock. Daniel Fripp took Pinney inside (where Alderman Fripp had been ensconced for two hours) and led him upstairs. The Mayor started writing a letter, stated just where he could be contacted, when Daniel Fripp intimated that his wife was extremely nervous about having His Worship as a guest. Mrs Fripp, it seems, was partly reassured—probably on the understanding that knowledge of Pinney's location would be restricted. Indeed, his exact whereabouts was then unknown to all but a few, which helped give currency to accusations that he had fled the city.

Whatever shortcomings Mayor Pinney may have been guilty of that night, at least he remained in Bristol.

Chapter Six

COMINGS AND GOINGS

JUST AFTER half-past nine that Sunday night, a fifty-seven-strong troop of the Dodington and Marshfield Yeomanry Cavalry entered the riot-torn city. At their head rode Captain Christopher William Codrington, the twenty-six-year-old son and heir of Sir Christopher Bethell Codrington and a nephew of Admiral Sir Edward Codrington (1770–1851), commander of the victorious fleet at the Battle of Navarino on 20 October 1827.

Captain Codrington would later engage in the political arena with a long spell of service as MP for East Gloucestershire (from 1834 until his death in June 1864) but, for the moment, he probably anticipated the cut-and-thrust of a different kind.

His troop, founded only ten months earlier, had experienced no real action. On getting Pinney's requisition at half-past two that afternoon, Codrington summoned the yeomanry (no easy task at short notice as members lived throughout the neighbourhood) and, to his credit, an almost full muster left for Bristol at seven o'clock.

It was a dark journey but, as the contingent neared the city, they were spotted by James Bush who, having delivered the Mayor's dispatch to Codrington at Dodington Park and since been to Tetbury, was returning home. On reaching Bristol, he searched in vain for someone in authority to give news of the approaching unit. Not until two hours later did the persistent Bush track down a couple of magistrates—by which time an unfortunate crop of complications and misunderstandings had arisen.

When they jogged into Bristol, the part-time soldiers must

have been somewhat overawed for, as Codrington himself subsequently wrote, it was 'on fire in many places, the gaols
emptied and the town in the greatest confusion'. Apparently
unhindered, and certainly doing nothing to hinder, the yeomanry trotted about the streets for the best part of an hour and
called at the Council House and the Guildhall; they were also
unable to make contact with a magistrate and doubtless
assumed (for a time, at least) that the city fathers had sent away
all troops and constables before themselves quitting the region.
In view of what they saw (and, equally, did not see), it was
a very understandable error.

At the Council House eventually, Codrington received notifi-
cation emanating from the City Chamberlain to report to Lt-
Col Brereton at College Green—presumably the first indication
the young captain had of any other military personnel in the
area. At about this time the troop was seen by John Cossens
(chief constable, Castle Precincts Ward), who, according
to him, asked for a few of the soldiers to help disperse some
roughs who had broken into a gin shop. He said Codrington
explained that his troops could not act until he had heard the
Riot Act read and, in any case, they were already on their way
for orders.

When the yeomanry got to the Recruiting Office—it must
have been towards eleven o'clock—Brereton was not there.
Some minutes later he arrived on foot, having been 'patrolling
the streets', and the captain asked him if a magistrate was avail-
able. Brereton replied there was not, nor did he know where
to find one. Precisely what happened then remains obscure. It
appears that after calling at two houses in Park Street in an
abortive search for a magistrate Brereton, accompanied by
Codrington, returned to College Green and the waiting troop
not far from the blazing Bishop's Palace. Codrington pointed
out that his own lieutenant was a magistrate for the County
of Gloucester who could remove his red tunic and read the Riot
Act, to which suggestion Brereton demurred: 'Oh no, that
won't do.' Again according to Codrington, his proposal that
Brereton take them to Queen Square (where most of the mob
and watching crowd were now concentrating) was also turned
down by the colonel, who bade the troop repair for the time
being to Fisher's Repository.

77

Brereton later contended that he went with the yeomanry to the stables and intended to issue further orders after finding a magistrate, but Codrington 'held a short conversation with his officer and marched directly from Bristol'. However the captain claimed there was insufficient room at Fisher's for his unit and, doubtless angered by the all-round lack of proper direction and liaison, immediately departed protesting: 'This is too bad; I will not be humbugged in this manner any longer.'

What an extraordinary situation: nearly sixty armed cavalry-men quietly clopping about the streets for some two hours and, despite the chaos around them, never called into action. All for the want of a magistrate, it seems.

The very next day, Codrington wrote to no less a personage than Lord Melbourne. He told him the yeomanry had been fully prepared to act, but 'having paraded through the principal parts of the city for more than two hours without being able to find a Magistrate, hearing that they had in fact left the town after withdrawing both His Majesty's troops and the police—finding ourselves thus unsupported, and without a hope of being in any way serviceable, the city being actually in the uncontrolled power of the populace, I had no alternative but that of withdrawing also my men, and we returned home at about five o'clock this morning'. [Before doing so, the troop had apparently waited in vain for about two hours at Downend, just outside Bristol, for some communication from the authori-ties. It would seem, however, that no-one else even knew they were there.] It is significant, perhaps, that Codrington made no mention of Brereton at this stage.

At about noon the same day, Codrington received a letter from the Mayor. In it, Pinney politely informed the captain that the magistrates 'deeply regret that their absence from the Council House last night, in the performance of an arduous duty, in heading a body of their fellow-citizens to a distant part of the city, should have deprived them of the pleasure of seeing you on your arrival and thanking you for the prompt attention to their request in bringing your troop to Bristol. As soon as the magistrates returned from the duty alluded to, a deputation immediately repaired to Colonel Brereton to make the neces-sary arrangements for the accommodation of your troops and billets, signed by the Mayor, were made out and sent to Colonel Brereton in the expectation that you would immediately have received them.' Pinney went on to assure Codrington that 'no disrespect was intended to you; on the contrary, the magistrates duly appreciate your kind intentions and they hope they may yet have the benefit of your valuable services. If you should determine to come again to Bristol, they beg to suggest your sending on a serjeant, or other non-commissioned officer, to apprise them, in order that billets may be ready on your arrival.'

The Mayor later put out a statement (published in the Press and, in effect, replying on behalf of the magistrates to Codrington's letter to Melbourne which had been reproduced in newspapers). Pinney pointed out that Codrington's troop arrived in Bristol not long after the firing of the Bishop's Palace where some of the magistrates had gone from the Council House and had as a result 'been separated by the rush of the mob'. Even so, he said, a messenger went to the Council House to announce the yeomanry's approach and a magistrate at once began making arrangements for billets (later delivered to Brereton's office in College Green). Meanwhile, he added, Codrington and his men had gone to Fisher's with Brereton in whose presence accommodation was offered, but 'whilst the lights were being placed in the stables, they went away and left the city'.

Codrington himself maintained that his troop could not discover a magistrate but when, after equally unsuccessful attempts, a messenger duly returned to the Council House 'he did find a magistrate who, although thus prepared for our speedy arrival, appears to have taken no measures for our accommodation, or enable us to act'.

In this account, which took the form of a letter to *The Bristol Mirror*, the captain agreed that Brereton took the troop to Fisher's but 'the gas pipes having been cut, and the people being consequently in a state of confusion, we were told we could have no accommodation; and having paraded through the same streets till we again arrived at the Council House, and still no magistrate appearing, we retired as before stated to a place called Downend, about four miles from the city'. Codrington ended on a high note, revealing that he possessed a personal letter from the Mayor who (said the captain) regretted 'the absence of the magistrates at the time of our arrival and showing that up to the date of our leaving the city, they neither had returned to the Council House nor made any preparations for our reception'. [This, presumably, was the one he received at noon on 31 October and referred to above.]

Of course, these conflicting views and developments (and others) did not emerge for general consumption until after the riots, although it is convenient to mention them here—out of chronological context—if only to indicate the kind of disorder and lack of official co-ordination that evidently existed. The fact that the civil and military authorities had not set up a joint operational headquarters added to the muddle, particularly during that crucial night. Brereton seems to have been confused by the whole affair, Pinney had taken temporary refuge in Berkeley Square and some of the other magistrates and corporation officials were apparently darting hither and thither to no obvious constructive purpose or cohesive plan.

Be that as it may. Not long after the Dodington troop left the city, Brereton entered No. 2 Unity Street [the lodgings of his adjutant, Lt George Francis, about 200 yards from the Recruiting Office and where he stayed during the crisis] and —went to bed. The colonel explained later that it became 'impossible in the absence of any magistrate or indeed the smallest appearance of a civil force, to be of any service with the then few exhausted troops I had . . .'[1]

Another volunteer contingent would have reached Bristol that night but for a disturbance—at Bath. Captain Charles Wilkins, a millowner, who was commander of the city's troop of North Somerset Yeomanry Cavalry, had donned regimentals and ridden from his Twerton home into the centre of Bath at seven o'clock in the evening to mobilize his unit. Recognized by some 'loose characters', he was followed to the *White Hart Inn* and there threatened with violence if he attempted to lead his men to Bristol. The captain told the mob that although a reformer himself it became his duty as a soldier to help suppress riots and, evading dirt and stones, backed into the hostelry and behind bolted doors.

Rocks were hurled at windows, heavy sticks used to break

[1] PRO HO 52/12.

shutters and the mob roared their intention of wrecking the entire building. Some ruffians got into the coffee-room and destroyed furniture before being ejected by hotel staff, aided by a few constables who had rushed to the scene. Wisely taking advantage of the melee, and 'disguised' in civilian clothes, Captain Wilkins made good his escape.

News of his departure did nothing to pacify the attackers who, now totalling nearly 300, marched to the Town Hall and smashed windows. After several pitched battles, reinforcements of special constables restored order just short of midnight. Because of the fracas, however, the Bath yeomanry did not get to Bristol until the following day.

A small detachment of the Bedminster Troop, North Somerset Yeomanry Cavalry, commanded by Captain Henry Shute, were reportedly armed and waiting in Bristol for much of that Sunday—but never called upon. Stationing himself and his men at a riding school in Portwall Lane [between Temple Street and Redcliffe Street], Shute apparently sent a note at about noon to the magistrates to advise them of his unit's position—and then awaited orders. According to him, none came. The soldiers went home.

So, for various reasons, there were no organized military or civil operations that night and the rioters capitalized to calamitous effect.

Meanwhile the Mayor, secure in the haven of Daniel Fripp's house, spent his second successive night without sleep. Shortly before midnight, Pinney was visited by William Brice (on behalf of Alderman George Hilhouse, now back at the Council House) and asked to sign some billets sanctioning accommodation for the Dodington troop. This he did. Then Ebenezer Ludlow and Daniel Burges turned up—obviously the Mayor's whereabouts were not entirely secret—and, after chatting for a while, took their leave. The Town Clerk, understandably anxious about his own family, then went home to Durdham Down, Clifton, returning to the city at about 9.30 the next morning.

Charles Pinney sent two vital notes to Brereton but, by the time the colonel could have received either or both (they were delivered first to the Recruiting Office and thence taken by an NCO to Unity Street), Codrington and his troop had already vacated Bristol. This helps partly to clarify contradictions which arose afterwards. The messages read:

The Mayor of Bristol desires Colonel Brereton to consider himself fully authorized to take whatever steps and give whatever orders he, as the military commander of the troops in this city, may think fit to restore and preserve, as far as possible, the public peace. The Riot Act has been read three times to-day. Colonel Brereton will have the goodness to consider this order to apply not only to the troops at present under his command, but to any which may subsequently arrive in the city.

Mr Daniel Fripp's, No 30 Berkeley Square,
Sunday Night, 12 o'clock, 30 October, 1831.

The Mayor of Bristol begs to inform Colonel Brereton that if he should have occasion for the orders of a magistrate, either the Mayor or some other magistrate will be found at No 30 Berkeley Square, Mr Daniel Fripp's, the second house on the right-hand on turning into the Square from Park Street.

Berkeley Square,
12 o'clock, Sunday night.

In view of the first communication, the second would seem almost unnecessary, but it resulted apparently because a 'Lieutenant Macclesfield' had called at the Council House asking for a magistrate. Presumably the notes were dispatched together (one complementing the other); the time on each is identical. Whatever the case, Brereton was later accused of ignoring them and retiring to bed while 'the whole of Bristol might be said to be illuminated by the conflagrations which were vomiting forth uncontrolled in different quarters of the city'.

Captain Warrington might also have been in bed at that time had he not been compelled to raise the troop of 3rd Dragoon Guards at about eleven o'clock to deal with some young rowdies who began stoning the Reeves Hotel. The throwers were driven off but, in case of further attack (though none came), the captain stayed at the head of his men. It was then that Thomas Kington, a merchant, applied to him for military assistance in Queen Square, where a number of buildings already blazed. Warrington said he would happily oblige, but could not move without directions from Brereton whose whereabouts he did not know.

Charles Pinney did know where his wife was and had written to her that evening: 'I am perfectly safe and believe me I will not put myself in any danger, but I think it is uncertain whether I can return to-night'.[1] The Mayor, who sat up with Alderman Fripp awaiting some reaction to those two midnight dispatches to Brereton, passed a few minutes penning another letter to the Mayoress:

To Mrs Charles Pinney,
Clifton Hotel, Mall
My dearest Love—Keep yourself as calm as possible, and if there is the slightest anxiety in your mind you had better go to Mrs Olive's, for the mob will not attack a private ladies, and keep yourself as quietly as possible and the servants had better not say where you are or where I am. I will not place myself in danger—Pray for Divine aid to help and preserve us in this trying occasion, and enable us to do our duty—God bless you my dearest love.—Yours ever Affect., Charles.
30, Berkeley Square,
Monday morn 2 o'clock[1]

Frances Pinney and her mother were later asked to leave by the hotel proprietor because other guests became nervous about having them there during the crisis. The two women moved from the Mall to Rodney Place, about a furlong away, to stay with a Mrs Olive.

The Mayor, whose direct links with the outside were surely only tenuous, did something positive at three o'clock on Monday morning when, at Alderman Fripp's dictation, he wrote a further note to Brereton. Even this decision was prompted by the unheralded arrival of Samuel Oviatt Goldney, a surgeon by profession, and Wintour Harris. They had come from Queen Square and, like a fast-growing proportion of citizens, were now heartily sick of the whole ghastly business. Searching for a magistrate, they knocked at 30 Berkeley Square and asked Daniel Fripp, who cautiously poked his head from a bedroom window, if he knew where one might be found. Fripp disappeared for a while before opening the front door and saying that the Mayor was within. He then went upstairs. Returning to the hall a few minutes later, Fripp handed over a letter and

---

[1] Pinney Papers.

commented: 'This is what you want.' As the two men departed, he added: 'Don't say where the Mayor is.'

Goldney and Harris went directly to Leigh's Horse Bazaar and saw Captain Warrington. He seemed reluctant to open a communication intended for his senior, but was eventually persuaded to do so. It stated:

31st Oct, 1831
Bristol, 3 o'clock, Monday Morning
Sir: I direct you, as commanding officer of His Majesty's troops, to take the most vigorous, effective and decisive means in your power to quell the existing riot and prevent further destruction of property.

To Col Brereton, or the Commanding   CHARLES PINNEY
Officer of His Majesty's Troops.
Per MR GOLDNEY
   MR W. HARRIS, Jun.

Warrington, once more expressing a wish to co-operate, recited his now familiar piece about having a magistrate present although, this time, he held the requisite written authority right there in his hand. He was nevertheless against acting without permission from Brereton whom, he now revealed, he didn't expect to see again until six o'clock. Despite towering tongues of flame and cascading sparks which illuminated the stricken city, Warrington took no steps to contact the colonel or to initiate any action himself. Goldney and Harris felt unable to help; they said they had no idea where to get hold of a magistrate (other than the Mayor whose location they were urged to keep secret).

Warrington, who voiced his regret at the departure of the Dodington yeomanry as well as the sending from Bristol of the 14th Light Dragoons, complained of the lack of specific instructions and also referred to the tiredness of his men and horses. 'There's a great screw loose somewhere,' he concluded. When Goldney and Harris left, the captain made no move other than to stuff the vital letter into his pocket.

An hour later Alderman Camplin, accompanied by three other citizens, sought out Warrington, explained he was a magistrate and exhorted him to take his troop immediately to Queen Square. Warrington faltered, but agreed to send some men as there was now a magistrate to proceed with them. 'Don't talk of sending,' bristled Camplin, 'but go yourself—a man of your experience.' The cornered captain hedged yet again; the soldiers really ought not to turn out without Brereton's knowledge and, anyway, he doubted if they were strong enough to have much effect on the rioters.

After further exchanges Camplin and Warrington, joined by a few others, walked the 200 yards to No. 2 Unity Street where they roused Lt-Col Brereton. He had proved none too difficult to trace after all although, reportedly, a couple of women leaned from a bedroom window and denied he was in the house. The colonel shortly appeared, but seemed loth to call out the troops. Alderman Camplin insisted, however.

So, at five o'clock that Monday morning, Brereton himself headed a detachment of just twenty-one dragoon guards [Cornet Kelson second-in-command] and, with Thomas Camplin and a group of plucky followers, entered the holocaust of Queen Square. Captain Warrington, with time to ponder on his part in the night's events, remained in quarters with a reserve of eleven men . . .

Chapter Seven

THE HORROR OF QUEEN SQUARE

THROUGHOUT THAT long unguarded night, Queen Square had been the focal point of fire-raising. Rioters ranged free on a rampage of wrecking and intimidation; homes and businesses were looted and burned, protesting occupants threatened and, in several instances, assaulted. Some perpetrators perished in the inferno of their own creation, while more than a few drank themselves stupid. The Attorney-General (Sir Thomas Denman) was to declare that offenders reduced 'to a mass of shapeless ruins what had recently been the abodes of comfort, respectability and hospitality'.

Trouble and the crowd had increased as darkness descended on that damp Sunday evening. As dragoon guards patrolled in front of the Mansion House, people burst in at the back and made for the wine cellars. Intruders broke bottles at the neck and drank copiously, heedless of the scarlet mixture of blood and liquor which flowed from lacerated mouths. Others went to upper rooms, struggling to snatch the best bargains or hurling out furniture to splinter on the ground below.

The well-stocked larders were raided: one man emerged with a side of bacon slung over his shoulder and a big piece of pork tucked under his arm; a small boy safely wedged a joint of beef high in the branches of a tree before returning for more booty.

The soldiers left and, as word spread of easy pickings, empty carts and trucks from far afield began to arrive. The hard core of rioters looked more intent on destruction than theft, however, and lighted faggots flared inside the Georgian building which had been the official residence of the city's mayors for more than half a century. Within minutes, flames spurted through the roof.

The Bristol Gazette said: 'Not a fire engine was present, nor do we hear that any made the attempt. The firemen of the different companies alone, armed with their fire-hatchets would have been more than sufficient to have routed the mob at this or any subsequent time during the evening. But every class seemed to be seized with the same apathy; not the slightest protection to property or molestation to the spoiler was offered . . .'

Queen Square was gripped by a kind of evil revelry. Occasionally, it seems, someone remembered to shout 'Reform and the King' as if that alone justified the commission of unlimited depredation. The nightmare scene of the mob at the Mansion House was described by *The Bristol Mercury*:

The infatuated creatures, no less intoxicated with their successful career than with liquor, pressed forward to the windows and waved their handkerchiefs, cheering at the same time, in exultation of the final accomplishment on that ill-fated building. We are almost certain, however, that many of them paid the forfeit of their lives for their criminal temerity. From the rapidity of the progress of the flames, it is supposed that some were cut-off from a retreat and that they thus met with an untimely end. The fire spread with most surprising quickness and, within about twenty minutes, the roof fell in and, together with the whole front, came down into the street with a tremendous crash.

The Custom House, a few doors away, was ransacked and set on fire, resulting in some deaths. Flames swept in upon a party of rioters having a meal in the second-floor kitchen; several panicked and (it was reported) leapt to scorching graves, while others escaped by sliding down structural pillars. There was, too, the tale of a madcap quartet who overstretched their luck by remaining on the portico of the building until the protective lead covering became 'actually in a molten state in which, being fixed, they were seen writhing in the agonies of death'. The Excise Office, at the north-western corner of Queen Square, was also burned down.

So far attacks had been restricted to official property, but when the mob switched their attention to private homes the watching crowd became far less enchanted. The first houses threatened included that of Captain Henry T. Parfitt, but here the attempt was foiled; although Parfitt was away at sea, his wife and family and their home were protected by a man named

Cooke [believed to be a member of Bristol Political Union] and two friends, Jones and White. After windows had been broken, the trio called on the attackers to stop and pointed out forcefully that they could pay with their lives for such outrages. Despite another volley of stones, Cooke and his colleagues refused to be daunted and the mob moved on.

A vast crowd, many of whom appeared respectable and well dressed, continued to stand and stare. Dwellings were often stripped of contents before being fired, furniture being piled in the open like a high-class jumble sale. Some rioters set up shop. For a table worth seven guineas, a mere sixpence was asked; bottles of superb wines sold at a penny a time and good blankets for tuppence a pair. When one man failed to sell an elegant mahogany chair for a florin, he dashed the article to pieces. Another instant vendor proved equally unsuccessful in disposing of a silver teapot and tray for fourpence, while the modest flat rate of a shilling was introduced by a rival selling feather mattresses and polished tables. Not surprisingly, there were few buyers. It was just as easy to pick up valuable items for nothing. Groups of rioters, guzzling wine and munching food, squatted on the littered grass or sat more comfortably on stolen chairs at stolen tables.

Each house to be demolished provided fresh drama. Sometimes the mob gave arrogant warning of their intention to return in, say, twenty minutes to burn the place, thus allowing occupants time to quit. Served with one such peremptory notice William Cross, a wholesale stationer, shepherded his family to safety and went back to retrieve some belongings. As he handed a chimney glass to a friend, a rioter smashed it to smithereens. Cross was so enraged that he bodily hurled the vandal through a window. A newspaper reporter commented: 'It is only to be regretted that the circumstances did not occur at a sufficient elevation to ensure the destruction of the villain.' [Cross's servant, Martha Davis, who tried bravely to dissuade the mob, was knocked senseless and at a subsequent court hearing awarded £10 'in consequence of the great courage and intrepidity displayed by her in defending her master's property'.]

Some rioters went on an alarming pub-crawl and induced innkeepers to give them gallons of ale and bottles of spirits. To refuse was often to invite disaster, although several landlords

88

and late-night customers did eject small bands of toughs. No such luck for William Holder, publican of the *White Horse Inn*, Horse Fair, who, according to *The Bath Chronicle*, was made to 'get up in the middle of the night and serve three hundred men with beer. They allowed him only three minutes to dress himself and threatened to burn his house down if he did not comply.' He complied.

James Coleman, a prisoner freed by the mob from the New Gaol, raised some buddies and visited the Maryport Street home of his former employer, Thomas Blethyn, a woollen draper. Coleman demanded £4 which, he contended, was owed him in wages. His mates promised to fire the house if the money wasn't forthcoming, although Coleman apparently urged them not to harm the man, who had been a good master. Blethyn, who strove to deter them with offers of beer, finally parted with the cash. Ironically, when later arrested in Ireland, Coleman complained he had been 'short-changed'.

By the small hours of Monday morning, flames engulfed most of the north and west sides of Queen Square. Buildings in adjoining streets were also burning. James Room, an accountant and a churchwarden of St Stephen's parish, who lived at 61 Queen Square, reputedly possessed one of the finest private libraries in Bristol; about 1,700 volumes became charred flimsy. A gold watch and money were among the personal effects of the Rev Charles Buck stolen from St Stephen's Rectory before that place was also ablaze.

Fire neared the house in which Madame Marie Tussaud and her family were staying. Although they walked unscathed into surrounding scenes of fearful illumination and crashing masonry, their overriding concern was for the safety of precious wax figures currently on exhibition at the Assembly Rooms, Princes Street. The most-prized effigies were removed beyond the range of radiated heat but, in the event, the hall remained unharmed—rather more than could be said for the Madame's constitution.

Also in Princes Street, the warehouse of Bickley and Company went up in smoke (as did the house in Queen Square of the unfortunate owner, Benjamin Bickley, a member of Bristol's Common Council) yet, amazingly, wooden casks in the cellars containing fifty tons of seal oil did not ignite. A large stock of cocoa owned by the well-known firm of Joseph S. Fry was ruined [the company being awarded the biggest 'riot compensation paid to a private claimant of £2,400, although they had sought £6,900].

A river of flaming rum gushed from James Johnson's warehouse in King Street; it seemed likely a row of dwellings, isolated by this sizzling 'hedge of fire', would be enveloped and housewives appeared in the doorways screaming for help. Several even dashed through the blaze to emerge like human beacons, but were saved from serious injury by some merchant seamen who smothered the women's clothing. The rum continued to flare brilliantly for over an hour, volunteer firefighters preventing any spread to adjacent property by keeping walls of the blistering end-house liberally douched with water. That 'truly generous and disinterested devotion to danger' by the sailors and others, said *The Bristol Gazette*, helped a little to offset the 'brutal and barbarous character evinced at almost every part of the unhappy scene that night'.

Among those ready to defend their livelihood were employees at a sugar refinery run by the Guppy family. Not only had the men duly armed themselves with staves, but gallons of water were kept on the boil to give a scalding reception to any approaching rioter. None came. Thomas Richard Guppy, an engineer and a man of many parts, became a business associate and loyal friend of Brunel. Then thirty-three, Guppy was to be involved in a number of memorable projects, including the Great Western Railway and those renowned ships, *Great Western* and *Great Britain*.

At the Theatre Royal, in King Street, the Ducrow company of players also prepared to deal sharply with unwelcome visitors, but there was no attack—further indication, perhaps, that the mob gave a wide berth to even a small display of resistance. Unexpected resistance of a different sort confronted Samuel Waring, thirty-six-year-old merchant, whose business premises were ravaged by fire. With generous assistance, he rescued barrels of Irish porter (his main stock in trade) and also broke into a nearby warehouse to save liquor belonging to others. Kegs of brandy, rum and beer were rolled to a point outside the public library in King Street, but the proprietor of a neighbouring firm refused permission for them to be stacked temporarily in his yard. Entreated to show a little fellow feeling, he replied there was already 'too much public spirit and liberality for me'—a reference to the fact that Waring and his friends were 'popular supporters of the people's rights'. When told the gates would be forced anyway, the reluctant owner unbolted them and was galvanized into active co-operation when he discovered part of the salvaged stock belonged to Sheriff Joseph Lax—his own brother-in-law!

Contrary to later assertions, the rioting appears to have followed no preconceived plan. The mob were systematic (probably more by accident or convenience than by design) in that they restricted the worst of their activities in Queen Square to only two sides, although undoubtedly they would have tackled a third (and most likely the fourth as well) but for the eventual intervention of the military. No single property, it seems, was disregarded for any specific reason.

Whatever recognizable and understandable motives there may have been for the earlier demonstration against Sir Charles Wetherell, the destruction of half of Queen Square resulted almost certainly from the indiscriminately dangerous work of an uncontrolled mob. Sightseers and petty crooks, who treked away with barrowloads of loot, added to the chaotic horror of the night which roared with fire and echoed to excited yells and crashes. Fiery reflections could be seen in Frome, Newport and Cardiff.

Estimates of the crowd in the square went as high as 20,000. According to Latimer's *Annals*: 'Almost the entire population was afoot and, in spite of a continuous drizzling rain, every eminence dominating the burning Square was crowded with a terror-stricken multitude of all ages.'

Charles Kingsley, then a twelve-year-old pupil at a boarding school on St Michael's Hill, had a commanding view and years later recalled: 'The flames increased—multiplied—at one point after another; till, by ten o'clock that night, one seemed to be looking down upon Dante's Inferno, and to hear the multitudinous moan and wail of the lost spirits surging to and fro amid that sea of fire ... dull explosions down below mingled with the roar of the mob, and the infernal hiss and crackle of the flame.'

Buildings collapsed as the furnace raged. The homes of

accountant J. S. Broad and bookseller William Strong were fired almost simultaneously; a warehouse rented by Bartlett and Mogg, wine and spirit merchants, flared into the darkness. Professor Chaillou, a teacher of the French language, of 43 Queen Square, fought a desperate lone battle to save his home. He lost. A boarding school for young ladies, run by the Misses Vigor at 6 Queen Square, was also set alight; another resident girls' school, of which Mrs Phillips was principal, and a dancing academy (under the tutelage of Miss Cecilia Giroux) suffered a similar fate.

Businesses gutted or seriously damaged included those of liquor merchants—in King Street, Princes Street and Queen Square—conveniently situated near the Custom House and The Quay. Respectable lodging houses also fell to burning rubble and, in one, local thespian Mr Woulds was seized by ruffians and robbed.

Most rioters made no attempt to conceal their identity and some, in an alcoholic haze, wobbled about their work and chatted incoherently to anyone who wanted to listen (and to many who didn't). The mob doubtless regarded themselves forever beyond the reach of the law; living for the heady brew of the present, they gave no thought to the distinct probability of ultimate arrest and legal requital.

It must have been terrifying for the occupants of a house under attack. Next door but one to the Custom House was the home of Fulke Tovey Barnard, an accountant. His manservant, William Furlong, had helped to remove ledgers and cash from the building, the entrances of which were barricaded with furniture. He and others struggled to hold the front door, but were trapped when rioters crashed in through rear windows. Furlong was struck down in the hallway and then savagely thrown outside; a friend, John Russell, after being beaten with sticks, received a nasty leg wound from iron hurled at him. With fifteen minutes, the place was ablaze.

For upwards of ten hours, Queen Square remained in the undisputed possession of the mob. Despite casualties from drink and other causes, the revelry and wrecking flourished until the small detachment of 3rd Dragoon Guards, led by Lt-Col Brereton, approached at 5 a.m. The soldiers experienced no serious opposition as they rode into the Square, which nevertheless framed a bacchanalian picture: steep banks of flame, mushrooming smoke, tumbling walls, jagged ruins, seared trees and widely-scattered debris. Some rioters lay on the scarred grass 'in the last stage of senseless intoxication and with countenances more resembling fiends than men'.

The pent-up troops charged down Princes Street and across Queen Square, reining-up on the south side opposite No. 42, which had just been entered by some of the mob. Ironically it was the residence of Christopher Claxton who, it will be recalled, made himself unpopular with reformers by prophesying at the sailors' meeting that dire consequences would attend the Recorder's public entry. Claxton was away but his home and most of the contents were saved by his negro servant, Robert Hopton, and several civilians who, backed by the military, drove out intruders. Fires started upstairs were soon doused, damage being relatively slight. Like Guppy, the forty-one-year-old Claxton would be concerned in commercial undertakings with Brunel and with whom he enjoyed a long personal friendship.

According to Sgt-Major John Martin, the soldiers 'could not refrain from cutting some of the mob as they came out' [of the house] whereupon Brereton 'immediately ordered that no violence should be used'. Then, said Martin, up came Major Mackworth shouting 'cut them down' and, during further charges across the Square, the cavalrymen made 'full use of their swords'.

Mackworth reckoned that when he arrived about a thousand rioters were in Queen Square, some of them trying to burn a corner house:

It immediately struck me [he wrote in *A Personal Narrative*] that if this house were fired the shipping which is close by and thickly moored in the heart of the city, would soon be in a blaze and nearly the whole city must inevitably be burned. It was no longer time to consider numbers or to await magistrates' orders. I called out 'Colonel Brereton, we must instantly charge' and without waiting for his answer—he could not but approve—I called out 'Charge men and charge home'. The troops obeyed with the utmost alacrity, Colonel Brereton charging with great spirit at their head; and I trust in God every man there injured was actually engaged in plunder or in burning and that not a single innocent person there fell beneath our sabres.

Numbers were cut down and ridden over; some were driven into the burning houses, out of which they were never seen to return, and our dragoons, after sabreing all they could come at in the Square, collected and formed and then charged down Princes Street and again returned to the Square, riding at the miserable mob in all directions; about 120 or 130 of the incendiaries were killed and wounded here.

The major had not finished. He got Brereton's permission to recall the 14th Light Dragoons: 'As I was the only person in plain clothes and probably none else could, under existing circumstances, have penetrated through the city, I rode myself to Keynsham, begging Colonel Brereton to keep the Square with the 3rd as long as it was in his power.... As for the 3rd Dragoon Guards, nothing could exceed their devotedness, activity and good disposition; to speak of gallantry in attacking such poor wretches, however numerous, would be misplaced; they received us with volleys of stones, with one or two discharges of firearms (by a shot from which one dragoon was wounded in the arm) and a few, including myself, received more or less contusions.'

Brereton and the dragoon guards continued to patrol the area and, periodically, to repel persistent rioters. Captain Warrington, with the tiny reserve, had now reached the Square and took part in the action.

Having left the sanctuary of Daniel Fripp's house, Charles Pinney got to the Council House just before six o'clock. Others were beginning to assemble. The previous evening, after consultation with magistrates, the sheriffs had decided (albeit somewhat belatedly) to summon the *posse comitatus*. This could not be accomplished unduly quickly anyway, for the law required it to be done by precept. The sheriffs' officers had been engaged for hours in their respective parishes calling upon citizens to report at local churches and elsewhere early that Monday morning. Despite initial setbacks, the response proved heartening.

The marked change in public attitude can be attributed to several factors. When the mob began demolishing private property, for example, the horrifying possibilities became all too clear. This realization, coupled with news that the military were at last acting positively, as well as the knowledge that army reinforcements were at hand, undoubtedly now persuaded many hundreds of inhabitants to enrol as special constables. Under-Sheriff Hare was authorized by the magistracy to seek William Herapath's help in recruiting members of the Bristol Political Union—an apparent necessity which must have gone very much against the Tory grain. It is intriguing to note that whereas a shilling a day was paid to other 'specials', the union men each received a daily rate of 3s 6d!

A formidable civilian force prepared to march into the streets; fresh troops began entering the city. The rioters had enjoyed their final fling. The weighty pendulum of retribution started unerringly to swing...

Chapter Eight

ROUTING THE RIOTERS

MAJOR WILLIAM BECKWITH, of the 14th Light Dragoons, arrived by post-chaise. Having journeyed through darkness from Gloucester—and now some three hours ahead of an urgently-needed troop of cavalry, led by Captain Ambrose Congreve—he reached Bristol as early light unveiled a huge umbrella of black smoke hovering above the centre. It was about seven o'clock when the thirty-five-year-old major strode crisply into the Council House.

Beckwith—'every inch a soldier'—brimmed with confidence. He had been blooded young, entering the army in January 1813 soon after his sixteenth birthday; he joined the 16th Light Dragoons as a cornet and, before the end of that year, saw action in the Peninsular campaign. Beckwith also fought at the Battle of Waterloo, shortly following which he was promoted to lieutenant. He attained the rank of captain in 1822 and that of major [with the 14th] in 1828, subsequently rising to become a general. A strict disciplinarian and a fine horseman, Beckwith expressed his views bluntly and was equally resolute in the performance of duty. Extremely useful to have around in a crisis, one imagines, and certainly not an individual to be cowed by any rabble.

The major reported to the Mayor and magistrates who, in his opinion, appeared 'bewildered and stupified with terror'. Outlining the situation, they lost no time in referring adversely to Brereton's behaviour and to the exit of the squadron of dragoons. Beckwith requested some aldermen to accompany him on horseback to Queen Square, but they declined, saying they did not ride. He nevertheless succeeded without difficulty in obtaining written instructions to restore peace and with his adjutant, Lt Patrick Leary, went to the devastated area.

Brereton rode up, told Beckwith the 14th were on their way back from Keynsham and 'then directed me to wait upon him at No 9 College Green in an hour'. The colonel was not there at the appointed time, but Beckwith eventually 'found his dressing' at 2 Unity Street. The two men discussed the position. Brereton's version of what had led to the present appalling state naturally varied a lot from that advanced by the magistrates. He complained of being unable to get proper orders and must have been shaken to discover the major had encountered no problem on that score. The unhappy Brereton then said that with so few troops it was impossible to do much anyway.

Mackworth returned with the 14th, plus a small detachment of the Bedminster Yeomanry Cavalry which had joined them just outside the city. Major Beckwith met them and claimed from that moment he gave all material orders although Brereton, as senior officer, was still nominally in charge. After scattering rioters rummaging in the ruins of the Bishop's Palace, and also dealing summarily with other missile-throwers on the way, Beckwith and the cavalry proceeded to their main objective of crushing all opposition in and around Queen Square. Special constables, identifiable by a strip of white linen tied to the left arm, were there to help disperse the crowd.

For two hours, a series of charges was executed with great vigour and little mercy. No half-measures this time: the recalled frustrated men of the 14th exploded into action and, said Beckwith, a 'great number' of civilian lives was lost. Exact casualty figures will never be known, but it must have been a terrible spectacle as people scattered like demented things in frenzied attempts to evade slashing sabres. Retribution was severe and, unquestionably, some innocents suffered.

Beckwith had this to say: 'On Monday morning, everything was done at the gallop and with the sword and, in consequence, for one that was killed a hundred were wounded. The greater number of our opponents did not belong to Bristol as was evident from the number of broken heads that were to be seen on almost every road leading from the town.'[1] The army's tactics were roundly condemned in some quarters and Thomas

[1] PRO HO 40/28

John Manchee, horrified by them, wrote that 'resistance having ceased, the magistrates became right valiant, and respectable citizens (not the "miserable mob") were given up to the unbridled passions of the 14th'.

Major Mackworth declared that the 14th commenced charging at about ten o'clock and 'in the most spirited manner cut down all the mob they met with and pursued with one troop the Kingswood colliers, who had been very active in the riots, some miles on the Gloucester Road, leaving the other troop to perform the same office in the city, and I think I saw at least 250 rioters killed or wounded in these affairs'.

Allegations (not only by Mackworth) that Kingswood miners were involved evoked strenuous denials particularly from Samuel Whittuck, the proprietor of extensive coal workings in that area, and from H. H. Budgett, a Kingswood resident for more than thirty years. Whittuck was convinced none of his employees was implicated and also believed other colliers in the district 'utterly incapable of such conduct as that ascribed to them'. The Kingswood men had an unfortunate history of violence and some probably did participate in the latest disturbances; however, it seems likely that rumour and their previous record, rather than substantiated evidence, now wrongly linked them *en masse* with the riots.

At the magistrates' request, Mackworth arranged for a military unit to 're-take' the New Gaol and also organized 250 army and navy pensioners into sections under retired and half-pay officers. 'Thus', he said, 'we were enabled to protect distant points such as the gaol, the docks and their gates etc., while I occupied every outlet of the city with cavalry and yeomanry, who arrived rapidly from all quarters; these I directed instantly to charge all bodies illegally assembled and so preserved the inhabitants in peace.'

Not everyone was enamoured with Major Digby Mackworth, nor impressed by his account published soon after the riots—*A Personal Narrative of the Late Events in Bristol*. One journalist wrote acidly: 'The Great Pronoun knows very little about the matter; he vastly overrates his services; and in giving his book away *gratis*, he has a very accurate conception of its value.' Even so, Mackworth and Beckwith both figured prominently in the restoration of law and order, not least by their audacious assumption of responsibility from a demoralized Brereton. Writing to Fitzroy Somerset that Monday, Brereton made no mention of either major and obviously regarded himself as still effectively in command. He could have hardly intimated otherwise.

By midday, things were much quieter, the streets being patrolled by the strengthened military and by redoubtable groups of special constables (about 5,000 citizens answering the call, it was reported). Shops were shut, businesses at a standstill and the people bewildered. Bristol presented a besieged appearance. During the day, these notices were issued:

Council House, Bristol, Oct 31, 1831

The *Posse Comitatus* of this City and County, having been called out to act in conjunction with the Military to endeavour to restore the Peace of the City and, as the most severe measures must be adopted to accomplish that object, the Magistrates earnestly caution all Persons not engaged in official duties as Constables to keep within their respective Dwellings as they will otherwise be exposed to the most imminent peril.   C. PINNEY, Mayor

Bristol, October 31, 1831

It will be of the utmost importance that the Inhabitants should place Lights in the Windows of their respective Houses as soon as it becomes dark, and the Magistrates again earnestly entreat that all Persons will strictly confine themselves within their respective Dwellings.   C. PINNEY, Mayor

The second placard was distributed after a rumour that rioters planned to cut off gas supplies, thus plunging the city into darkness. Any such intention (if there was one) did not materialize.

Following the mob's outrages, it became ominously predictable—and virtually unavoidable—that initial retaliation would involve some grim acts. Stringent operations were necessary to a degree but, for all that, they proved no more palatable. *The Bristol Mercury* objected: 'We are sorry to have to record another piece of folly—wanton cruelty we would call it—if it had not, as we believe, originated in the utter ignorance of the Magistrates of the state of the city. The shops remained unopened and the military were ordered to clear the streets—an

99

order which was fulfilled to the letter by a party of the troops which had experienced some rough treatment and had in consequence fired upon the people the previous day. The sight of this useless piece of duty was peculiarly distressing; nothing was to be seen on every side but unoffending women and children running and screaming in every direction while several men, apparently on their way to work, were deliberately cut at, several seriously injured and some killed.'

Felix Farley's Bristol Journal took a different view: 'The soldiers and inhabitants generally seemed to be of the opinion that the time had come for the most severe measures: those who stopped in the streets did so at their own risk and have none to blame but themselves. There was no excuse for their being on their way to work, for it was notorious that every shop was shut and business completely suspended.'

Some thought, however, the army re-established order as indiscriminately as the mob had destroyed it. Surely, they argued, it was not too difficult—especially in streets well away from principal trouble spots—to distinguish between the innocent and guilty. One man claimed the troops slashed at nearly everybody and 'in some cases, they rode their horses upon the pavement and aimed at terrified individuals who had sought refuge in some corner'. Whatever else the military were accused of doing (and there is little doubt some soldiers over-reacted), they could not be reproached for being ineffective. Within a short time, they uncompromisingly smashed the riot. Special constables helped to pick up the pieces.

It had been a little more than forty-eight hours since Sir Charles Wetherell entered Bristol. Allowing that honours between the lawful and the lawless were fairly even until the assault on the Bridewell, it meant the mob had enjoyed a free run for something like twenty hours. During that period, rioters fired three gaols, burned down the Mansion House, the Bishop's Palace, Excise Office, Custom House and four tollgate houses, while in Queen Square and adjoining streets nearly fifty houses, warehouses and offices were destroyed or badly damaged. *The Bristol Gazette* grieved: 'Our columns this week are stained with an account of the most disastrous and destructive rioting and incendiarism that ever disgraced any city or town in the most civilised country in the world.'

What was the cost in civilian casualties? The only semi-official list to be published put the deaths at 12 (two shot, two from sword cuts, six burned and two from excessive drinking) and the injured at 94 (10 shot, 48 with sword cuts, two suffering from drunkenness and 34 from 'other causes'). Those figures, referring only to people taken to hospitals or dispensaries, surely represent but a modest proportion of the total.

Various overall assessments were attempted. Major Mackworth, for instance, told Fitzroy Somerset 'the numbers of killed and wounded by the dragoons, which I estimated in a former letter at 400, is considerably under the truth. So many killed have been ascertained that the usual proportion of wounded ... could amount to almost double that number.'[1] It seems an inflated aggregate, but 'A Citizen' (the Rev John Eagles) managed somehow to calculate that no fewer than 500 rioters had died! This was certainly a monstrous exaggeration. Mackworth might have been nearer the mark with his first estimate if any credence is given to a report from Bristol appearing in *The Dublin Evening Post*: 'The deaths and maimed are stated by the authorities here at 348, of which they have reports, but those who were taken off into private houses may swell the number to 400 or 500.' Still too high, perhaps, but the truth will never be known—no accurate returns exist.

Some deaths got more publicity than others, a case in point being that of twelve-year-old Thomas Morris—killed while standing innocuously in an avenue near Queen Square. Apart from the victim's tender age, what made the incident controversial was that the fatal shot was fired by a special constable on duty that Monday morning. The constable—John Cossley Lewis, a tall half-pay army officer (56th Regiment of Foot)—struggled with a 'desperate character' whom he had ordered to move on. In self-defence, Lewis maintained, he drew his pistol to frighten the man and it promptly went off, mortally wounding the youngster nearby. Pounced on by incensed witnesses, Lewis had to be rescued by fellow constables.

Captain Lewis, as he was known [the Army List describes him as a lieutenant], had arrived home from Devon with his family to King's Square, Bristol, on the day preceding Wetherell's entry, because of a summons to serve on the Grand Jury.

[1] PRO HO 40/28.

Instead, an inquest jury returned a verdict of 'Manslaughter' against him but, at the resultant trial, Lewis was found 'Not Guilty'—by no means to everyone's satisfaction. He told the judge that much as he lamented 'this most unfortunate occurrence, I shall ever console myself with the reflection that at the time I was acting in aid of the law and not in opposition to it'.

As little Tommy Morris lay dying in an infirmary bed and cavalry charged amid burning ruins the Mayor's forty-five-year old widowed sister, Mary Ames, was riding in an open carriage from Bath to Bristol. Having watched from twelve miles away the intense glow in the night sky, the worried woman left home early Monday morning 'to see if possible once more my dearest brother'. As it proved 'quite impossible' to pass through the confused city, her driver went by way of Bitton and Redland and on to Clifton. Mrs Ames outlined what happened in a letter to her sister-in-law, Frances, the wife of John Frederick Pinney:

> On the road we enquired of the Mail Coach man what state he left Bristol in. His answer was, most dreadful beyond description; he passed four and twenty dead bodies in various groups on the road ... proceeded to Rodney Place where I found poor Mrs Charles and mother in comparative peace, as Charles' life at that time was out of present danger.... On the day of terror, Mrs Charles did not leave the Mansion House till nearly three o'clock.... In a few minutes longer, it would have been impossible.... My feelings have been of such an acute nature that my nerves are so unstable, that I can scarcely hold any command of myself, but God is merciful in allowing my mind to be more calm this morning [Thursday, 3 November].... We are obliged to stay with Mrs Olive for the present, as the man at the Clifton Hotel obliged them to leave as their presence was likely to cause its being burnt down.... Pray for dear Charles, that God may continue to protect him. I am sick at heart; it feels as if it would burst.[1]

Charles Pinney, for whose divine protection his sister appealed, was busily engaged in the city throughout that melancholy Monday. Although there would be yet another night before he could enjoy his first proper sleep for nearly ninety-six hours, the Mayor wrote reassuringly to his wife: 'Do

[1] Pinney Papers.

not be alarmed for me, there is no apprehension of any recurrence of riot.'[1]

His Worship had other letters to write and sign, among them one to the Home Secretary...

---

[1] Pinney Papers.

Chapter Nine

THE GREAT ROUND-UP

BRISTOL BEGAN to lick painful wounds. An uneasy calm prevailed as the military, augmented at frequent intervals by fresh detachments, clamped down on the shocked city. In a combined security operation, the soldiers and the civilian posse patrolled near-empty streets, guarded buildings and winkled out not only riot suspects but also recaptured prisoners liberated from the gaols by the mob. Armed sentries stood by at hospitals in which several of the injured patients were wanted for questioning.

In and around Queen Square, crumbling masonry and flaky blackened timbers were all that remained of some property. Smoke continued to spiral from a few houses, but now fire-fighters could at least work uninterrupted under the protection of the army units. A number of special constables and firemen was identified as having been active rioters, a matter soon relayed to the authorities.

Charred rubble was combed for possessions and, less hope-fully, for trapped survivors. Grisly sights met the eye including, it was said, almost indistinguishable human forms cooked to cinders. A sickly stench pervaded the air. The seemingly omni-present Major Mackworth quietly dispersed an inquisitive group viewing, in his words, 'the mangled remains of some of the poor wretches who were cut down and burnt on Monday and whom they were dragging out of the ruins'.

When the wreckage of the Mansion House was probed a man, with an arm burned off at the shoulder, apparently arose like a phoenix from the ashes and, 'to the surprise of the bystanders', shook his dazed head and walked away! Remnants of the night's horror—innumerable tables, chairs, beds, household utensils, linen, books and clothing—littered a large area. 'For such trifles', commented *The Bristol Liberal*, 'the greatest risk had been run and one half of the finest square in England destroyed.'

During that edgy Monday, rumours were rife. Fresh uprisings were forecast and, because of a fear that shipping might be attacked, the *Earl of Liverpool* was fitted with guns and moored in mid-river. Crews on other vessels also prepared for action. Nothing happened, but such precautions mirrored a marked improvement in official organization. According to postmaster John Gardiner, the *posse comitatus* now numbered 'many thousands' and they 'guarded every avenue and paraded the whole of the city and allowed no person to pass who could not give an account of himself, while the military kept all the roads around the city clear'.

Towards evening a few smoking buildings again burst into flames and, although firemen quickly dealt with the outbreaks, gave rise to an erroneous report that rioters had re-grouped in Queen Square. A portion of pavement in King Street was forced up by heat from a cellar. The cause? Blazing brandy! As night fell, citizens heeded the magistrates' edict to keep candles burning in their homes; the interiors of churches were also illuminated and utilized as constabulary depots.

Mayor Pinney had written to the Home Secretary, describing the sad state of the city. 'No doubt', he concluded, 'you have received the fullest information from the commanding officer of the district, but I can safely assure your Lordship the aspect of affairs has been most serious and alarming, the plans of the operation well organized and carried into effect in the most complete manner of the destruction of property to a very large amount including the Mansion House, Custom House and Excise Office etc.' Under-Secretary of State George Lamb replied by return that Lord Melbourne 'greatly laments' the riots and would be 'glad to receive a report of all these unfortunate transactions; and further he requests to be informed particularly when no defence was made of the Gaols, which his Lordship presumes are strong buildings, by those who are charged with the custody of the prisoners'.[1] The magistrates had some explaining to do.

[1] PRO HO 40/28.

Major-General Sir Richard Downes Jackson (the Deputy Quartermaster General) was appointed to command the troops in Bristol, his instructions being to concert with the magistrates 'upon the means to be adopted for the restoration of order and tranquility [*sic*]'. A few hours after arriving in the city on Tuesday, 1 November, the major-general wrote to Fitzroy Somerset: 'Everything has been tranquil all day. Prisoners made and plundered property brought in, but the alarm has not subsided.... Great apprehensions are entertained here of an attempt to rescue the prisoners and certainly there would be every inducement to the attempt if we had not some infantry, as the gaols are destroyed and our cavalry weak though victorious.'[1]

The infantry referred to was a 170-strong detachment of 11th Foot from South Wales which Lt-Col Love led into Bristol at about six o'clock the previous evening. There had been opposition on the way. Having reached Newport, where Love requisitioned a steamer, the soldiers faced a mob who, sympathizing with counterparts across the channel, 'violently attempted' to prevent embarkation. Love promised them an unpleasant time at the hands of the troops if they did not desist. They withdrew, but 'their fury found vent in execrations, and wishes for the sinking of the vessel, ere her crew should trouble their confederates in Bristol'.

The military contingent got safely to their destination and when they marched down Park Street, according to *The United Service Journal*, inhabitants called out 'Thanks, thanks, brave fellows, you are come to save us from pillage and death' and blessed the soldiers as 'deliverers'. Love and his men remained a few days before being replaced by six companies of the 52nd Foot (commanded by Lt-Col James Fergusson) which, after a tour of duty in America, had only just landed at Portsmouth.

Search parties continued to retrieve stolen goods. The Exchange building, in Corn Street, became a vast repository for thousands of articles. Offenders now realized only too well the consequences and, gripped by panic, scrambled to hide, plant or dispose of the booty. For once, the authorities were quick off the mark and dispatched constables and troops to scour the most likely districts.

[1] PRO HO 40/28.

The enormous amount of property recovered—'to an extent beyond belief', said postmaster Gardiner—included furniture of all kinds, china, glassware, knives and forks, pots and pans, clothes, cash, linen, wines and spirits. Two large wagon-loads of loot were collected from a single house in Host Street; one man was arrested for illegally possessing £200, while an equally impecunious-looking individual had pockets bulging with shiny sovereigns. Sudden raids on 'almost all the lowest and dirtiest parts of the town' revealed all manner of things secreted under heaps of coal, stuffed up chimneys and jammed into roofs. Buried treasure was unearthed from beneath freshly-turned ground.

Newly-lighted bonfires were discovered as the guilty strove desperately to eliminate all clues and, sad to relate, at least one cask of brandy was poured down the sink. While the fronts of some homes in the Pithay were being checked, occupants tossed 'the most elegant furniture' out the back and into the grubby water of the River Frome. One devoted housewife prepared to serve her husband with steaming broth when a constable called, but diligent examination disclosed that the ingredients of that bubbling brown liquid contained silver cutlery! Books and papers purloined from the Bishop's Palace were found; so, too, were valuable records belonging to the Custom House.

Some of the worst trouble-makers, it may be safely assumed, were never brought to book and numerous lesser fry also escaped punishment. In fact, those arrested and subsequently arraigned represented only a fraction of those who, in varying degrees, perpetrated the outrages. After being interrogated and charged, prisoners were remanded in custody at the damaged New Gaol—now under strong military guard.

Bristol returned to something like normal on the Wednesday. Shops re-opened, men went back to work and people generally could venture outside and go about their daily business without fear. Tongues began to wag. Major Mackworth felt sure the city 'is chiefly engaged in mutual recrimination, the authorities under public odium and each throwing the fault of the late painful events upon one another'. Criticizing the 'wretched police' and public indifference during the riots, the major informed Fitzroy Somerset that 'nothing effectual was done by the good citizens till their houses were burnt and the mob cut down by the dragoons. Then we had two or three thousand of the most active and zealous special constables in the world and enough to have eaten the mob if they would have come forward a day sooner....'[1]

Crowds naturally tended to congregate in the worst-hit areas to see the sights, but they were warned not to do so:

Council House
Wednesday, Nov 2, 1831

The Magistrates most earnestly desire that all Persons will avoid assembling in Crowds in different parts of the City, as such assemblages are likely to promote disturbances and interfere with arrangements now being made for the recovery of property and detection of offenders.

C. PINNEY, Mayor

There was no disturbance of that sort, but much heat simmered under some collars and the magistracy and military soon came in for the full treatment. Although the corporation wisely banned the sale and traditional letting-off of fireworks on Guy Fawkes Day—as the 'greatest mischief and danger may at this time be apprehended'—they were quite powerless to stop a barrage of verbal rockets from being launched in their direction.

On that very Wednesday, a meeting of citizens agreed to press Lord Melbourne to enquire into all aspects of the riots. The precise framing of the resolution was postponed until the next day when an even larger number of merchants, bankers, tradesmen and 'other respectable inhabitants' turned up at the Commercial Rooms to register their disapproval of the alleged ineptitude shown by the authorities. Two condemnatory motions related to the magistrates in general and the 'highly reprehensible' conduct of Brereton in particular. One fair-minded gentleman prudently suggested that unless such a prejudicial accusation against the colonel was withdrawn, they might just as well 'shoot him through the head'. After accepting the point and also watering down other wording, those present finally decided to send Lord Melbourne the following memorial:

We, the undersigned, Merchants, Bankers, Traders and other inhabitants of the City of Bristol, deeply lamenting the riotous and dis-

[1] PRO HO 40/28.

graceful proceedings that have recently occurred in this city, and the
sad destruction of property resulting therefrom, bearing in mind that
the lives and fortunes of the Citizens were for a considerable period
entirely at the mercy of a desperate mob, and firmly convinced that
all this might have been prevented if proper precautions had been
adopted, do earnestly request your Lordship will be pleased to cause
an investigation to be instituted, as the only course that will satisfy
the minds of the public and restore confidence in future.

An accompanying letter was addressed jointly to Bristol's
MPs, James Baillie and Edward Protheroe, asking them to
impress upon Melbourne the importance of an enquiry. Baillie,
back at his London home after a seaside holiday, knew nothing
of the riots until they were over and now learned his parliamentary partner was out of town. In view of the urgency, however,
he went alone to tender the memorial to Melbourne, who
already had relevant reports and letters and, only a day or so
earlier, interviewed Wetherell. The Home Secretary promised
to raise the matter at Cabinet level where it would receive 'immediate and serious consideration'.

Due to Melbourne's indisposition, developments were slightly
delayed but, on 16 November, he replied (through Baillie):

. . . It is impossible not entirely to agree with the memorialists that
the fullest and strictest investigation, which the law authorizes and
empowers, is required to be instituted into the conduct both of the
civil and military authorities. If there is reason to presume that these
unfortunate events have had their origin in supineness, neglect of
duty, or delinquency, they should be inquired into by the due process
of law, and according to the established forms of legal proceedings. . . .
His Majesty's Government will be most anxious to receive all the information which can be collected relating to the late calamitous disturbances at Bristol and to give it their most attentive consideration,
to submit it to those advisors who are the most competent to decide
upon its import and bearing, and to adopt upon it such measures as
may be required, either of animadversion upon the past or for the
precaution of the future.

This cautious reply contained no actual promise of a Government investigation but a well-attended meeting of Bristolians,
composed largely of prominent Liberals, decided to elect a
committee to collate data for a riot dossier. There was some
straight talking and much dissatisfaction when it was felt the

magistrates, already accused of gross mismanagement during the riots, were now contriving to throw the whole blame for the catastrophe on to Lt-Col Brereton. Thomas John Manchee told the assembly that while respecting some magistrates as individuals, he still held to his conviction that 'Bristol owes all the calamities we deplore to the system under the predominance of which they have taken place'. That and similar sentiments were enthusiastically cheered. There were calls, too, not to prejudge.

While the magistracy came under fire at this period, there was a measure of sympathy for the Mayor. Even Manchee agreed that at times in the disturbances Pinney 'appears to have conducted himself with great personal courage, as long as he received or expected the slightest assistance from his brother magistrates and the citizens.... But Mr Pinney was a young magistrate, having only just entered on his office; and he has great reason to complain that he did not receive more judicious advice from his older and more experienced coadjutors.' However, this was an isolated concession by Manchee, who waxed anti-corporation down to the final full-stop of his scathing pamphlet.

There were people who believed Pinney had fallen political prey to a confidence trick by Tory magistrates who, sensing some kind of trouble in the near future, pushed him forward as Mayor and thus created a ready-made Whig scapegoat. William Henry Somerton, of *The Bristol Mercury*, was among those who alluded to such a set-up: 'Indeed, there have not been wanting many to affirm that there are members of the Magistracy who were far from being anxious to prevent a *slight* disturbance; that they even courted it, for the sake of the argument it would furnish against Reform; and that the Whig Mayor was, in a political sense, the victim of Tory Aldermen.... It certainly offers a plausible solution to their conduct, but we are loth to ascribe unworthy motives to them.'

It was none the less a theory subscribed to by John Ham, a prominent member of the Bristol Political Union, who later wrote that the corporation wanted 'to throw upon the Mayor the onus of quelling what they called a Reform riot'.

Mary Ames entertained similar suspicions (doubtless based on what brother Charles himself told her) and, writing from

Rodney Place, Clifton, on 8 November, to her niece, Fanny Smith, who lived at Blandford, said this:

... He being the head of the Magistrates must bear the whole of the abuse of the Reformers and Tories, having during the office of Mayor conscientiously declined entangling himself with Politics, thinking any other line of conduct may throw suspicion on his character as judge ... the whole of the Magistrates with *one* or two exceptions with himself are principal Tory families which renders the Corporation as a body specially hateful, and what still increases the critical nature of his situation is the perfect hatred of the whole Tory party to him, having always been prominent for Reform ... notwithstanding the trying and singular position in which he is placed as a mark for the fire of both sides, I believe ... that he acted in the best way he possibly could have done under the existing circumstances, that God in his good providence will place the blame on the right shoulders. I did not see Charles till Tuesday, that was the *first* time he had left the city, not having changed his clothes or been to bed since the fatal entry of Sir Charles on the Saturday.... [1]

Mrs Ames had earlier told Fanny Smith's mother, Mrs John Frederick Pinney, the Mayor revealed to her 'as a secret' that the magistrates were sending a report to the Government, as well as urging an investigation, and 'he says Brereton is either a traitor or a coward. You must not let a word of this drop.'[1]

Indeed the magistrates had not been slow to record their version of events and two very long statements, in the form of letters signed by the Mayor and dated 4 November, went to London— one to Lord Melbourne, the other to Lord Hill. They put themselves in a good light, of course, and intimated Brereton was largely responsible for the breakdown of law and order. When those statements were released to newspapers ten days later, the Mayor attached a prefix:

A fortnight has now passed since the distressing scenes took place in the city of Bristol.... It is hoped that the candour of by far the greatest part of their [the magistrates'] fellow-citizens has, in the meantime, spared them from the censure and reproach which others, in ignorance of the facts, and without materials for judgment, have thrown upon them; their complete vindication must be left to that

[1] Pinney Papers.

full and fair enquiry which, whether it be called down on them by adverse application, or may take place under any other circumstances, they feel that justice will eventually be done to all, and by the result of which they are intent to abide....

National and provincial newspapers added their influential weight to the controversy and, in due course, the matter received an 'airing' in Parliament. Convinced the riots were but a segment of an organized and extensive plot, *Felix Farley's Bristol Journal* laid the blame squarely at the door of Reform and local radicals. Equally predictably, *The Bristol Mercury* castigated the magistrates for precipitating the riots by bringing in cavalry and swearing-in hireling constables which was 'more calculated to excite tumult than to allay it'.

The leader-writer of *The Bristol Mirror* asked: 'But are we quite blameless ourselves? When it was clear that we were in the hands of the mob, ought not the citizens instantly to have formed bands in every parish and at least endeavoured to have arrested the hands of the incendiaries and robbers? ... There were many intervals wherein a hundred citizens, armed even with clubs, might have prevented the greatest part of the mischief, if not entirely dispersed the ruffians, but all were panic struck.'

A weightier injunction had come on 2 November from King William, who 'thought fit, by and with the advice of our privy council' to issue a Royal Proclamation condemning the 'outrages of the most violent description' recently committed in 'divers parts of Great Britain and more particularly in the towns of Derby and Nottingham and the city of Bristol'. Whereas 'all the restraints of law and order have been overborne and trodden underfoot by such lawless multitudes' to the 'great disturbance and danger of the common weal and the subversion of established government', it was firmly determined 'vigorously to exert the powers which we possess for the protection of all our subjects, in the entire enjoyment of their rights and liberties'. His Majesty therefore commanded municipal and judicial bodies throughout the country to "effectually repress all tumults, riots, outrages and breaches of the peace' and bring to justice the perpetrators of such acts and, furthermore, commanded 'all our liege subjects' to do their bounden duty by assisting the authorities 'in enforcing the law against evil doers and in protecting their fellow-subjects in the enjoyment of their property, and the exercise of their rights, against all forcible, illegal, and unconstitutional interference, control or aggression'.

Chapter Ten

COLONEL ON THE CARPET

THROUGHOUT THE AFTERMATH of the riots, Lt-Col Brereton consistently maintained the troops had not been strong enough to deal effectively with the serious situation which arose and, moreover, that the magistrates had given him neither sufficient support nor specific directions. Even so, he undoubtedly realized the gravity of his present position and, in a long letter to Fitzroy Somerset on 3 November, sought to justify himself:

I hope I shall stand excused if under the feelings excited by your Lordship's letter of the 31st ultimo I again intrude myself upon your notice respecting that paragraph which conveys the disapprobation of Lord Melbourne upon my sending the 14th Dragoons as a temporary removal to Keynsham, permit me to say my situation was a peculiarly distressing one, between an overpowering infuriated mob and a magistracy from whom no essential aid could be procured; I was left in a very unenviable position ... to have attempted anything against the mob at that moment would have been putting too much to hazard; supposing we had shot many of them and dispersed them for the instant, they would have re-assembled with considerably augmented numbers which I could not have prevented for I had not force to occupy the many outlets of this large city. Men and horses would have been exhausted, and so exasperated were the mob previously that they had determined to attack all the houses for arms to destroy the Dragoons in their quarters when they went to refresh; would it have been right under such circumstances to hazard the troops being repulsed; for, if they had, the mob flushed with their victory would have had possession of the whole city and *fired the shipping*—of this intent they made no secret, nor of their plan to attack the banks; and then throw all the surrounding countryside into confusion.

At the same time they very cheerfully, and with the greatest earnestness, promised to return to peaceable conduct if the 14th were removed—now at this moment I had also an impression upon my mind that I might reasonably expect a further military force would be ordered to this station; it would be judicious to use every means that might abate their fury until further aid was obtained. On the morning of Monday, they had become so fatigued by their diabolical exertions and partly broken by drunkenness that I could then use the 14th Dragoons with advantage and the magistracy having then commenced what they should have done originally, the city was placed in *safety*.

It is necessary also that I should observe I did not remove the 14th without the concurrence of the Mayor. I also beg leave to assure his Lordship of my incessant endeavours during this calamitous business, as can be sufficiently proved by respectable persons, not suffering under it or connected in any way to bias their opinions, for I was equally, day and night, exerting myself in every direction for the public welfare and the best execution of the duties committed to my charge.[1]

Bristol now abounded with troops. In addition to sizeable units of cavalry and infantry, there was a small detachment of artillery, although most of the volunteer yeomanry contingents [from Gloucestershire, Somerset and Wiltshire] had departed within a week of the riots being crushed. On 15 November, the regulars paraded in Queen Square to hear Major-General Jackson read a communiqué from the Commander-in-Chief. In it, Lord Hill expressed pleasure that a member of his personal staff, Major Mackworth, had 'materially assisted the Magistrates of Bristol with his exertions and advice', and noted the 'admirable conduct' of both Captain Gage and Cornet Kelson. The C-in-C also commended the 'altogether excellent conduct' of the NCOs and privates of the 3rd Dragoon Guards and 14th Light Dragoons and assured Major Beckwith that, although he reached Bristol only on the Monday morning of the riots, his services were 'by no means less important' than those of the other officers named.

Jackson told the assembled troops he had been particularly happy to convey Lord Hill's message on the very ground where the deeds were performed and also in the presence of two such distinguished corps as the Royal Horse Artillery and the 52nd Light Infantry.

[1] PRO HO 40/28.

Two officers went without tribute—Lt-Col Brereton and Captain Warrington. Fitzroy Somerset had previously informed Jackson that Lord Hill 'sincerely wishes' he could have included Brereton in a commendation, but was 'precluded from doing so by circumstances which imperiously call for early and minute investigation'. Having read Mayor Pinney's statement on the colonel's alleged conduct, Hill was 'persuaded that Lt-Col Brereton will at once see that it is under the circumstances due as much to his own feelings and character, as it unquestionably is to the interests of public service, that his case should be fully enquired into and understood'.

It became Jackson's unenviable task to pass on those observations to Brereton, whose behaviour during the disturbances formed the subject of a Military Court of Enquiry[1] [held behind guarded doors at the Merchants Hall, Bristol] which opened on Thursday, 17 November, and lasted a week.

Basically, this private examination set out to ascertain whether or not a *prima facie* case against Brereton existed. The man appointed to preside over the proceedings was Major-General Sir James Charles Dalbiac, the Inspector-General of Cavalry, who was advised by Lord Hill that the investigation should be 'conducted with great caution and deliberation' and Brereton 'afforded the fullest opportunity to meet and remove the unpleasant allegations thus set forth against him'. Dalbiac sat with four other officers: Col Sir Edward Miles (89th Regiment), Col James Fergusson (52nd Regiment), Lt-Col Lord Loughborough (9th Lancers) and Major Edmund Yeamans Walcott (Royal Horse Artillery).

The Mayor, two aldermen, the Town Clerk and several soldiers were among those giving evidence. Brereton missed hearing much of it because he was absent 'through indisposition' for no fewer than three consecutive days although, by arrangement, a half-pay army friend—Major Henry Ellard, of the 65th Regiment—attended on his behalf. When the colonel reappeared on the final day [Thursday, 24 November] he declined to call witnesses, but confined his defence to the presentation of a comprehensive document which was read to the court.

In it, Brereton said that judging from the tone of the letter

[1] Proceedings: PRO HO 52/12.

from the Horse Guards advising him that cavalry had been ordered to Bristol he wasn't to be 'entrusted with anything like an independent command'. While doubtless intended the magistracy should direct operations through him, it still appeared 'the troops were not the less to consider the magistrates rather than myself as the authority from which such orders emanated'. The colonel explained that he mentioned the point 'to show under what impression I acted in declining to assume the serious responsibility of firing upon the mob without express directions to that effect'.

Towards the end of his written testimony, which ran to twenty-three foolscap pages, Brereton complained bitterly that while he scarcely rested or ate during the rioting 'the magistrates who now come forward to sully and, if possible, to destroy my character with a view to screen themselves from a part of their palpable and gross neglect in the performance of their duty, never failed to retire at a given hour to some comfortable home, and many of them to their country houses'.

The colonel emphasized that his small military force were 'left totally unaided or supported' by the civil authorities, whose orders were of the 'most vague and indecisive nature'. During his thirty-three years in the army, Brereton wrote, he had held 'highly responsible commands' and received the utmost approbation from superior officers and the Government concerning his services, but at no time 'did I ever feel greater anxiety or more strenuously exert myself day and night for the public good than during the three days of the late dreadful events in this city . . .'.

In the court's considered opinion, however, Brereton had sent the squadron of 14th Light Dragoons from Bristol without justification and against the wishes of the magistrates and, furthermore, 'did not display that degree of judgement, activity or firmness' generally required of him during the riots. Among other things, the court noted that the magistrates 'appear to have neglected to take sufficient measures for the organization of a Civil Force, to co-operate effectually with the military at their disposal for the suppression of disorder and the protection of property'. The court's conclusions, plus a separate report on the alleged conduct of Captain Warrington, were forwarded to Lord Hill.

Less than a week later, Major-General Jackson was instructed by the C-in-C to tell Brereton he would be tried by court-martial. Lord Hill said on the evidence before him it became 'utterly impossible' to reach any other decision, although it was with 'earnest regret' he had 'adopted this course towards so old an officer'. Brereton had to 'consider himself in arrest' and report daily to Major George Gawler, of the 52nd Regiment, who was instructed to take charge of the Bristol Recruiting Office until further notice. [Gawler was to be Governor of South Australia—October 1838 to May 1841.] Captain Warrington, also due to face a court-martial, was similarly told to regard himself as under arrest. Both officers now had to wait six weeks before the hearings began.

To some extent, Brereton's case had been prejudiced already by the release to newspapers (and reproduced prior to the Military Court of Enquiry) of copies of the Mayor's letters to Lord Melbourne and Lord Hill. The Commander-in-Chief, plainly cross that Pinney 'thought fit to publish', informed Melbourne: 'As each of these reports contains serious matter of charge against Lt-Col Brereton and as the natural consequence of such communications was the institution of an enquiry into the conduct of that officer, I cannot but lament and even reprobate a proceeding which will have the effect of magnifying the question and of inducing the public to form a view of it as unfavourable to Lt-Col Brereton without his having an opportunity of stating anything in vindication.'

Lord Hill admitted not notifying the Mayor the enquiry was to be held, but 'it had for many days been a matter of notoriety that such a measure was in contemplation and, on the other hand, nothing had transpired to cause Mr Pinney to believe that his representation would be unheeded'.[1]

Sir Charles Wetherell was also displeased—in his case with the composition of a Special Commission, headed by the Chief Justice of the Common Pleas, Sir Nicolas Conyngham Tindal, appointed to try the Bristol rioters in January. When Parliament reassembled on 6 December (after its prorogation on 20 October), he took advantage of the Commons debate on the King's Speech not only to refute the 'gross calumny' perpetrated by some newspapers in maintaining the riots resulted

[1] PRO HO 40/28.

from his insistence to hold the assizes, but also to challenge the legality of excluding himself and the Mayor and aldermen of Bristol from the commission. Was it not imputing personal feelings would influence his impartiality as a judge? Wetherell also asserted that the omissions could be interpreted as recognizing the condemnation the Bristol Political Union had heaped upon him and the corporation.

Replying, George Lamb denied that the Government had been swayed at all by the union in nominating the commission. How could any concession be made to judges who claimed a right to act as such in their own cause? He believed Wetherell would have declined to serve anyway, but that was insufficient reason for inserting his name as it would have furnished a precedent for others not possessing the same high sense of honour as Sir Charles.

The advent of the Special Commission presented the magistrates with a headache. Although a repeat of the recent horror was beyond belief, the possibility of some demonstration could not be ruled out. The military in the city were now powerful enough to put down almost any disturbance but, in the interests of public morale, it would be infinitely preferable to keep the soldiers in the background and to ensure the peace with an organized civil force. There was the rub. As yet, Bristol had no full-time paid constabulary—though a Bill to establish one was under way. So, to augment the 114 constables and 115 night-watchmen from the twelve wards, it was proposed to call out a hundred service pensioners and arm half of them with muskets. In addition, there existed a 'fluctuating body' of nearly 1,700 volunteers of whom (by the end of November) only 682 had consented to be sworn-in as special constables.

Major-General Jackson, while acknowledging the 'great readiness' of the magistrates to co-operate with him on matters of public welfare, was disappointed with the recruitment and also told Lord Melbourne the constables and night-watchmen were 'reported to me as being ill-composed and inefficient'. Nevertheless, he added: 'Mobs are speedily collected from a population so ill-composed and uncontrolled by authority as that of Bristol and there are persons here endeavouring to keep up popular excitement, but they are not calculated to become leaders or the mob likely to follow any. With common vigilance on the part of the magistrates, disturbances that cannot be immediately quelled are not, I think, to be apprehended in Bristol.'[1]

Also keeping Lord Melbourne informed of developments was Mayor Pinney, who believed 'a very efficient body will be in readiness to act' and, on the day before the opening of the commission, reported that 1,390 special constables had been enrolled. They would be under the direction of a Metropolitan Police superintendent whom the Home Secretary had dispatched to the city.

The eminent judges were already on their way to consider the cases of more than a hundred prisoners.

[1] PRO HO 40/28.

Chapter Eleven

'YOU WILL BE TAKEN HENCE...'

For the second time in nine weeks—on 2 January 1832—a judicial procession made a ceremonial entry into Bristol. Of course, the situation was quite different from that existing when Wetherell came in. Having experienced the fear, bitterness and grief emanating from a collapse of law and order, as well as the rigorous measures to restore calm, citizens were now generally more disposed to co-operate with the municipal authorites. Even so, an understandably apprehensive magistracy took no chances.

Nearly 1,800 constables and special constables, each wearing an identity marker, were to maintain a round-the-clock vigil during the fortnight's stay of His Majesty's judges and a carefully-chosen squad, dressed in uniform 'similar to that worn by the new police in the metropolis', assigned as personal bodyguards. Security arrangements also provided for military detachments to assemble discreetly near St Thomas Street, Portwall Lane and Broad Street.

The cavalcade proceeded without incident from Totterdown to the city centre, the route being lined by 'perhaps the most respectable as well as most numerous civil force ever witnessed out of the metropolis'. In fact, comparatively few citizens even turned out to watch. This time there was no seething scrum at the Guildhall where, preceded by the Duke of Beaufort (Lord Lieutenant of Gloucestershire), the three robed judges entered the courtroom and took their places on the bench: Mr Justice (Sir William Elias) Taunton sat at the left-hand of Chief Justice Tindal, upon whose right were Mr Justice (Sir John Bernard) Bosanquet and the sixty-five year-old duke. The proclamation of the Royal Commission was read, the calendar of cases presented to the Chief Justice by Sheriff George Bengough and the court then adjourned until that Monday afternoon.

The judges were driven in state—via Corn Street, Clare Street and College Green—to No. 6 Park Street, where they were to reside, and from there to Bristol Cathedral for divine service. The Rev Henry Lee ended his sermon by exhorting all to trust in the Almighty and by quoting 'though weeping might endure for a night, joy cometh in the morning'—a sentiment unlikely to have found much favour among prisoners currently awaiting trial!

Back to the Guildhall, where the Grand Jury were sworn-in before being addressed at some length by the Chief Justice. Spectators sat in a temporary gallery rising in tiers from the middle of the room and this special accommodation, plus the unfamiliar absence from the bench of local magistrates, 'rendered the scene peculiarly novel'.

Tindal stressed that common law empowered a citizen, on his own authority and without the advice of a magistrate, to suppress a riot or to disperse, or assist in dispersing, a tumultuous assembly. More than that—it was his bounden duty to do so to the utmost of his ability. If a riot was dangerous, a citizen might also arm himself for its suppression. It was more advisable to have a magistrate present, because it provided a check on the intemperate use of arms but, if immediate action was demanded, it was the duty of every subject to preserve the peace and, whatever was done with that object in view, he would be upheld in common law. Neither was there any difference in law, Tindal explained, between the soldier and the civilian: the soldier was also a citizen and similarly obligated to repress violence. If a salutary check on arms was requisite on the civilian the same ought to operate, in greater degree, on the soldier but, overall, both were bound to employ the most effectual measures for the preservation of the King's peace.

There was no vestige of disturbance throughout that day and night; the magistrates, conscious of the nation's eyes upon them, had made much effort to prevent any possible repeat of events two months earlier. On Tuesday morning, prisoners arrived at the Guildhall under heavy escort. When the judges entered the courtroom at precisely nine o'clock, a large crowd rose respectfully and, although there was intense anticipation, little more than the rustle of legal papers broke the solemn silence.

First to be put up was William Clarke, a strongly-built sawyer in his early thirties and attired in a blue frockcoat, white waistcoat and blue trousers. His personal appearance was 'far beyond' that of the five others accused with him: James Courtney, of similar age, John Mecay, Patrick Kearney ('an itinerant vendor of Irish linen') and James Williams, all in their twenties, and Daniel Higgs, said to be eighteen. They were together charged with riotous assembly, 'pulling down' the New Gaol and firing the governor's house. Evidence was given as to Clarke's threatening and violent behaviour at the gaols; he egged-on other rioters, was frequently seen carrying an iron bar and also identified as being in several inns boasting of setting fire to the prisons. The prosecution patently regarded him as a leader.

Clarke, who fainted during the hearing, had lived for the past fifteen years in Bedminster where his mother kept a public house. He was stated by friends to have respectable connections and, when sober, to be of good disposition; he sustained a head injury at work some years previously and, since then, had been easily affected by drink and liable to get inflamed. A number of people swore to his polite and honest nature but alcohol, it seems, constituted a main factor in his downfall. Close acquaintances and employers also came forward to provide 'alibis' and character references for the other prisoners: Kearney, for instance, was described as 'peaceable and well-disposed' and Higgs as a 'quiet, civil and obliging young man'.

That first case lasted nearly twenty hours: It went on until half-past eleven on Tuesday night, Chief Justice Tindal began summing-up after ten o'clock the following morning, the jury retired at two o'clock and, after taking about three hours to reach a verdict, found all but James Williams guilty as charged. Two days later Clarke and Kearney, along with John Towell (aged twenty-two) and Matthew Warry ('little more than a lad, a journeyman baker'), were convicted of assembling riotously and fire-raising at the Bridewell. As he left the court, Kearney spiritedly retorted: 'That's not fair play; I'll be damned if it be.'

Considering the many involved in attacking the Bishop's

Palace, it is astonishing to find that only two persons—Thomas Evans Bendall and James Sims, aged nineteen and eighteen respectively—were actually indicted on the capital charge of destroying it. Bendall, among those seen burning books, was recognized by witnesses as having been in the Old Market during the week before the riots collecting signatures for a Reform petition; he was said to be a 'downright honest lad' but of weak intellect. Both youths were found guilty.

So it went on—a succession of charges, denials, identifications and a few acquittals. Thomas Gregory, a labourer of twenty-nine, was among those convicted of destroying houses in Queen Square; another, Richard Vines (twenty-one), who made a living hauling boats up the river from Pill, contended he was as innocent as an unborn child but was pronounced guilty, with butcher's assistant William Reynolds (twenty-nine), of demolishing the rectory home of the Rev Charles Buck. Reynolds, remembered by witnesses because he wore a distinctive blue smock-frock during the disturbances and was 'very much intoxicated', had been heard to shout: 'Damn it, now for the bloody parson of St Stephen's.' Joseph Kayes, the Cardiff-born son of a shoemaker and the same age as Reynolds, was a groom with a slightly superior air about him. On that night of destruction in the Square, he was dressed sufficiently neatly in a black-and-white striped waistcoat and a fustian jacket to draw attention to himself. Although his employer testified to seeing him at work on the Sunday evening at eight o'clock and again the next morning at seven, the jury decided that during part of the interim Kayes engaged in rioting and helped to destroy the home of Charles Bull. The prisoner protested that he had been framed.

One of many cases of theft concerned James Ives, a 'respectable looking' man of forty, who was transported for fourteen years for stealing Mr Buck's gold watch and also a silver salver belonging to Bristol Corporation. Ives, employed as a shopman by ironmonger Samuel Luxton, of 31 Wine Street, was rumbled when he tried to dispose of stolen articles to a jeweller who became suspicious and informed the authorities. When arrested, Ives had a gun in his pocket. According to Latimer's *Annals*, the sixteenth-century salver had been cut into no fewer than 169 pieces to avoid detection: all but two fragments were recovered and 'so successfully riveted together that its original beauty remains intact'. The story goes that years later Ives, on returning to Bristol a free man, visited the Council House to inspect the restored salver and, what is more, generously voiced his approval of the craftsmanship!

William Christopher, an 'ill-looking dirty fellow' of thirty, was also transported (for seven years) for filching clothes he found lying on the ground, while William Mason got twelve months' imprisonment for 'lifting' a gold watch and a silver pin. Because of his youth and previous good character Thomas Lane, who stole a brass chandelier owned by the Mayor, was recommended for mercy and shared [with Mary Parker, for larceny of a sofa] the dubious distinction of receiving the lightest sentence imposed at the riot trials—a month in prison. John Jones, who had suffered a head wound when the troops charged, was discovered on admission to hospital to have a military jacket stuffed under his coat. It cost him a year's hard labour. Thomas Brimel had six months behind bars in which to do penance for his sin—thieving a bible.

The case attracting most attention—held on Wednesday, 11 January—featured Chrisopher Davis. Aged forty-nine, he lived at Counterslip [off Temple Street] where 'he has for many years carried on an extensive and lucrative business as carter'. One report said he had recently sold out as wharfinger and carrier for £2,000 and, in addition, enjoyed 'an independence' of £300 a year. By no means, the normal run of riot prisoner.

Davis, well known locally for his generosity to the poor and as a champion of the under-privileged, seldom missed an opportunity at public meetings to express his disapproval of bishops, anti-reformers and Bristol Corporation. It seems he was also something of a tap-room orator and, boosted by a few drinks, could become quite vehement. In short, Mr Davis had a problem. He couldn't keep his mouth shut.

The inoffensive-looking man was accused with 'divers other persons unknown' of tumultuous and riotous assembly and of being involved in the attack on the New Gaol. The Attorney-General sought to prove Davis had been the instigator and leader of the outrages committed by the mob on Sunday, 30 October, although 'he had himself cautiously abstained from employing his own hand in the work of devastation'.

During the hearing, it emerged that Davis was seen at most of the places assailed by rioters. Early on the Sunday afternoon, outside the Mansion House, he held a silk umbrella aloft, waved his hat and cursed both the Church and the corporation. He shouted to an old acquaintance, John Gilbert, 'this is the end of your damned magistrates and bishops', adding that if he had his way those 'robbers' would be hanged by chains in Queen Square. When spotted later at the New Gaol, Davis appeared to be inciting the mob to further violence. His mouth was still working overtime: 'Now, damn ye, we will have Reform; this ought to have been done years ago.'

Shortly after the Bridewell had been attacked George Phipps, who lived in King Street, saw Davis at the head of a group of nearly 150 men and boys coming along Back Street, swinging his umbrella and declaring: 'Damn their eyes—burn them—down with them.' From the rear of his house, an alarmed Phipps called out 'For God's sake, Mr Davis, do come in' but Davis, who may not have heard and looked 'tipsy', strode on. Phipps seemed affected by emotion as he told the court that Davis, whom he had known for twenty years, was a 'highly humane and respectable' gentleman.

Davis was described as being drunk when he unburdened his radical soul on that fateful Sunday. He turned up near the Bishop's Palace, again yelling his condemnation of bishops and saying it was criminal they should pocket so much money when there were so many thousands of poor people in the country. Christopher Davis, it was evident, welcomed the chance to broadcast his views. Regrettably for him, the sobriety of his attire—'black coat, drab breeches and boots'—was not matched by his general demeanour during the riots.

In the ghastly realization of the morning after, Davis became a frightened man. He had a hunted look—as well he might—for law officers were seeking him and, on the Wednesday following the disturbances, he called at the Trenchard Street home of William Perry, a wharfinger's clerk, to whom he confided: 'I fear I'm in an unpleasant situation.' He remained Perry's uninvited guest for four days before going under cover of darkness to Hill's Bridge, from where a gig took him from the city.

Nearly two months later, the court also heard, he was discovered by attorney Thomas Crosby hiding in the attic of a

house at Sutton Montis, near Sherborne. Davis then exclaimed:
'You have found me, then. I'm not here for stealing or murder;
I'm glad you've found me. I'm happier now than at any time
since I left Bristol; I should never have left but on the advice
of my friends.' The remorseful prisoner added: 'There is one
thing against me—it is what I said.'

Now the reputable businessman with the runaway tongue
was on trial for his life. Even some prosecution witnesses
appeared reluctant to paint a dark picture, while those called
on his behalf emphasized that Davis was peaceable, honest and
benevolent by nature and, although inclined forcefully to speak
his mind on occasions (hardly a unique trait), became raucous
only after drinking. A number testified to meeting him during
the disturbances and claimed he told them he utterly disapproved of the violence.

It must have been difficult to imagine the doleful individual
now arraigned being involved in rioting at all, let alone as a
mob leader. *The Times* thought 'his physiognomy was that of
a weak and inoffensive man and very far from indicative of the
passions that usually lead to a share in acts of turbulence and
outrage'. Indeed, one might get the impression of a rather path-
etic figure making a clown of himself by drunkenly parading
the streets, brandishing an umbrella and loudly dispensing
some injudicious observations.

The court took a much more serious view, however. After
a two-hour summing-up by Chief Justice Tindal, the jury de-
liberated for a further hour before bringing in a verdict of
'Guilty'. Davis showed no reaction. It was just past nine o'clock
in the evening.

There were harrowing scenes the next morning when some
of those convicted of capital offences learned of their fate. It
became horribly apparent that the intervening night had
wrought an incredible change in Christopher Davis who, trem-
bling and weeping, was scarcely able to walk to the bar. When
asked formally if there was any reason why sentence of death
should not be passed, Davis cried: 'Oh, my Lord, I am innocent; I did not intend any harm.' He sank whimpering to a
chair. William Clarke, Thomas Gregory, Richard Vines and
Joseph Kayes then emerged separately to face the bench and,
confronted with the same dreaded question, each man was also

overcome. Between shuddering sobs, Vines kept protesting he was not guilty and called out for mercy; so, too, did Gregory. There was less to be heard from Clarke who, apparently drained of strength, rested his giddy head on the bar. Kayes went into convulsions, screaming his innocence and repeating 'Oh, my wife and children', and had forcibly to be removed.

The whole piteous spectacle was enough to wrench at the strongest stomachs. A newspaper reporter wrote: 'The judges were visibly affected. The majority of the spectators were in tears. Every man saw his pale face imaged in that of his neighbour; and the deep-drawn breathings of the men and the half-stifled screams of the females were mingled with the yells of the wretched man below and the convulsive sobs and groans of the prisoners who remained at the bar.' On learning from a doctor that it would be some time before Kayes was sufficiently recovered to reappear, Chief Justice Tindal addressed the other men:

You have been convicted, four of you in number, upon evidence in each particular case, which can leave no doubt of your guilt upon any reasonable mind of crimes so deeply affecting the interests, even the very existence of human society, that your lives have become justly forfeited to the laws of your country. Assembled together with multitudes of others, evildoers like yourselves, you have by threats and acts of violence thrown the peaceful and industrious inhabitants of this city into a state of panic and alarm; you have deprived many of their only means of livelihood. You have carried fire to public buildings, and to private dwellings, and have exposed the property of all to pillage and the lives of many to destruction. Human society cannot be held together if crimes like these are not put down by the strong hand of the law.

What motive could lead you to the commission of these crimes it is impossible from the evidence brought before us to judge with any reasonable certainty. It was not the pressure of want or misery; it was no grievance, imaginary or real, under which you laboured. I fear no other purpose can be assigned that will apply to the greater number of those who shared in these wicked transactions than that of giving up this city to the flames that it might become the object of universal pillage. You stand each of you a striking and awful example to others of the wickedness which men commit, and the misery which inevitably follows it, when they throw off the restraint of the laws of God and man and give themselves up to their own un-

9. Queen Square became the main centre of revelry and destruction

10. *Above:* Ruins of the Excise Office

Below: Ruins opposite the Assembly Rooms

11. *Above:* Ruins of the Mansion House, Custom House and other buildings

Below: Ruins of the Bishop's Palace

12. *Above:* The west side of Queen Square

Below: The north side of the Square similarly destroyed

COUNCIL-HOUSE,

FRIDAY MORNING,

11th of November, 1831.

The **MAGISTRATES** request that Persons who may be able to identify any of the Prisoners now in the Common Gaol of this City, on charges of Riot and Felony, will immediately attend at the Gaol, where the Magistrates are sitting for the purpose of investigating the Cases, and taking the Informations of Witnesses.

MILLS AND SON, PRINTERS, GAZETTE OFFICE, BRISTOL.

13. Poster calling upon inhabitants to identify prisoners

SIR N. C. TINDAL.

C.J. OF THE COMMON PLEAS.

Published by A.Maxwell

Printed by Graf & Soret

J.F.Bird del.t &

14. Sir Nicolas Conyngham Tindal

PETITION

TO

The King,

To Spare the Lives of the Five Men

UNDER

SENTENCE OF DEATH.

𝕿𝕺 𝖙𝖍𝖊 𝕶𝖎𝖓𝖌'𝖘 𝕸𝖔𝖘𝖙 𝕰𝖝𝖈𝖊𝖑𝖑𝖊𝖓𝖙 𝕸𝖆𝖏𝖊𝖘𝖙𝖞.

The humble Petition of the undersigned Inhabitants of the City of Bristol.

SIRE,

WE, the undersigned Inhabitants of the City of Bristol, beg to approach your Throne with the most sincere and ardent expressions of our attachment to your Majesty's Person and Government. We yield to none of your Majesty's subjects in our love of social order, in our desire to uphold and obey the laws, and in detestation of the criminal violation of them, which lately disgraced our City; and we are at all times ready to support your Majesty's Government, in any measures necessary to prevent the recurrence of tumult and crime.

It is with grief and horror we reflect on the loss of human life which has already occurred in this City; and we are animated by the strongest feelings of detestation against the perpetrators of those tumultuous and disgraceful proceedings. So appalling was the sacrifice of life on that melancholy occasion, that we are most anxious to submit to your Majesty's serious consideration any mitigatory facts, in the cases of those convicted, which may afford the slightest chance of saving their lives: and we beg further to call your attention to the remarkable absence of those circumstances of aggravation, by which the carrying into effect the extreme penalty of the law is justified.

We beg leave to point out to your Majesty's notice the entire absence of any testimony showing a guilty premeditation; that it has been made evident that the excesses of the mob arose from the impulse of the moment; and that, amid the excitement and the devastation of property, they restrained themselves from outrages affecting personal safety.

We beg also to call your Majesty's most gracious consideration to another important fact. The guilty conduct of most of the criminals capitally convicted began at a late period of the riots, when the unrestricted access to intoxicating liquors, which accidentally and unfortunately fell in their way, and the impunity that attended the first outrages, involved them in a depth of crime, which, in all probability, would have been prevented, had the proper measures been taken to check their mad and criminal career, and to restore the peace of the City.

We are fully sensible of the enormous guilt of the prisoners; but we earnestly implore your Majesty to exercise your royal clemency, by sparing the lives of these unhappy men, and by commuting their punishment, and thus afford them an opportunity of repenting of the injuries they have inflicted on society.

And your Petitioners, as in duty bound, will ever pray.

The above Petition lies for Signature at Mr. Manchee's, Quay - Street; Mr. Bingham's, Broad - Street; Mr. Rootsey's, North-Street; Wright & Bagnall's, 18, Bridge-Street; and at the Arcade.

T. J. MANCHEE, Printer, Quay-Street, Bristol.

15. A petition to the King

16. A caricature of Lt-Col Thomas Brereton

bridled passions. I can only pray that your unhappy example may be the means of preventing all others from treading in your steps.

You, Christopher Davis, are proved to have been present at the greater part of the lawless acts which have been committed within this city. You appear to have stood amongst the foremost of the multitude in their various acts of devastation. They were at once encouraged by your presence and example, and excited to further acts of outrage by your violent and inflammatory language. It is indeed a grievous and unhappy sight—a man, respectable from his age and station in life as you appear to be, bringing misery upon his friends, and destruction to himself, by yielding to the turbulence of his passions.

You, William Clarke, have also been proved to have been one of the foremost in the work of destruction. By you, a violent and tumultuous mob were instigated and led on to the attack and the destruction of the bridewell and the gaol. Your previous condition and habits of life now only serve to aggravate your crime beyond that of many others, who were reduced by your example to the commission of these enormities.

You, Thomas Gregory, formed part of that riotous mob which plundered the dwelling house of William Strong, and are proved to have been one of the persons who actually carried into the house the flaming papers by which it was afterwards burned to the ground.

You, Richard Vines, after you had broken and entered into one house with a tumultuous assemblage of people, are proved to have fed the fire, by which it was afterwards destroyed, with the books and furniture belonging to the owner. You are also proved to have called upon the mob to come on and, with such unlawful aid, you broke into another house which you first assisted in plundering and then in consigning to the flames.

There was an appalling quiet. Then followed the absolute sentence, the Chief Justice directing: 'Every one of you will be taken hence to the place from whence you came and thence to a place of execution, where you will be severally hanged by the neck until you are dead and may the Lord, in his infinite goodness, have mercy on your guilty souls.'

The graveyard stillness was broken by Davis, who lamented: 'Oh, my Lord, I hope you will have mercy. I never was in any depredation; I never meddled with any one thing; I never meddled with the fires; I never threw a stone or nail; I was never in a gaol before...' His voice tailed off, trapped in a parched throat. Such pleas proved unavailing, of course, and the four prisoners were taken from the courtroom 'in the greatest possible agony'. [Later that day Kayes, who had regained a little of his composure, was also sentenced to die and left ardently proclaiming that he had been wrongfully judged.]

Next to appear at the bar was a row of nineteen ashen faces, the owners of which had been convicted variously of riotous assembly, demolishing buildings and robbery—in fact, offences similar to those for which their predecessors were condemned to death. The Chief Justice declared:

You have, with many others who for the present have escaped the hands of justice, devoted to plunder and destruction the city in which you live—the place which has afforded to all of you subsistence and protection. You have reduced parts of it to a state of ruin and desolation more complete than any foreign enemy, unless the most mercilous, could have inflicted upon it.... You now stand at the bar of justice—a sad proof to yourselves and a monument and warning to all others, that the triumph of injustice is short-lived and that the law of your country is too strong to be assailed by such vain attempts as yours.

Under the commission of offences so aggravated, I know not that any just exception could have been taken if the full measure of the punishment, in some of your cases at least, had been allowed to take its course. But the earnest hope we entertain that the sad fate of those upon whom the sentence of law has been just passed will operate as a sufficient warning to all others, induces us to join in a humble recommendation to His Majesty that your lives may be spared.

I would not however lead you to expect that by escaping the bitterness of death you have avoided all punishment for your offence. You will pass the remainder of your lives in a foreign and distant land, separated forever from parents, relations and friends, and in a state of severe labour and constant privation. Thus will your perpetual absence from your own country prevent you from disturbing again the peace and happiness of society, and will operate as a warning to all others to avoid the example of your crimess For the present, the sentence of death must be recorded against you.

Colour returned to pallid cheeks and Kearney 'actually leapt for joy', although it is unlikely the prisoners had much conception of just what transportation entailed. However, they doubtless reflected it might well be far more acceptable than rotting in an English gaol or prison hulk and infinitely preferable to the hangman's noose. Indeed, conditions had so greatly improved since the establishment of the first convict colony 'Down Under' [at Port Jackson, in Sydney Cove, in January 1788] it was even said men and women openly committed petty crimes to obtain a free ocean voyage to this new land in the confident belief that, after completing sentence, better opportunities awaited them.

Nevertheless, this was by no means a penal picnic the judges were recommending instead of the scaffold. Life could still be unimaginably grim in that remote vastness on the underside of the globe—an unceasing purgatory for some—and, moreover, it was a one-way only ticket.

Those convicted (their sentences commuted to transportation for life) were George Andrews, Patrick Barnett, Thomas Evans Bendall, Benjamin Broad, Timothy Collings, James Courtney, Stephen Gaisford, Henry Green, Cornelius Hickey, Daniel Higgs, Patrick Kearney, John Mecay, William Reynolds, James Sims, James Snook, Michael Sullivan, John Towell, Matthew Warry and Charles Williams.

Short terms of imprisonment were later substituted for 'sentence of death' recorded against seven others found guilty of theft: David James, Henry Krinks, Joseph Thomas and James Walker (two years each), James Coleman (eighteen months) and James Dyer and James Price (twelve months apiece).

Seven more convicted of stealing were ordered to be transported: James Ives (for fourteen years) and William Christopher, Charles Huish, Joseph Keates, Aaron Martin, Richard Neville and James Street (seven years each).

Nineteen of these 'riot' men were aboard the prison hulk, *Justitia*, moored in the Thames at Woolwich, by 25 January and a further seven arrived two days afterwards. Most were entered in the register as 'Not Known' (no previous convictions). A few received more attention: Benjamin Broad, for instance, was marked down as 'conviction before, bad character and connections', while Gaisford and Hickey were similarly noted. For a different reason, James Ives also rated a special mention—'well behaved, gave the court much useful information, good connections'.

And so, in the fusty confinement of the forbidding hulk, the convicts awaited a transport ship...

Chapter Twelve

LAUNCHED INTO ETERNITY

IN BRISTOL, five other men waited. Condemned to die, they languished in separate cells at the New Gaol which, despite much repair work, still bore deep scars from the rioting. Time was fast running out. The date fixed for the executions was Friday, 27 January, just fifteen days after the ultimate penalty had been pronounced.

Sections of the community, shocked by the severity of the sentences, campaigned to save the victims and an estimated 10,000 inhabitants signed a petition to the King 'praying for a commutation of the punishment'. There were also independent representations to the Home Secretary on behalf of individual prisoners, notably an appeal for William Clarke's reprieve which was accompanied by fifteen 'exculpatory affidavits'.

In favour of the five hapless men, it was strongly argued in some quarters that their actions were unpremeditated and exacerbated by drink, that they had taken no-one's life in the process and, moreover, that the riots would not have occurred but for the ineptitude of the authorities.

Particularly was there remonstrance in the much-publicized case of Christopher Davis, whose offence, according to many people, amounted to no more than vociferously expressing his opinions. That the loquacious Davis had uttered 'a hundred ridiculous things to his friends' was not doubted by one sympathizer, who added: 'The great wonder is, not that a man should have acted thus, but that his friends—friends, some of twenty years' standing—should have come forward to give such evidence against him and the greater wonder still that, on such evidence, a jury of twelve men should have found him guilty of riotously destroying the gaol.'

The newspapers joined in. *The Sun* declared: 'Their guilt was that of infatuation, of phrenzy, rather than of cold, studied, methodical malignity. Had the civil power done its duty, these misguided men would never have had an opportunity of effecting mischief. . . . If the Bristol rioters are guilty, the Bristol magistracy was doubly so; if the one party had a right to stand at the bar of justice, the other had an equal right to stand there beside them; nor do we know any earthly reason why the brave military and the misguided populace should have been made the victims of a slothful, chicken-hearted magistracy.'

After pointing to the difference between crimes of impulse and those of deliberation, the *Morning Herald* said: 'We do not say enough, but too much, blood has been shed already in consequence of the Bristol riots. Many perished in the fires—many have been slaughtered by military execution and many more maimed for life. The judicial destruction of five more human beings in cold blood will not be of the least advantage to the interests of society—justice does not demand their lives. We implore the *kingly prerogative of mercy* to interfere, lest the country may believe they were immolated on the altars of revenge.'

On the day before the hangings were scheduled, there was a dramatic development. A reprieve came through for Richard Vines, the youngest of the five, reportedly because of statements filed in proof of his alleged 'idiotcy' and also suspected perjury by a prosecution witness at his trial. [Vines was transported for life.]

The remaining four doomed men were said to have received the news with stoicism and that Thursday evening relatives and friends visited the gaol to say their final melancholy farewells, the scenes being 'afflicting and soul-harrowing beyond description'. Then the prisoners, who had been attended daily by priests, were again exhorted to earnest prayer.

A crowd began to assemble on both sides of the New Cut early on the bitterly cold Friday morning and, by noon, had increased to several thousands. A solitary sentry paced the exposed platform of the gallows erected at the top of the lodge at the front of the gaol and the lower portion of which was draped with black cloth. About 700 special constables were on duty in the vicinity, the military guard at the prison strengthened and detachments of infantry and cavalry, though screened from public view, at the alert in the city. Blinds were drawn in some shop windows.

Ministers had been with the prisoners since dawn, moving from cell to cell offering words of comfort and reading from the scriptures. Soon after midday, in the awful privacy of the condemned room, the agonized quartet were freed of leg-irons. Preceded by the prison chaplain (the Rev William Day), who intoned the burial service, the funeral procession of sheriffs, the four victims, clergymen, city officers, turnkeys and the governor (William Humphries) edged slowly across the yard when some of the other convicts, drawn up to watch, were said to have burst into tears.

In a small room beneath the gallows, the chaplain delivered an address during which he 'called on the prisoners to trust alone in the Lord Jesus Christ as the last and only hope here and hereafter'. It was a dreadful moment. The condemned men embraced each other, thanked the governor and the ministers for their consolation and kindness, continued to 'utter ejaculations to heaven' and, somehow, prepared themselves for the inevitable. As *Felix Farley's Bristol Journal* put it, 'the utmost attention was paid to the wretched men in every respect that could at all tend to soothe the last moments of their sojourn in this world'. Some of those with them wept.

With arms pinioned and the fatal ropes around their necks, the four men were helped to ascend an interior spiral staircase to reach the scaffold. Christopher Davis, the first to emerge, surveyed the huge hushed crowd spread out below. Thomas Gregory, Joseph Kayes and the burly William Clarke followed. There was no bravado, no hysteria and, from a distance at least, they must have appeared remarkably calm and resigned. Nevertheless, the whole macabre business seemed shrouded in horrifying unreality.

The four climbed a ladder to the platform of the 'drop'. Affixing the ropes to hooks above, the executioner—'a poor, dirty, wretched looking being, whose self-apparent poverty was a sufficient reason for his undertaking the revolting office', said *The Bristol Mercury*—shook so violently that he nearly fell from the scaffold and had to be steadied by a turnkey. He was still shivering when he adjusted white caps over the heads of the prisoners, cutting from them the light of that bleak day.

CHRISTOPHER DAVIS.
(From a Sketch, taken in Court, by Mr. W. Hazard).

The Bristol Mercury.

TUESDAY, JANUARY 17.

Condemned to hang: Christopher Davis

At five minutes past one o'clock, 'the fatal bolt was then drawn and the prisoners were launched into eternity'. An observer described the sickening finale: 'At the time the drop fell, the prisoners were in the act of fervent prayer and the sudden jarring sound it made in descending, with the equally sudden cessation of four human voices in the midst of half-breathed supplications for mercy, was peculiarly appalling.'

An uncomfortable shudder swept through the massed crowd, which was strangely subdued (in marked contrast to behaviour seen at some other public executions of the period), and people quickly and quietly dispersed. Gregory and Clarke had died instantly although Kayes, it was reported, suffered for a short while. Life lingered for a moment in Christopher Davis, the mouth which had led to his downfall silenced forever.

According to *The Bath Chronicle*, the body of Davis was removed by hearse from the New Gaol to 'the house of his wife's father' in Shepton Mallet and later interred in a chancel vault of the parish church in the presence of 'many respectable individuals'. Clarke and Gregory were buried at Bristol and Kayes taken to his native Cardiff for interment.

The absolute penalty of the law had been seen to be done. Those thousands of signatures so hopefully appended to petitions had failed in their merciful objective and *The Bristol Liberal* had this to say:

The forfeiture of their lives has left a memorable example of the dreadful influence of popular frenzy when uncurbed by civil or military power, or even the menace of it. By the death of these men, the law has indeed been avenged but it is impossible to deny that, although there cannot be much abatement of the ignominy attaching to the criminal who makes his exit upon the scaffold, yet a very large share of public sympathy has fallen to the lot of these individuals, from the peculiar circumstances of their case, and especially from the fact that they were not villains by premeditation, but became the victims of a sudden stimulus, the vigour of which was heightened by impunity and by the immediate means of intoxication.... If ignorance, coupled with intoxication on the one hand, led to crime, overweening confidence and presumption prepared the field for it on the other, and unparalleled imbecility crowned the whole ... the odium which attaches to certain parties not yet placed on *their* trial, while they are made instrumental the conviction of others there is, we have no hesitation in saying, a large measure of justice to deal out before public opinion can be satisfied.

Of course, this was but one view. At the other end of the local press spectrum *Felix Farley's Bristol Journal*, which unswervingly maintained that radical agitation was at the bottom of the riots, commented in this manner on the executions:

Another scene of the Reform-Tragedy—God grant it may be the last—was enacted in this city yesterday, when four of the criminals condemned at the late special commission, suffered, and most justly, an ignominious death. Human society (as the Lord Chief Justice

WILLIAM CLARKE.

THOMAS GREGORY.
(From a Sketch taken in Court, by Mr. W. Hazard.)

RICHARD VINES.

JOSEPH KAYES.

Condemned to hang: William Clarke, Thomas Gregory, Richard Vines (reprieved at the eleventh hour) and Joseph Kayes

observed, in passing sentence) could not be held together if crimes like theirs were not put down by the strong arm of the law;—unless others were deterred from the commission of similar enormities by the just severity of their sentence; all that makes life valuable to man, the free enjoyment of the fruits of his honest industry, and protection from personal violence, must be altogether given up; the innocent and weak would become a prey to the wicked and the strong; and brutal force would take the place of order and of law.

Indeed, the Special Commission which tried the rioters of Bristol (or, more precisely, the proportion actually apprehended) had inscribed an awesome mark. Of the 102 prisoners appearing before the judges, eighty-one were convicted and twenty-one acquitted; indictments involving a dozen or so others were not proceeded. Considering the amount of destruction and damage caused in the city, remarkably few were finally charged with causing it. In fact, the majority of cases concerned stealing.

Early reports that several hundreds of rioters had been arrested turned out to be far from accurate, but might be accounted for to some extent if one included recaptured convicts released from the gaols by the mob. Be that as it may, many people actively engaged in the lawlessness unquestionably got away with it.

For those who did not, requital was often severe and in some instances, as we have seen, absolute. Death was recorded against thirty-one men and youths, but the sentence carried out on only four; of the remainder, twenty were directed to be transported for life (either to Van Diemen's Land or New South Wales) and seven sent to prison with hard labour. The fifty others convicted were sentenced as follows: seven transported (one for fourteen years; six for seven years apiece); forty-three imprisoned with hard labour (eleven for two years; seventeen for one year; seven for six months; three for four months; three for two months; two for a month).

The military, too, had been striving to balance the books...

Chapter Thirteen

TO BE OR NOT TO BE?

L IEUTENANT-COLONEL THOMAS BRERETON was so much affected by the riots and their consequences that his personality underwent a melancholy change. Disturbing memories of those three dramatic days preyed upon a tortured mind, which reflected in his haggard face. The unhappy colonel became agitated and preoccupied, found it distressing even to discuss the events and, moreover, continued to suffer the gnawing unpleasantness of a liver complaint doubtless aggravated by recent tension.

Now came the humiliation of appearing before a court-martial, with its attendant glare of newspaper publicity, in the very city where he had made his home and friends. The trial—held in the Merchants Hall, King Street, close to some of the worst scenes of destruction—opened on Monday, 9 January 1832. The president, Lieutenant-General Sir Henry Fane, sat with four major-generals, six colonels and four lieutenant-colonels. Captain Arnold Thompson (Paymaster, 81st Regiment of Foot) had been appointed to act as deputy judge advocate. The important case 'excited the greatest possible interest'.

Standing to attention in front of the impressive tribunal, Brereton answered 'Not Guilty' to each of eleven charges which collectively alleged a 'great want of vigour and decision requisite for the duties in which he was engaged, are highly disgraceful to his character as an officer and prejudicial to good order and military discipline and tend to destroy the confidence of the troops in their officers and reflect dishonour on His Majesty's service'. Major-General Sir Charles Dalbiac, who prosecuted, submitted that some of the indictments carried with them the culpability of a nature 'altogether unprecedented and unheard of in the case of a British officer'.

At the end of each day's hearing, Brereton returned to his home, Redfield House, at Lawrence Hill, a mile or so from the city centre on the Upper Bath Road. Ostensibly he lived in considerable material comfort, his needs being attended to by several servants. An elegant drawing-room was graced by dark moreen curtains, with matching couches and chairs, a rosewood card-table, a handsome French-polished pianoforte, a gleaming sideboard on claw-feet, sparkling cut-glass bowls and a number of paintings. The colonel (in less trying times) usually ate well from richly-coloured blue and white plates, his meals being served from silver dishes in a dining-room where curtains of scarlet blended harmoniously with a set of chairs and a table of solid mahogany. Dominated by a sturdy four-poster, the principal bedroom was also furnished with a flat-fronted chest of drawers, Pembroke tables and some chintz curtains of floral design.

The colonel was proud of his fine collection of shotguns and of his wine cellar stocked with more than 400 bottles of madeira, vintage port and a selection of choice 'reds' and 'whites' from the vineyards of South Africa. In attractive grounds outside, the livestock included a milch cow and a yearling calf; there was, too, a splendid bay saddle horse and the stables also housed a pony and a phaeton, two small carriages and the colonel's private gig. When Brereton's wife was alive they lived first in Hambrook [about four miles north-east of Bristol] and then at Clifton Wood House, but he subsequently moved with his children and domestic staff to rent this more suitable—and, one suspects, less expensive—residence.

Brereton doted on his two daughters (Catherine Letitia was nearly six and Mary Sarah Coghlan just over three) and most evenings would visit the nursery to see them tucked into bed; if home late, however, he always peeked in and watched for a while with fatherly affection as they slumbered. This, then, was the man now called upon to defend his military honour. Here dwelt the 'scapegoat'.

The family's faithful housekeeper, Miss Mary Ann Pitchforth, was among the first to notice a marked alteration in Brereton's disposition. He looked nervous and distracted and, on occasions, rang for her and asked to be brought some familiar object which was plainly visible and within easy reach. Then, sometimes, he knocked things about. James Wilson, the young footman, who normally found his master 'very cheerful', also witnessed a transformation. Dejected and head down, Brereton would pace the floor for long spells. The anguished colonel, it seems, was fighting a grim battle not only for his reputation—but also for his mind.

Somehow he managed largely to disguise his distraught emotions at the court-martial where, among various misdemeanours, he was accused of temporizing in a manner encouraging to the rioters; sending a squadron of the 14th Light Dragoons from Bristol, falsely stating their condition and refusing to recall them; contrary to magistrates' instructions, neglecting to protect the New Gaol; remaining inactive when the Bishop's Palace was attacked; not utilizing the services of the Dodington Yeomanry; retiring to bed, despite an order from the Mayor to restore peace in the city, and showing reluctance to dispatch troops to Queen Square at four o'clock on the morning of 31 October, notwithstanding a direction from the magistrates.

They had thrown the book at him and among those present to peruse the open pages were many citizens. The man from *The Times* reported:

The upper part of the room was occupied by benches filled with ladies whose appearance and manners were in the highest degree prepossessing. The table for the Court ran down the centre of the room, and there were two other tables at the sides, near the President's end, one for the defendant (Colonel Brereton), his counsel (Mr Earle), and his solicitor (Mr T. M. Evans); the others for papers, &c, connected with the prosecution. A barrier was erected at the lower end of the room, to keep out the crowd, which was very numerous, and, indeed, the whole interest of the community here seems exclusively directed to the proceedings of this court, the trials before the Judges now being matters of minor consideration. A few minutes after 11 o'clock the members of the court took their places, and the list was called over.

After preliminary formalities, and the pleas had been recorded, attention focused upon the prosecutor. Dalbiac, a perceptive man in his mid-fifties, had seen considerable active service in the Peninsular War and spent much of his military life with the 4th Light Dragoons. He had marshalled his facts well and presented the case with forthright lucidity.

The riots, he said, had excited discussion and speculation in all sections of the Press and at every level of society throughout the land. The true facts had never been publicly stated, but seldom was there a matter about which the public were more entitled to know the full story. Some apportioned much blame for the 'disgraceful consequences' of the disturbances to the civil authorities; others held the military entirely responsible. The only undisputed question, he declared, was that a high degree of fault attached to some quarter—hence the absolute necessity for the present investigation.

With a shrewd sense of occasion, Dalbiac outlined the relevant circumstances. His apparent honesty of purpose, subtly shaded with a contrived dash of personal modesty, must have appealed to the court, especially when he confessed to a deep awareness of his own 'deficiencies' in carrying out the important task and craved indulgence for his 'humble abilities'. However inadequate he felt about successfully discharging the heavy responsibility entrusted to him, he added with telling humility, he had never shrunk from his duty. The fifteen high-ranking officers sitting in judgment may well have interpreted the allusion to 'duty' as being an oblique reference to the defendants alleged conduct during the riots.

Dalbiac stated that on being summoned to the Mansion House in the early evening of Saturday, 29 October, cavalry units quickly formed up at the alarm post [recruiting office] in College Green where Brereton ordered them to load firearms. Having reached Queen Square, the same soldiers were expressly instructed not to fire, nor to use undue force, but merely to 'ride through' and 'walk away' the rioters. Brereton was seen shaking hands with some of the mob, acknowledging the cheers of the crowd and feebly attempting to disperse them.

Such clinical recapitulation put Brereton in the worst possible light, of course, and must have seemed to him far removed from the confusion and clamour of the episode at the time. In the cushioned comfort of hindsight, perhaps even Brereton himself now wondered just why he had not adopted a much firmer line with the populace. Dalbiac recounted how effectively Captain Gage—on his own initiative—had led a charge against those attacking the Council House later that Saturday night. There had been an unfortunate death or two and a few injuries but, surely, Gage was now being shown by the prosecutor to have employed the tactics expected of an army officer faced with such a situation.

Describing events outside the Mansion House on the Sunday morning, Dalbiac spoke of the mob's 'outrageous' conduct towards a detachment of the 14th Light Dragoons who suffered 'indignities' until Brereton, apparently blaming them for the disturbance, directed Gage to withdraw his men from Queen Square and subsequently instructed the whole squadron to leave the city.

In retrospect, Brereton's decision to dismiss the dragoons while the rioters grew in both strength and defiance was probably regarded by the court as little short of madness. Dalbiac pressed home his advantage. He referred to the colonel's refusal to recall those troops, despite sharp protests from the magistrates, and also told how young Cornet Kelson was sent with a small unit to the New Gaol and given strict orders by Brereton not to use force. At this juncture, Dalbiac could not refrain from voicing his utter dismay. 'His Majesty's dragoons, and I speak it with shame,' he asserted, 'looked patiently on whilst the rioters were busily and deeply engaged in their work of demolition, the gaol gates having been already forced. The detachment remained for a minute or two in front of the gaol and then turned back to Queen Square.'

Members of the tribunal, steeped in the traditions of bravery and invincibility of the nation's military arm, doubtless drew mental pictures of the incident. Any suggestion of the British Army (however small the unit) 'retreating' from an undisciplined rabble (however large) would have appeared to them as unthinkable and repugnant.

The court then heard that a detachment of 3rd Dragoon Guards, under the personal command of Brereton, watched passively as rioters attacked the Bishop's Palace and, even when appealed to, gave no assistance to constables and others trying to overcome the mob. Brereton, it was further alleged, headed the cavalry to the already burning Mansion House, but soon afterwards ordered all troops back to quarters.

From about half-past nine that Sunday night until almost five o'clock the following morning, Dalbiac maintained, not a single soldier was dispatched to combat the mob; indeed, Lt-Col

Brereton 'thought fit to retire to bed' and ignored an urgent directive at midnight from the Mayor calling upon him to put down the rioting. Dalbiac also related how Alderman Camplin eventually persuaded Brereton to lead a party of dragoon guards to Queen Square before dawn, the mob then being repeatedly charged in a 'decisive manner'. The later arrival of reinforcements and success of resultant actions ensured that 'perfect tranquility reigned' by midday.

'This', declared Dalbiac, 'was chiefly effected by that very squadron of the 14th Dragoons which exactly 24 hours before had been pronounced by Lieutenant-Colonel Brereton, and reported by him to the municipal authorities assembled in the Guildhall, to be utterly insufficient to restore the public peace or to offer any effectual check to the outrages of the rioters or to the deplorable and disgraceful destruction of property which followed the removal of that squadron from the city.'

In conclusion, Dalbiac said he trusted Brereton would not regard his prosecution as a personal attack and would surely understand that there 'can be little but unmixed bitterness in the discharge of a duty, which tends to bring down punishment or dishonour upon the head of a fellow soldier'. Brereton cannot have derived much consolation from that.

Eleven letters which had passed between the defendant and the Horse Guards were produced as evidence. Among them was one of Monday, 31 October 1831, to Lord Fitzroy Somerset in which Brereton, referring to several recent developments, wrote:

... the mob proceeded to the work of devastation without it being possible to give them the slightest check, for our military opposition, as I have before informed your Lordship, could be but trifling and the magistrates I may say had *no* Civil power. The consequence was that a regular organized body of men proceeded deliberately to put their wicked intentions into effect, and I am sorry to say they succeeded as the following melancholy list will show [*Brereton here detailed buildings destroyed or damaged*]. I have drawn the squadron again from Keynsham; another troop of the 14th from Gloucester is on the march and will be here before I close this. Half a troop of the Bedminster Yeomanry have joined, and are now patrolling, previous to which I cleared all the streets with the squadron of the 14th Dragoons.[1]

[1] PRO HO 40/28.

Another letter considered by the court was from Major-General Pearson to Brereton, forwarded to Fitzroy Somerset on 1 November. In it, Pearson agreed with sending the 14th from Bristol because, he said:

... the continued presence of that small force who had brought on themselves the fury of the populace, by having killed one man and wounded others, would have endangered the safety of the whole body whose weak numbers were too small to enable them to act with any effect against the excited population—independent of which there is no doubt but, by their continuance on the spot at the moment, the loss of private property would have been much greater than it unfortunately was, and could not have been prevented by their longer continuance; on the contrary, from the almost exhausted state of the horses this squadron, at the time of being withdrawn, required both rest and feeding to render them again efficient for service.[1]

Many witnesses were due to be called and on that first day just enough time remained to hear some of the Town Clerk's evidence. Ludlow said although magistrates in the Mansion House on the Saturday ordered the military to clear the mob in Queen Square, he could not swear Brereton was told explicitly to open fire; neither did he recall any magistrate telling the colonel *not* to do so. However, the Town Clerk remembered Brereton saying a precise requisition would be necessary if fire-arms were to be used; on the other hand the magistrates, whose authority the colonel never disputed, naturally expected the most effective measures would be adopted.

On the second day of the court-martial, Mayor Pinney claimed that Brereton was directed to commence firing if circumstances demanded but the officer generally favoured employing as little force as possible. He would not accuse Brereton of 'positive disobedience' at that time—'I should rather call it non-compliance with the orders'. Brereton frequently intimated the crowd were good-humoured and ought not to be antagonized, the Mayor said, but the magistrates' impression was that the colonel's conduct in Queen Square that Saturday evening was 'feeble and temporizing'.

Alderman Abraham Hilhouse and Captain Gage were examined in turn, the latter referring to Brereton's initial instructions that swords were not to be drawn and neither were carbines

[1] PRO HO 40/28.

or force to be used against the crowd. When it was decided to charge in Queen Square, he stated, the colonel insisted on only the 'flats' of sabres being employed.

On the third day, another officer (Lt James Dawson) and two NCOs were among those who recounted what occurred on the Saturday in Queen Square and at the Council House. Occasionally faint glimmers of extenuation appeared such as when Sergeant Edmund Deane (3rd Dragoon Guards), while confirming Brereton waved his hat as the crowd cheered, explained that rioters reached up to shake the mounted colonel's hand and 'I supposed it was against his will'. Nevertheless, there was no dodging the snowballing weight of emerging evidence that, however noble his reasons, Brereton had displayed uncertainty and weakness.

The relentless Dalbiac presented the prosecution's case charge by charge, which meant some witnesses reappeared. The Mayor was now asked about the Sunday, when he and others had hurriedly to leave the unguarded Mansion House, and of meetings held that day—particularly when Brereton reported his intention of sending the 14th Light Dragoons from Bristol. Despite objections, Pinney declared, the colonel later refused to call them back, adding that to do so would mean their certain destruction. The Mayor said he never regarded the troops as being under his own command, nor were his fellow magistrates sufficiently experienced to say exactly how the soldiers should be deployed, but he reminded the court that the military were there expressly to assist the civil authorities and to carry out their general directions.

Town Clerk Ludlow deposed that when he exclaimed it was 'a dreadful thing' to leave the city virtually unprotected, Brereton said the men and horses of the 14th were tired and unfit for duty. Ludlow also recalled telling the colonel he would report the matter to the 'proper place' and further asserted in court that when the 14th departed a state of 'very great confusion' existed with the mob 'in possession of the city'.

Much of the evidence on the fourth day also related to the exit of the 14th Light Dragoons. Asked about the state of his troops and horses at that time, Captain Gage replied that they were capable of performing any duty required of cavalry and, in his view, the livery stables (where they were quartered) could have been defended easily by half-a-dozen soldiers against any mob.

Final testimony that day [Thursday, 12 January, the same on which—in another courtroom—Christopher Davis and four other rioters were sentenced to be hanged] came from Cornet Charles Kelson, who stated that he had led a small detachment of 3rd Dragoon Guards to the New Gaol and, without taking steps to check the mob, then returned with his men to College Green where he reported to Brereton that he had obeyed orders—and done nothing. 'He told me I had acted perfectly right,' Kelson further alleged.

At that stage of the court-martial, the prosecution had still to call a host of witnesses concerning six more charges and the whole of the defence yet to be heard.

It had been a particularly depressing day for Brereton and a marked change in his temperament after the hearing was apparent. He did not go home immediately, but spent the evening with a few friends including Major Ellard and Augustus Lewis Loinsworth (Army Medical Officer for the Bristol District). The doctor, who had in the recent past noticed Bereton say and do the 'most inconsistent' things, realized the colonel's general condition was now rather worse. The edgy Brereton made some inconsistent assertions and wanted his counsel (William Erle) to propose matters to the court which, in Loinsworth's subsequently expressed view, 'as a military man, or a man in his senses, must have known would never be acceded to'.

Brereton left the Reeves Hotel at a quarter to eleven, shaking hands with Loinsworth and Ellard before climbing into the gig (dutifully brought over by his gardener) and setting off for Redfield House. His two friends experienced some misgiving as he disappeared into the darkness.

At about the same time, William Erle called by arrangement at 18 The Mall, Clifton, where Captain Thompson, the deputy judge advocate, was staying during the trial. According to Thompson, the lawyer pointed out that Brereton's feelings had been 'so much hurt' by the turn the evidence had taken against him and the apparent hopelessness of contradicting it, that he wished to plead guilty to the remainder of the charges and confine his defence to a few observations on the evidence already adduced, provided his further attendance in court could be dispensed with, and no further evidence examined.

Thomspon also reported later that he refrained from expressing a personal opinion but referred Brereton's legal advisor to the *Rules and Regulations of the Army* which, the captain observed, said when a prisoner pleaded guilty 'it is the duty of the court-martial notwithstanding to receive, and report in their proceedings, such evidence as may afford a full knowledge of the circumstances, it being essential that the facts and particulars should be known to those whose duty it is to report on the case, or who have discretion to carrying the sentence into effect'.[1]

It is reasonable to suppose Thompson's reply was soon made known to Brereton, who had arrived home just after eleven o'clock—an hour past his normal bedtime—and started fretfully to pace the carpeted floor of the sitting-room. He twice rang for his housekeeper and on the second occasion, somewhen before two in the morning, she saw him writing at his desk and then throwing papers into the fire. Before bidding her 'Good Night', the colonel handed Miss Pitchforth a letter telling her to ensure it was delivered to his uncle, Lt-Col Andrew Coghlan [a former long-serving officer of the 45th Regiment of Foot who, as a captain, first took an enthusiastic young Brereton to the West Indies in 1797]. Coghlan now lived at Bath, maintaining his association with the army in the 3rd Veteran Battalion.

An overwrought Brereton failed that night to take even a peep at his sleeping daughters, but left the desk and went straightway to his own bedroom. It was about a quarter past two. A few minutes elapsed ...

A loud bang shattered the stillness. Thomas Brereton had shot himself through the heart.

[1] PRO WO 71/280.

Chapter Fourteen

'THE INJUSTICE I HAVE BEEN DONE'

THE STARTLED HOUSEKEEPER, who heard the report clearly, ventured briefly into the colonel's room before arousing the other servants.

Brereton was lying on the bed, his eyes staring lifelessly at the ceiling and his mouth wide open. Blood saturated his shirt; he also wore trousers and was in stockinged feet. His divested jacket and waistcoat hung over a chair, while his watch, spectacles, purse and comb lined the mantelpiece. As though at supine attention, the colonel's right arm ran stiffly down his side; the left arm was slightly bent towards his head and the fatal pistol, one of a pair he kept loaded in case of intruders, on the floor.

The tremulous flame of a candle on the bedside table cast shaky shadows upon the walls. Nearby was an opened bible, on the front fly-leaf of which has been penned: 'Died at three o'clock on the morning of the 14th of January 1829 my beloved wife, Olivia, at Clifton Wood House.' That Brereton had taken his life almost exactly twenty-four hours before the third anniversary of her death prompted some speculation that, in his confused mind, he mistook the date and intended his own exit to coincide precisely with the time of day and month of his wife's. Perhaps the superstitious even noted it was now Friday the Thirteenth!

A messenger sped to Bath for Lt-Col Coghlan who, on being awakened at five o'clock, 'thereupon instantly proceeded' to Redfield House which he reached as dawn struggled to escape the wintry shackles of night. Miss Pitchforth gave him the letter [later sworn-to as Brereton's only will]:

My ever dearest Uncle: My unfortunate mind is not now in a state

149

to enter into particulars and I can therefore only hope yourself and my dearest aunt will not forsake my innocent and helpless babes who will be but little sensible when they awake to-morrow of the injustice done to their unfortunate father and which deprives them forever of his protection. Let me request that you will immediately write to Mr Ross who will not fail to give them his protection and let him know the injustice I have been done. Do not let poor Pitchforth want, she has been a faithful creature to me. I cannot say more. God in heaven bless you both. T. B.

Captain Phillips[1] will have in his hands upwards of five hundred pounds which includes two stock receipts for about four hundred given to him this morning in order to sell them out for me. There is one more stock receipt in my desk for upwards I believe of six hundred. I scarcely owe anything but half a year's rent to March £50, for the newspapers about £5, Messrs Moss in London about £5 10s, Mr Evans and Mr Earl their charges respecting my unfortunate business. Pitchforth will give you all the receipts for the last year or you can find them in my writing desk. If not expensive, let my unfortunate remains be placed beside poor Olivia's. I request that no expense will be incurred that it is possible to avoid for my funeral as in my opinion that is a waste of money. Every allowance must be made for my present state of mind and which must account for the incorrectness of this last address.

T. B.

[On 2 April Coghlan, as great-uncle and guardian of the orphaned girls, was to be granted administration 'with the will annexed of the goods chattels and credits of Thomas Brereton ... for the use and benefit of the said infants'. Five years later on 31 March 1837 the old soldier, then seventy, finally succumbed to a 'long and painful illness'—a mere seventeen days after making his own last will and testament, which included bequests to his wards. Sadly the elder child, Catherine Letitia, died within five weeks—on 2 May, her eleventh birthday—so only her sister, Mary Sarah Coghlan, figured in the administration papers transferred on 18 December 1837 to the attorney of their maternal grandfather, Hamilton Ross, then a Cape businessman.]

A stunned and uneasy air was apparent when the court-martial reassembled later that morning. Sir Henry Fane, the fifty-three-year-old president, rose formally to state that those

---

[1] William H. Phillips (Paymaster, Bristol Recruiting District).

present were probably already aware of the 'most distressing' reports concerning the defendant, adding that Major Mackworth and the District Military Surgeon had gone to ascertain the truth. When confirmation of Brereton's death arrived, Major-General Dalbiac appeared extremely moved and said if the court was pained 'how much deeper must that pain be to the individual who has had the task assigned to him of conducting the prosecution. I do assure you that I rise with a degree of distress and embarrassment such as I never remember to have felt in the course of my life.'

Fane immediately sent a brief note about the tragic development to London, where Fitzroy Somerset reported to the Commander-in-Chief: 'You will be shocked to hear that Lt-Col Brereton has destroyed himself.'[1] In a follow-up letter the same day, General Fane was more illuminating. After referring to the 'catastrophe', he pointed out to Lord Hill that the evidence given by both Captain Gage and Cornet Kelson was 'so completely condemnatory of the conduct of Lt-Col Brereton and placed him in such a view that it produced a feeling of incapacity to meet the further proceedings of the court and he consequently at a late hour last night sent to the judge advocate to desire to know if he could be permitted to plead Guilty to the remainder of the charges at once and thus avoid further exposure. The judge advocate very properly referred him to a specific clause on this subject which is in the General Regulations of the Army. . . . He must have received this communication toward's 12 o'clock at night and I am informed that he committed suicide at about three a.m. . . . It is a melancholy termination of our proceedings, but I am inclined to think from what I hear of the individual that it will have saved him from utter destitution and ruin!'

Sir Henry went on: 'Fortunately, the proceedings of the court have advanced so far as to show to the public that amongst the military no fault existed, except on the part of this individual, and the civil authorities will have had the satisfaction of having been able to show that they were neither backward, nor inactive, in the discharge of their duties—at least, after the tumult had gained head.'[1]

The inquest was held the next morning at Brereton's home

[1] PRO HO 40/28.

by order of W. Joyner Ellis, a coroner for the County of Gloucestershire. At one time, so many people were in the bedroom viewing the body that there was danger of the floor collapsing. Members of the jury and others beat a hasty retreat downstairs where they found a large crack extending the length of the parlour ceiling.

Among the witnesses were the colonel's housekeeper and his footman, both of whom wept as they gave evidence. On leaving the room, the former fainted. Dr Loinsworth told the coroner that Brereton, whom he attended years earlier in the West Indies and also for some time recently, had a severe liver disorder and during the riots was suffering from the effects of an acute attack. Consequently, he was 'not in a fit state of health for the performance of the arduous duties that devolved upon him' and since then had been extremely agitated.

Asked why he had not remained with Brereton, who was obviously in a bad way on the Thursday night, Loinsworth said the merest mention that he needed care would have increased his complaint tenfold; the thought something drastic might happen did cross the doctor's mind but he genuinely believed the presence at home of the two children, whom the colonel adored, would act as a strong deterrent. Dr Loinsworth described Brereton as 'an exceedingly fond father' and, in general disposition, 'a most kind, benevolent and humane man'; as to his principles of honour he had, if anything, 'almost too high a sense of it'. He was, too, a man of temperate habits.

Death had been instantaneous and the jury returned a verdict that it resulted from 'a pistol wound, inflicted by himself, under temporary derangement'.

In a suicide note (not revealed at the inquest), Brereton attributed the principal cause of his death to the 'gross neglect' of the Government in sending an inadequate force to Bristol and 'now wishing to screen themselves' employed Major-General Dalbiac 'to conduct the infamous and cruelly unjust prosecution instituted against me in order to show to the world that *Eighty Dragoons* was sufficient to protect this city against the countless thousands of an infuriated mob and without the smallest assistance from the magistrates or civil authorities'. The colonel accused Dalbiac of prosecuting with the 'most malignant and heartless perseverance' and hoped he would 'meet his reward for being the chief cause of *depriving my innocent and helpless babes of their only protection in this world*—supported by the most gross perjury it is possible to imagine...' Brereton alleged that the Mayor, the Town Clerk, Alderman [Abraham] Hilhouse and others had 'sworn to the most dreadful falsehoods in order to screen themselves and brother magistrates' and further declared that 'Cornet Kelson's evidence this day as to the orders he stated to have received from me upon going to the new jail is *false in the extreme* but which I have no doubt he gave with a view to screen himself from the blame he highly deserved for not having as far as possible performed his duty upon that occasion'. Brereton ended the note (dated 12 January 1832): 'I leave this hasty and badly expressed statement as some proof of the cruelly *unjust* manner I have been used throughout the entire of the proceedings and which I wish to be published to the world at large as the only satisfaction my friends can have for my untimely end.'

From what we know of Brereton, he was normally a kindly soul of high principle and not given to spite or calumny. Nevertheless, it would seem wholly unfair to conclude that any of the cited individuals, although differently motivated and obviously holding a dissimilar view of preceding events, were not also men of integrity—albeit, like him, humanly prone to prejudice and fallibility. A question-mark remains.

Whatever the truth the colonel, by his own final tragic act, robbed himself of any possible chance of refuting in court the testimony he deemed perjurious and also of calling a large number of defence witnesses. Sadly, in his distraught state, he evidently could not contemplate even that prospect.

[Brereton's request that his declaration 'be published to the world at large' apparently went unheeded at the time. A distant kinsman of his provided me with a typescript copy of the note and it may be that, until now, even extracts have never appeared in print. It appears likely that Thomas Brereton himself would not have objected, however.—Author].

Although the funeral was intended to be private—a small cortège left Redfield House at seven in the morning on Thursday, 19 January—a 'considerable number of the populace' spontaneously joined the principal mourners as the procession moved slowly through the quiet streets. Many hats were doffed and heads bowed in silent tribute. The colonel was laid to rest, alongside his wife, in the crypt of Clifton Parish Church.

Reduced to a nervous ruin and then to self-destruction by a tragic chain of circumstances, Lt-Col Thomas Brereton was now beyond the misery which had beset him. Paradoxically, an endearing brand of homespun courage seemed to issue from his bumbling efforts during the riots. He appears earnestly to have had a very high regard for the lives of his fellows and yet, for whatever reasons, there can be no doubt that it was partly his failure to act decisively which led to a dreadful escalation of exactly the trouble he had attempted passively to prevent. How much subsequent human suffering and material destruction would have been avoided had he shown a forceful hand at the beginning? There were those who obviously considered he lost his nerve, clearly shirked his responsibilities and failed in his duty as a soldier.

Brereton plainly felt himself handicapped by the small military unit at his disposal and also by the absence of any sort of organized civil force for most of the time. Furthermore, he bitterly believed that the magistrates had schemed and misrepresented to throw the entire blame upon him in order to shield themselves. The magistrates, for their part, claimed that Brereton refused to co-operate and left them in the lurch. The colonel was evidently physically unwell, causing him agitation, before and during the rioting. Who can measure just what effect such illness might have had upon his judgment and mental capacity?

There developed a fresh surge of pro-Brereton feeling after his death and, with his dramatic exit from the stage, the probing spotlight of discontent from some quarters beamed with renewed power on the magistrates. Press reactions varied, but most commentators were generally at pains to distinguish between Brereton the Soldier and Brereton the Man.

Commented the *Morning Advertiser*: 'Colonel Brereton, no doubt, knew his duty well and no doubt saw clearly what ought to be done, but he neither possessed the energy to enable him to carry his views into effect nor the talent that was necessary to persuade others to the adoption of more vigorous measures.

He was beset by a stupid and vacillating Corporation, which had drawn upon itself difficulties and dangers which it was unable to encounter.' *Morning Herald*: 'It is lamentable to think that a generous aversion to take the lives of others should have placed him in circumstances which drove him to lift his hand against his own. But why has Colonel Brereton, of all the persons whose duty it was to protect the peace of Bristol, been made the scapegoat to bear the sins of so many who were recreants to their trust?'

The Times regretted the absence of sufficient civil and military forces to put down the riot in its early stages, while *Bell's Weekly Messenger* recorded: 'The error of Col Brereton seems at once the most excusable and most venial in a military man. He erred from extreme humanity—from a desire to spare the effusion of blood—from a wish to deter the infuriated mob rather by menace of slaughter and attack than by actual military execution. It was not cowardice or fear but, it appears to us, an indisposition and hesitation to act from the mildest and purest of motives.' The *Albion and Star* believed that 'no man of common-sense and impartial mind, who has read the evidence, will deny that his humanity extended to an omission of that duty which, had it been properly fulfilled, would in all probability have caused the Bristol riots to stop very far short of the disastrous consequences to which they reached'.

The Morning Post had no reservations: 'Colonel Brereton all along persuaded himself it was consistent with his duty to cause the King's troops to retreat before the face of a lawless rabble, to seek to gratify a lawless rabble by familiar condescension, to submit to their caresses and to caress them in turn, to disregard the representations of the magistracy and to attempt to silence the remonstrances of the civil authorities by misrepresenting and depreciating the efficiency of the troops under his command.... That his ignominious dismissal from the King's service would be demanded loudly and violently could not for a moment be doubted.'

A piece of almost heroic pathos appeared in *The Bristol Mercury*:

The articles of war differ materially from the best feelings of mankind, and it is more than probable that the humanity which must have made every kindly heart honour him, would have served his cause in a very trifling degree at the Horse Guards. There are some men who would spill human blood like water, though it were only for the protection of a hen-coop. We reverence Colonel Brereton for his aversion to this, and however culpable the soldier might be, we think much better of the man. At the same time, we admit that there may be a season in which the employment of military force is not only excusable, but absolutely essential—a time, indeed, in which it would argue not only a highly culpable neglect of duty, but even in-humanity, in an officer to shrink from his task of dispersing a mob, however repugnant such a task might be be to his feelings.

Speaking, however, to what we saw—and, throughout the whole of this melancholy affair, our opinions have been grounded solely on our personal observation—speaking to what we saw, we are decidedly of opinion that the conduct of Colonel Brereton was not only most honourable to his feelings as a man, but most praiseworthy to him as a soldier.

Poems lamenting the colonel's death soon circulated, among them a piquant offering by 'C.C.' whose partiality was unmis-takably reflected in these opening lines:

> Brereton farewell! thou victim to the arts
> Of ledger-plodding merchants—base upstarts:
> Gifted with nothing, save the love of rule;
> Forgetting half they stole from Colston's school.

The writer claimed in an explanatory footnote that 'some of the Bristol Corporation have had a cheap education in Col-ston's School, which was intended by the founder for poor freemen's sons'.

So Thomas Brereton, long since forgotten yet once an unfor-tunate figure of national controversy, passed from the scene—respected for his restraint, branded with blame. The colonel, said *The Times*, was 'not made of stuff stern enough for the late crisis. The professional habits of the officer were over-powered by the benevolent feelings of the man.'

Indeed he had fretted, though not strutted, his final hour.

Chapter Fifteen

THE CASE OF THE CAUTIOUS CAPTAIN

THE COURT-MARTIAL reconvened three days after Brereton's death, formally to wind-up proceedings. Next morning—Tuesday, 17 January—Captain William Henry Warrington, of the 3rd Dragoon Guards, who had been 'in arrest' for two months, appeared before the same tribunal.

He faced a number of charges: failing to turn out his troop or to notify his commanding officer on receiving intelligence that the Custom House was about to be fired; not acting upon a letter from the Mayor directing the military to quell the riot, nor communicating that requisition to Brereton; being absent from his quarters and neighbourhood when a detachment of his troop were summoned 'to protect the palace of the Bishop of Bristol from a violent attack made thereon by the rioters' and, on arriving back at the Reeves Hotel, did not attempt to join that unit nor await their return but, instead, retired to bed; twice remaining inactive in quarters after sending out a detachment under the sole command of a young cornet of only sixteen months' service.

Such conduct by the captain, the indictment ended, evinced 'a lack of vigour and activity requisite in the situation in which he was placed, being highly unbecoming and disgraceful in his character as an officer and calculated to bring dishonour to His Majesty's Service'.

As he had only just learned the precise nature of the accusations, Warrington explained, he sought time in which to prepare a proper defence 'notwithstanding the melancholy event of the death of Lieutenant-Colonel Brereton which deprived me of the principal witness in my favour'. An adjournment was granted and when the court again assembled at ten o'clock on Wednesday, 25 January, it was announced that twenty-two prosecution witnesses and nineteen for the defence were scheduled to be heard.

Captain Warrington, who pleaded 'Not Guilty' to all charges, was to assert several times during the hearing that he stood bound by the orders of his superior officer. Whether Brereton would have been able to help very much without, in some measure, incriminating himself, is surely debatable. Brereton was beyond recall, of course, and equally unable to contradict anything Warrington might now choose to say. Undoubtedly, the departed colonel's shadow hovered over the trial. Major-General Sir Charles Dalbiac, again in the role of prosecutor, regretted the necessity of treading 'the very same ground which is stamped with images of sadness; I must inevitably revert, at times, to those very proceedings which have been brought to so calamitous and so tragical a termination.'

As Inspector-General of Cavalry, Dalbiac said that Warrington was technically under his command although he hardly knew him personally. It was also coincidental that the captain belonged to the regiment which had once been brigaded with Dalbiac's own corps when 'I had the good fortune, for the first time in my life, to draw my sword against the common enemy of Europe in the field of Talavera, under the auspices of that gallant general who presides over this court'. Dalbiac recognized the value of an impressive opening address. What better than a timely piece of flattery, followed by references to military glory and the noble ideals embodied in the service?

Was there a member of that illustrious court, he asked astutely, who had not experienced 'the magic of that sympathy which binds those corps which have fought and conquered together, as it were, in the bond of sacred brotherhood?' Indeed, was it possible for him to aproach the court-martial with indifference when the investigation involved the honour of that corps or of any individual belonging to it? That honour was dear to him and, though feeling solicitude for the defendant, he would be failing in his duty if he did not strive to bring down 'the weighty arm of justice on all those whose conduct may have fixed a stain upon it'.

The prosecution evidence went on for three days. Cornet Kelson and NCOs gave straightforward accounts of Warr-

ington's behaviour during the riots, describing how he had
ordered out the troop (which went subsequently to the New
Gaol) while he remained in quarters, and remembered his
being absent when a detachment was summoned to the Bishop's
Palace. Charles Gresley, a timber merchant, stated that in consequence of the mob's attack on the New Gaol, and on behalf
of Aldermen Abraham Hilhouse and John Savage, he visited
Warrington in the Reeves Hotel and told him the magistrates
directed that troops be dispatched immediately. The captain
said he was himself fatigued, but ordered Cornet Kelson to
assume command then of ten soldiers, join up with the guard
outside the Mansion House and proceed to the prison.

Another merchant, Thomas Kingston, recounted how at
about half-past ten that Sunday night he urged Warrington to
take troops to prevent the Custom House from being burned
and to clear rioters from Queen Square; at that time Warrington and his men were on horseback in front of Leigh's Horse
Bazaar, but the captain declined to march without his commanding officer's permission and added he did not know where
to locate him. Kingston agreed that Warrington seemed eager
to act if only he had the necessary orders.

Cornet Kelson testified that on returning from the Bishop's
Palace on Sunday night he found Warrington at the Reeves
Hotel 'in the act of getting into bed'; an hour later when a gang
stoned the building, the troop were called out and Warrington
was then at their head. Cross-examined, Kelson conceded that
Warrington was only partly undressed when apparently climbing into bed and, furthermore, he himself had suggested the
captain should lie down for a while, saying he would let him
know if anything required his attention. Kelson also stated that
when he led the detachment to the New Gaol, Warrington had
directed him to report on the way to Brereton at College Green
for orders; he did so, and it was the colonel who actually instructed him to go to the prison.

There was evidence, too, from Samuel Goldney and Wintour
Harris on taking the Mayor's urgent letter at three o'clock on
the Monday morning to Warrington who, at their insistence,
read it. They claimed he did nothing more about the matter,
however. Asked if Warrington wanted them to deliver the
letter to the officer commanding (to whom it was addressed),

Goldney replied: 'I don't remember any such request.' He also answered queries raised by the tribunal:

Question: Did you observe any backwardness or unwillingness to act on the part of Captain Warrington?

Goldney: On the contrary, he expressed every willingness to do anything upon proper orders.

Question: When Captain Warrington stated to you that he could not act without a magistrate to go every inch of the road with him, did you make any reply or take any measures to communicate to the Mayor or the magistrates what Captain Warrington had stated?

Goldney: No, I did not. I did not know where to find any other magistrate than the Mayor; the Mayor had particularly requested me, through Mr Daniel Fripp, not to mention where he was.

Then there was Alderman Thomas Camplin, who succeeded where others had failed in rousing the military officers from their apparent torpor. He said that accompanied by several fellow citizens he went to Warrington at four o'clock on the Monday morning and persuaded him—later, Brereton as well—to make a decisive move. Camplin refused to be put off by the captain's plea that his men and horses were too tired nor by his assertion that he had no knowledge of Brereton's whereabouts.

Question (by the court): When you expressed to Captain Warrington, in such strong terms, that it was your opinion he should go himself with the dragoons, and not send an inexperienced officer, did he make any specific reply to what you said, or did he merely say the troops should not fire?

Camplin: He made no specific reply.

Question: You have stated that Captain Warrington said he did not know where to find the officer commanding the troops; at whose suggestion, then, was it you went to Unity Street to look for him?

Camplin: I had seen Mr Francis, an officer connected with the staff, some time ago accidentally, going into No. 2, Unity Street; that induced me to go there, thinking I might find Lieutenant-Colonel Brereton there, knowing that he lived some two or three miles from Bristol.

The prosecution appeared to establish that Warrington (for whatever reasons) was not with his troops when he should have been, that he failed effectively to liaise with his commanding officer and, moreover, remained quiescent while parts of Bristol were going up in flames and rioters rampaging through the streets.

Captain Warrington began his defence in a packed court-room on the morning of Monday, 30 January. It was, he said, the first time in his life he had spoken before an assembly and his embarrassment was heightened by hearing himself called 'prisoner at the bar'. He regarded the honour of his regiment most highly, especially as both his father and brother were soldiers while 'my grandfather and great-grandfather and almost every male relation and connection for centuries past have held commissions in the British Army'.

Referring to the late Lt-Col Brereton, who would have been his chief witness, Warrington voiced a noble-sounding senti-ment: 'I would sooner suffer any degradation, or bear all the odium of these charges, than I would place one blot on his escut-cheon.'

Warrington started well enough considering it was his maiden speech and, thus encouraged, plunged into the realms of grand simile and colourful phraseology: 'When I reflect upon the eventful circumstances connected with this inquiry—the immense loss of life and property at a time when my conduct is censured, the late awful catastrophe which still throws such a gloom over this city and the yet more recent and appalling sacrifice made within these few hours and within a short dis-tance of these walls as an atonement to the offended laws of the country—when I reflect that I myself am compelled, at this particular juncture, to launch my bark amongst the shoals and breakers that have proved destructive to so many others, I may well be unfitted for any struggle, however necessary for the pre-servation of my honour.'

The captain emphasized that from the moment he entered Bristol with his troop he came under Brereton's command and, in his submission, nothing less than the colonel's explicit in-structions, or the authority of a magistrate, permitted him to act against the rioters. Of the Mayor's vital letter which reached him, Warrington said he entreated the bearers [Goldney and Harris] to take it to Brereton; they refused, but he sincerely believed they had gone to apprise the colonel of the situation.

'I do, however, deeply regret that I relied upon those gentle-men to communicate to my commanding officer the contents of the letter, instead of taking the more military course of dispatching it by an orderly,' Warrington told the court. This suggests the captain did know where Brereton was then to be found, although some prosecution witnesses had already claimed he stated the exact opposite.

On the question of his delegating Cornet Kelson to command the detachment on the Sunday afternoon, Warrington maintained he was merely obeying Brereton's orders to send a small unit to College Green and that the colonel, in fact, told them to continue to the New Gaol. The captain conceded being absent from quarters that evening, explaining that he went to consult Major-General Pearson as to whether it was always necessary to have a magistrate in attendance when suppressing a riot. All appeared quiet when he left on foot for Clifton at about eight o'clock and, after a short discussion with the general, he arrived back at the Reeves Hotel just before nine. He had informed Kelson of his intended movements.

'I am ready to admit, strictly speaking, I had no right to absent myself for a moment,' he confessed. 'I trust, however, that this honourable court will see the anxiety I evinced to meet the exigencies of my situation and will not condemn the motive which induced my absence.'

Warrington denied retiring to bed on his return, but said he went to his bedroom to change into dry clothes and was partially undressed when Kelson reported to him. Although feeling unwell, he took command of his troop outside the hotel soon afterwards. At about five o'clock the next morning, Kelson accompanied Brereton, who headed a cavalry unit into Queen Square. Warrington stressed that in accordance with the colonel's orders he stayed in quarters with a small reserve; subsequently, they were summoned to the Square where he himself participated in charges against the mob. He also declared that Cornet Kelson, despite his short military career, was not without experience of riot assignments, having been engaged in putting down disturbances in Hampshire in 1830 and in the Forest of Dean in 1831. In conclusion, Warrington handed in nine commendatory references from senior army officers and respected civilians testifying to his honour, zeal and devotion to duty on similar occasions prior to the Bristol crisis.

Defence witnesses included several called earlier by the prosecution. Cornet Kelson and other soldiers confirmed that when the 3rd Dragoon Guards entered the city on 29 October, Brereton firmly forbade any action against inhabitants without his direct permission or a formal requisition signed by two magistrates. Kelson also stated Warrington told him on the Sunday afternoon that he felt ill.

Trooper William Denney proved mainly responsible for confounding the prosecution on one count when he told the court he heard Brereton order the defendant not to join the unit going to Queen Square early Monday morning, but to remain in quarters with a few men. Denny deposed: 'Captain Warrington said "I would much rather go off myself", but the colonel replied "No, captain, I think you are very much fatigued and want some rest, for you look very poorly." Captain Warrington said he was not more so than Mr Kelson and the rest of the troop. Colonel Brereton rode off instantly and desired him to take his advice.'

Brother officers rallied round. Major Mackworth said Warrington had shown great willingness to act and in strict compliance with orders; Captain Gage, too, stated Warrington exhibited no lack of vigour in doing what was required of him. The outspoken Major Beckwith agreed that the defendant appeared 'alert, zealous and desirous to do his duty', but thought he was 'in great measure paralysed by the imbecility and misconduct of those who ought to have directed him'. Asked if he was alluding to Brereton or the magistrates, Beckwith answered tersely: 'To both.'

On the morning of the seventh and final day of the court-martial—Thursday, 2 February—a big crowd waited impatiently for admission to the hall and, when the doors opened, surged forward to claim the limited number of places. Many were left outside. Some disappointed ladies gave up their efforts to see the attractive young captain, while 'the crushed bonnets and disordered dresses of others bore testimony to the struggle they had undergone'.

Warrington closed his defence by producing a copy of directions issued by Sir Colin Campbell, as GOC Western District, during agricultural riots in the latter part of 1830 when the captain served in those operations. Relevant passages were to the effect that an officer commanding a detachment called out by the civil power was invariably to require a magistrate to accompany him or to obtain a written order signed by two magistrates.

Major-General Dalbiac, who took an hour and fifty-five minutes summing-up for the prosecution, said the matter which alarmed him most was Warrington's erroneous assumption that the refusal of an officer to act in a riot without a magistrate accorded with army regulations. Referring to the document just put in by the defendant, Dalbiac revealed that he was very familiar with the directive therein because it conformed precisely with instructions given by himself when he commanded troops sent into Kent, Sussex and Surrey to deal with civil disorders in the winter of 1830–31. Such instructions were designed to save troops being summoned to every village disturbance, or expected disturbance, or 'whenever a private gentleman chose to fancy that an attack was about to be made on his house or premises'.

Dalbiac continued: 'But surely the position of an officer holding a detachment commanded in a disturbed district, under circumstances such as I have represented, is not to be laid upon a parallel with the position of an officer placed in command of a troop, under circumstances such as those in which the prisoner stood in this city, between midday of the 30th October till sunrise of the following morning, during which most awful period the rioters were proceeding in systematic progression from outrage to outrage and from enormity to enormity without check or control, and when the whole of this vast and opulent city was threatened, under the prisoner's own eyes, to be included in one general conflagration.'

While it might be advisable and even desirable to have a magistrate present, he said, it was certainly not essential in law—a point with which every army officer ought to be acquainted. If an emergency arose, as it had done in Bristol, were troops to stand idly by and take no action to deal with it? The case before the court 'affords a most deplorable illustration of the evils that may arise from a misconception of the principles by which the discharge of this duty should be regulated'. Had the King's rules and regulations issued for the guidance of the army in instances of riot become a dead letter? Dalbiac was in top gear:

Surely to God, it is time to raise my voice and put this question when an officer under my superintendence, who has now to answer before this court for having declined to act against the rioters under a distinct and written authority to do so from the Chief Magistrate of this city, has called upon another officer under my superintendence to speak to his conduct during the Bristol riots, which officer did not hesitate to act against the rioters under similar written authority to do so from the said Chief Magistrate of Bristol....

Shall the open rebel, the public robber and the midnight incendiary be suffered to stalk forth in our streets, to proceed from atrocity to atrocity and His Majesty's troops be told that they can lay no hand upon them but in the presence of a magistrate?... Shall our city be fired at all points and sacrilege be carried to the very thresholds of our altars and British troops be taught that they must stand by and look on, or be held fast in their quarters, till a peace officer shall arrive to command and to direct their exertions? Shall the aged and infirm, the sick and the helpless, the nursing mother and the nestling infant be torn from their beds at the dead of night to glut the reckless fury of the plunderers and the incendiary, and the British soldier be told that he must stretch forth no hand to save without the sanction of a magistrate? God forbid, I say, God in Heaven forbid.

That powerful speech did much to seal Warrington's impending fate. Dalbiac had totally rejected the contention that it was necessary to have an attendant magistrate before troops could act. Undoubtedly, the captain's extreme caution stemmed largely from his apparent ignorance on that point and yet, to some extent, he was left holding an explosive baby. The captain was to pay dearly for his own shortcomings, however, although the court unanimously and 'most earnestly' submitted an extenuatory recommendation. They did so, Sir Henry Fane wrote to the Judge Advocate General (the Rt Hon Charles Grant), upon the following considerations:

1) The very difficult and trying situation in which Captain Warrington was placed during the whole period of the Bristol Riots, between the Commanding Officer of the Troops and the civil authorities of that city. A situation, as they deem, well calculated to paralyse the energies of a young man, of no great military experience!

2) For that his crimes appear to them to have arisen from errors *of judgement*; and not to have been caused by any disinclination to discharge his duty, had his line been clear to him.

3) Because ample testimony had been given, by various witnesses,

as to his active and proper discharge of his duties, at the head of his troop, when under proper command; here and elsewhere.

4) On account of strong testimony as to his general character, which he has laid before the court; from several officers of high rank; and from others under, and with, whom he has served.[1]

Despite these reservations, however, the findings of the court-martial—promulgated during the final week of February—pronounced Warrington guilty on all counts but one. The exception was that alleging on the morning of 31 October he allowed a detachment, representing two-thirds of the troop, to proceed under the sole command of a young cornet (Kelson) to Queen Square to put down rioting while he himself remained inactive in quarters. In the circumstances, that isolated acquittal meant next to nothing.

Captain Warrington was sentenced to be cashiered—a decision confirmed by the King, who nevertheless extended 'his most gracious clemency to the prisoner' by allowing him to sell his commission. In the regiment's muster rolls, Warrington was recorded as having 'retired' on 15 March 1832.

While the dejected captain contemplated his fate and future, it was gazetted that Cornet Charles Kelson had become a lieutenant (by purchase) in the 3rd Dragoon Guards—a vacancy indirectly created by the enforced departure of his erstwhile troop commander. A few weeks later—on 24th May—Kelson was also noted as 'retired' which, considering the young man had been so recently promoted in such a distinguished cavalry regiment, does appear to be somewhat unusual. Maybe there was nothing whatever significant about it, but one cannot help wondering. Could there just possibly have been some link with Brereton's suicide-note allegations (and, almost certainly, we shall never know) regarding Kelson's evidence at the Colonel's court-martial? To speculate further would be unfair, perhaps.

Less than a year afterwards—on 22 March 1833—another cavalryman closely associated with events at Bristol 'retired from the service'. He was Captain Gage (14th Light Dragoons), who thus terminated an army career which had begun for him in 1817 as a sixteen-year-old ensign in the 3rd Foot Guards.

Two officers to emerge from the riots with official flying colours were Major Digby Mackworth and Major William

[1] PRO WO 71/280.

Beckwith, each being rewarded with a knighthood of the Royal Hanoverian Guelphic Order.

An unpleasant aftertaste lingered on the public palate of Bristol. The severe reckoning emanating from the October disturbances included four rioters hanged, twenty-seven others transported, the military commander killing himself and another officer kicked out of the army. To that must be added the loss of life, personal injury and material destruction caused during the actual rioting and its suppression. A growing body of opinion insisted that the city's magistrates should be charged with neglect of duty. The energetic Committee of Enquiry, claiming to represent an important cross-section of 'respectable' inhabitants, had collected much information and, thus armed, pressed Lord Melbourne to approve the institution of legal proceedings against Mayor Pinney and a number of aldermen.

Confirmation from the Home Secretary that such a trial would be held was announced in late February. *The Bristol Mercury* reacted: 'Hitherto the trials, whether civil or military, connected with the late riots, have been conducted with peculiar severity; we are prepared to expect that, in the case now pending, the same stern justice will be administered. After what has passed, we believe the country will scarcely be satisfied if the prosecutor be found to lack the rigour of Sir Charles Dalbiac.'

Chapter Sixteen

FINAL VERDICT

THOSE WHO LONGED to see the Mayor and magistrates arraigned before a judge and jury had to be patient. The trees in Queen Square burgeoned, blossomed into full leaf and then started to shed flurries of russet and gold by the time citizens received subpoenas to appear at the Court of the King's Bench in London on 25 October 1832, when the long-awaited case was scheduled to open.

By then, Charles Pinney had completed his term as Mayor, passions had somewhat cooled and recollections suffered from a little blurring at the edges. Events which had engendered such horror and outrage twelve months earlier were now a bitterly unpleasant, though gradually fading, memory.

Much can happen in a year and that particular Bristol crisis was nudged from the foreground by intervening matters of importance claiming both local and national attention. For example cholera, which swept the country, gripped Bristol during the summer and resulted in nearly 600 deaths from more than 1,500 cases reported in the city. Another significant event was the ratification of the Reform Bill, given the Royal Assent in June. It meant a much fairer system of parliamentary representation nationally but the direct effect upon Bristol, which had a comparatively wide franchise anyway and continued to return two MPs, was ironically almost nil. While initial advantages to be gained from an extended franchise went primarily to the country's middle classes, there was no immediate benefit for the poorer people who had called so loudly for Reform.

For Charles Pinney, his mayoralty could not end soon enough. 'I am happy to say I shall retire from office on the 29th', he wrote with relief on 19 September to Peter Thomas

Huggins, his best friend among the Nevis sugar planters. 'I have been much perplexed during the whole year and until after the trial of the magistrates next month I must be continually occupied; after that, I shall with infinite satisfaction bid adieu to public life forever....'[1]

So, on Michaelmas Day, Pinney handed over the gold chain of office to successor Daniel Stanton. That very morning *A Free Reporter*, a radical news-sheet published in Bristol by J. G. Powell (junior), contained these recriminatory comments about the outgoing Number One citizen:

> No man entered the Mayoralty with brighter prospects than Mr Pinney; he had been fostered by the people, he was in their belief one of themselves; he was a professed Reformer ... thus it was with him upon his being installed Chief Magistrate—but he deserted the people, he truckled to the Tories—his Mayoralty has been vacillation from beginning to end, he leaves it unregretted by any, but spoken of by all as being deficient in the policy and judgment so necessary to the Magisterial character.

Harsh and biased words maybe, but one imagines a public opinion poll at that stage would not have rated Pinney's civic stock unduly high. As the date of the trial drew closer, there was a marked resurgence of general interest; some, perhaps, regarded it as an opportunity to enjoy the unusual sport of magisterial head-rolling.

About 500 people crowded into the courtroom at Westminster on the morning of Thursday, 25 October. Many more were unable to get in. Shortly after ten o'clock the Chief Justice of the King's Bench, Lord Tenterden, took his place and was accompanied by Mr Justice (Joseph) Littledale, Mr Justice (James) Parke and Mr Justice Taunton, the last-named having been a member of the Special Commission at Bristol nine months previously. Lord Tenterden had but a few days to live; already fast ailing, the seventy-year-old judge was forced to retire after the trial's third day to his London home in Russell Square where he died on 4 November. By strange coincidence Sir Thomas Denman, who was to succeed him as Chief Justice, appeared as Attorney-General to lead the prosecution. Principal advocate for the defence was Sir James Scarlett, himself a former Attorney-General.

[1] Pinney Papers.

The case concentrated on Charles Pinney, who was the first and, as it transpired, only magistrate to be tried. To the charge which amounted to that of 'neglect of duty during the riots', the ex-Mayor pleaded 'Not Guilty'. He must have been heartened to find that the jury comprised country gentlemen, some of them also magistrates and likely to consider sympathetically the arguments advanced on behalf of a kindred spirit.

The trial itself produced very little startlingly new. Familiar ground was retraced, variations played on well-worn themes and old tales re-told. Even the outcome, one suspects, was never really in doubt.

Denman submitted that for nearly forty-eight hours when Bristol was in 'an alarming state of consternation' Pinney, as Mayor, neglected and abandoned his obligations and 'withdrew from being found by those who wished to discover him'. It appeared the Mayor held the view that having told the military to act at their own discretion, he had done his duty and was thus absolved from further responsibility. Although magistrates gave Lt-Col Brereton 'a sort of commission' to clear the streets, they did not accompany him to see it properly executed. The colonel could not obtain precise orders and that put a very great onus on him.

The Attorney-General accused Pinney not only of failing to act effectively, even when citizens offered their services, but also of being too concerned with his own safety. He contended that 'had the magistrates been at their posts and done their duty, the whole of the mischief having been done by small parties— many composing them being intoxicated and many others young—the outrages ought easily and soon to have been suppressed by a common civil force if there had only been resolution and vigour'.

More than thirty witnesses were called to infill the picture sketched by the Attorney-General. Instances of indecision by the magistrates were described: Father Francis Edgeworth, a Catholic priest, claimed that when he proposed to raise 200 'able and steady' men, one alderman alluded to their being Irish and liable to get drunk; a Baptist minister, the Rev Thomas Roberts, said the magistrates seemed to have no set plan for dealing with the crisis, although he confessed himself 'astonished' at the general apathy which prevailed in the city;

Edward Goss told the court he suggested to the magistrates the wisdom of transferring all firearms from gunsmiths' shops to a place beyond the reach of rioters, only to receive a reply from Alderman Thomas Daniel that the weapons might as well be thrown into 'The Float'; Captain Codrington, of the Dodington Yeomanry, recounted how he led his troop into Bristol during the height of the disturbances and was unable to locate a magistrate; Major Beckwith recalled asking aldermen to accompany him to Queen Square on the Monday morning of rioting, but one declined on the grounds that he was unpopular, another that he had too much regard for his own property and a third because he feared his ships would be fired by the mob.

The prosecution's case closed on Monday, 29 October, and most of that afternoon devoted to a lengthy address by Sir James Scarlett for the defence. The magistrates had suffered 'much obloquy, much persecution and much misrepresentation' because of riots they greatly deplored he said, and also the indignity of knowing that an investigatory committee of their own citizens, to which they had no recourse, was sitting in judgment on them.

Having been deserted alike by the military and most inhabitants, and confronted by a desperately dangerous situation, just what were the magistrates expected to do? They had zealously attempted to call out citizens to assist, Scarlett declared, and could hardly be blamed if so many blankly refused. The magistrates already had plans for the safe removal of firearms, but were unlikely to reveal those intentions for general consumption so that when Mr Goss raised the point, Alderman Daniel jokingly replied 'Oh, I think we'd better throw them into The Float' merely to put off such importunities.

Scarlett totally rejected any imputation that Pinney went into hiding at Daniel Fripp's house; his whereabouts were perfectly well known to his colleagues and he also notified Brereton where he could be found if a magistrate was required. During the riots, Scarlett maintained, the Mayor and magistrates had acted as best they could in view of the unprecedented and perilous circumstances.

The prosecution made no specific charges, Scarlett pointed out, but rather a vague one alleging neglect, which might be applied conveniently to any of nearly fifty different incidents and represented a wide net calculated to catch the innocent. If it was possible on the evidence to convict the magistrates of 'any defect of duty or abandonment of their posts to prevent what has taken place, I declare before God and heaven that this country would no longer be a land of liberty', he concluded.

Evidence by defence witnesses lasted for the best part of two days. Daniel Burges, the Mayor's clerk, said Pinney never lost his self-possession during the riots and at various times placed himself in 'situations of peril'. Under-Sheriff Hare agreed that Pinney showed no want of personal courage. Tribute to the Mayor's pluck was also paid by Ebenezer Ludlow, the Town Clerk, who believed Pinney did his duty to his utmost ability and could not have suppressed the riots with any force short of a military one. After describing his own sharp comments about the withdrawal of the 14th Light Dragoons, Ludlow said although he was then among many who thought Brereton a traitor or coward he now felt that opinion to be unjust. He added: 'I think he intended to act properly and meant honestly; I think it due to his memory to say so; I think he intended to gain time and thought he should be better able to cope with the mob when reinforced.'

Daniel Fripp deposed that he informed two callers not to disclose where the Mayor was (but did not tell Pinney this) because his wife was afraid their home would be attacked if the mob knew. Major Mackworth told the court that at the Mansion House on the Saturday evening when Brereton asked if armed force was to be used, the Mayor replied in effect: 'You must fire if the riot cannot be suppressed without it.' The major said he begged Pinney and Brereton not to permit this because 'firing was a bad mode for cavalry to act and that shots which were designed for active rioters would often reach innocent people and I was convinced, by the combined effort of civil and military force, the people might be dispersed in a few minutes'.

After the case for the defence, the Attorney-General announced that the prosecution withdrew accusations of personal cowardice against Pinney, who had, on the evidence adduced, conducted himself with 'spirit and courage and he was placed in a situation which deserved compassion'. It was also evident, however, that he and other magistrates displayed 'vacillation and irresolution', or rather a fixed determination to incur no responsibility at all, and were guilty of 'a terrible dereliction of duty'.

In his summing-up on Thursday, 1 November, Mr Justice Littledale said that during the riots Pinney had recourse to expert legal and military advice (through the Town Clerk, Lt-Col Brereton and Major Mackworth) but, in law, he remained responsible for the peace of the city and even if he acted on bad or illegal advice he did not stand acquitted. It should be borne in mind, however, the advice was offered on the spur of the moment when some new development occurred and the jury were to assess the defendant on what he did on specific occasions, not on what he might have done had he been able to foresee what was going to happen. They should not convict on the general charge of neglect unless all were agreed upon some particular instance of negligence.

The judge observed that the prosecution alleged the Mayor did not venture forth to give assistance, but it had been proved he did go into the streets, that he read the Riot Act and was in great personal danger. It was not his duty to be at the head of the special constables, nor was he bound by law to accompany the military, although it might have been wiser had Pinney stayed at a known place from where he could send help to various quarters when it was required.

The jury, who were out for only twenty minutes, returned the following verdict: 'We unanimously find Charles Pinney, late Mayor of Bristol, not guilty.' When applause from the public had subsided, the foreman continued: 'We are of the opinion that, circumstanced as he was, menaced and opposed by an infuriated and reckless mob, unsupported by any force, civil or military, and deserted in those quarters where he might most reasonably expect assistance, the late Mayor of Bristol acted to the best of his judgment with the highest zeal and courage.' More applause greeted this rider.

So, far from being chastised, Charles Pinney left the court-room with a glowing tribute from the jury. Charges pending against other magistrates would now be dropped and, for some of their sakes, it was surely as well Pinney had headed the list. By no means all of them, one imagines, would have survived— let alone received a verbal accolade for meritorious conduct!

Many people were convinced the trial was a package deal, neatly wrapped and tied by the Whig Government, to highlight deficiencies existing in such an unpopular system of municipal control. Said *The Globe*: 'There can be no doubt from the evidence that the Mayor had a most sincere and anxious desire to do his duty and that he behaved himself as well as a man plunged suddenly into a difficult crisis of business, with which he was altogether unacquainted, would be likely to do.... Has it been shown that there was an efficient and popular magistracy? It has been shown, on the contrary, and this was the Mayor's strong defence, that the magistrates as a body were so unpopular with the mass of the citizens that even men the most interested in the preservation of the peace would not co-operate with them till the danger of property had been proved by the actual destruction of a part of the city.'

Several newspapers regarded the case as little more than an absurd caper. *The News* confessed that the acquittal 'we were prepared to expect but when the presiding judge and the jury, for the most part composed of Berkshire Tory justices, talk of His Worship's presence of mind and *personal courage*, then we are tempted to laugh outright'. *The Examiner*: 'If this be the paragon of mayors, the sooner we have done with such worthies the better for the safety of our cities. There is probably not a common inspector of police who, placed in the same difficulties, would not have shown more resource and energy than Mr Pinney. But yet the acquittal seems to us right.' *The Spectator*: '... the jury stepped out of their legal way to pronounce a panegyric on his courage and zeal. This will probably be the last attempt in England to impose responsibility on a magistrate until the municipal system undergoes some very considerable reformation.'

To conclude this mini-anthology of comment from the Fourth Estate, hearken *The True Sun*:

Nothing would have given us greater surprise than to have heard that Charles Pinney Esq., some time Mayor of Bristol, had been found guilty of the charges brought against him. The finding of a magistrate guilty of doing anything that he ought not to do would have startled us in the extreme; nor should we have marvelled less had such a functionary been found guilty of not doing what he ought to do. Mayors are little monarchs and monarchs, we know, can do no wrong....

If our economy-and-retrenchment rulers cannot relieve us a little from the pressure of taxation, let them at least spare us the national humiliation of spending out money on such mockeries. It is not unreasonable to expect that such magistrates as have not already been brought to trial should purify themselves at the expense of their own pockets. Let us hope Mr Pinney may take the hint. Let him pay a thousand pounds towards the cost of the trial; he will have purchased his eulogium cheaply.

Charles Pinney doubtless viewed with acute distaste those and other uncomplimentary observations by sections of the national Press who, more than anything, appear to have used him as a topical example (not altogether unfairly, perhaps) to draw further attention to that iniquity which plagued so much of the country—an archaic, diverse, undemocratic and harmfully defective regime of municipal government.

Local newspapers were generally much kinder about what one called the 'most honourable' acquittal. Another, *Felix Farley's Bristol Journal*, found it 'scarcely possible' to describe the 'joy and satisfaction' felt in the city: 'So early as six o'clock yesterday morning [*Friday, 2 November*] the intelligence was announced by the ringing of some of our parish bells and at various hours throughout the day this demonstration of joy was repeated. The evidence on the trial has wonderfully changed the sentiments of many of our fellow citizens, and the colouring given to the conduct of the Magistrates by party feeling has taken a different hue.'

While it is impossible to picture Pinney as a fearless white knight in shining armour, he appears to have come through the dramatic events with more credit that most. Pinney—in private life 'estimable and exemplary', commented *The Bristol Liberal*—was a staid, well-intentioned individual of endeavour and probably handicapped by a fragile constitution although, moving as he did in a pretty select orbit, he was nicely cushioned against life's grimmer rubs by virtue of the privileged independence money and position can provide. He may well have been an uncompromising businessman, but he was also capable of amiability and understanding. It seems, too, he was a faithful and thoughtful husband. Such personal attributes by no means guarantee a commanding public figure or dominant leader, however, and Charles Pinney was just not cut out for the part.

As he himself confessed, he was 'much perplexed' during his year of office.

Of course, human frailties surfaced for scathing scrutiny when the city experienced such a riot crisis—the frightening like of which has faced no other Mayor of Bristol nor, indeed, any civic counterpart elsewhere in this country. Pinney was the 'junior' of the magistracy in the senior seat and, in only six weeks, had hardly accustomed himself to the mayoralty when the threatening storm broke. Confused not only by conflicting advice he was, in a political sense, also caught between the devil of the city's extreme radicals and the deep-blue sea of entrenched conservatism—and, furthermore, forsaken by the military at a most crucial time.

It is now easy to assert that firmer combined tactics initially by the civil authorities and Lt-Col Brereton (a tragic mis-alliance seemingly characterized by mutual mistrust from the outset) would have prevented the ugly eruption of violence that was to follow and, yet, this appears clearly to have been the case. It might be said that Pinney and fellow magistrates fiddled while Bristol burned for, surely, the principal charge levelled at them amounted to indecision and inactivity. The unhappy Pinney, who deserved better all-round support, found himself in an unenviable predicament and, despite his own inade-quacies, it is difficult not to feel a considerable degree of retrospective sympathy for him. Overall, he acquitted himself pretty well in the circumstances.

Although criminal and military courts spent weeks in adjudi-cation, the hearings produced nothing to establish beyond doubt any precise cause of the rioting. Parliamentary Reform, though commonly held to be the guilty godfather, barely re-ceived a mention when prisoners paraded in front of the Special Commission and citing a character like Chrisopher Davis as a 'ringleader' looks, on the face of it, to have bordered on the ridiculous.

Sir Charles Wetherell, the Bristol Political Union, the pro-vocative presence of the army, special constables, disruptive outside influences, the Kingswood miners, a Radical plot, Tory intrigue, Government manipulation—all were more or less accused of fomenting the riots at some stage. A partial case might be made out against several of them individually or collectively, but the fundamental reason for the disturbances would still appear to be in question.

Allowing that the Reform Bill was the immediate underlying factor, did not under-privileged sections of the community seize the opportunity to demonstrate also against an unpopular corporation? Was some sort of show-down inevitable? Did the disliked Recorder's ill-fated visit to Bristol conveniently furnish just the spark to ignite a long-smouldering resentment of the city's governing body? Certainly there had been growing opposition and agitation for years calling for major reforms in the local administration. In the end, perhaps, one might be persuaded that it was the corporation which represented the most culpable link in an explosive chain of events.

Nebulous all that may be but, sadly, for the sake of tidy analysis, there appears to be no single or simple explanation.

Chapter Seventeen

THE AFTER YEARS

THE AFTER-EFFECTS of the riots did not end with Pinney's trial, of course. A local commission of twelve members (each representing a ward and elected by ratepayers) had been empowered by Act of Parliament to negotiate with those seeking compensation for material damages arising out of the disturbances. When the commissioners began work no fewer than 121 actions, involving nearly £150,000, were already instituted against the city, but by settlements they managed eventually to slash that amount to £55,824.

The only private claimant with whom they failed to reach agreement was the Bishop of Bristol, who, accepting £2,040 for loss of furniture, wanted a further £10,000 in respect of the gutted palace. His case came up at Bridgwater Assizes where, on 8 August 1833, he was awarded £6,000. Although the commission effected big reductions on original claims, £7,424 in legal charges and an additional £4,960 for obtaining and operating the Act helped bring the aggregate expenditure to £68,208. Not until 11 January 1835 did the commission finally close their books on this long and costly business.

Meanwhile, a Royal Commission had been appointed in 1833 to enquire into the state of civic authorities throughout England and Wales and from their recommendations emerged the Municipal Corporations Reform Act, 1835. Bristol received a hammering. Edward J. Gambier and John Elliot Drinkwater, the commissioners assigned to investigate the city's affairs, left very few oligarchical stones unturned and their voluminous report, published in early 1835, included these conclusory observations:

It has been shown that the governing body of the corporation of the city of Bristol is constituted on the closest principles of self-election and irresponsibility and it seems to us to offer a very unfavourable specimen of the results of such a system. We think the corporation stands entirely clear of any imputation of clandestinely appropriating its public revenues to individual profit, but it cannot be so easily acquitted of mismanagement and extravagance. With a sinking and overburdened trade, its large revenues have been unprofitably expended in the maintenance of an overgrown establishment and in the display of state magnificence, which is satisfactory to contemplate only when it is the symbol of prosperity and defrayed out of its overflow.

The ruling principle of the corporation appears to have been, at all times, the desire of power and a watchful jealousy that nothing should be undertaken within the limits of the city over which they cannot, at pleasure, exercise control. Almost every one of the long list of legislative enactments which belong to their local history affords full proof of this assertion, makes good some questionable point and fences them round with some new privilege. . . .

As owners and conservators of the port, the behaviour of the corporation of Bristol appears to us to be altogether indefensible. The mildest charge that can be made against them is that they have been careless of its interest; there is much ground for asserting that they have been actually injurious to it. They have suffered burdensome charges of every description to be accumulated upon its trade, of which they are the last to see the impolicy; and when nuisances and obstructions are complained of, they then declare themselves to be without power to abate them. . . .

We are informed that the same political party has not always held the ascendancy in the council-house of Bristol and that some of the acts we find most objectionable have been in the time of a party opposed to that which is now supposed to be predominant there. We should not seek for a stronger proof that the fault is inherent in the system itself. Among all the quarrels and disturbances of which unhappily Bristol has at all times had more than her share, among all changes of political party, the corporation has always been the subject of attack and animosity and we are of the opinion that these feelings cannot permanently endure in any society, unless there is something essentially bad in the first principles of its constitution.

There it was—a stinging slap in the face for Bristol's strongly established closed-circuit administration. The new Act laid down a uniform and much-improved system of government for corporate boroughs and, among other things, extended the franchise to include all male ratepayers. When the fresh-look

Bristol City Council, which provided for sixteen aldermen and forty-eight councillors, officially became operative on New Year's Day 1836, familiar faces were missing. Charles Pinney's was not. Although failing to poll sufficient votes to get in as a councillor, he was democratically elected an alderman by those who did. William Fripp, who had stayed at his brother's house with Pinney during the rioting more than four years earlier, now had the distinction of being the first Mayor of the reformed local authority.

The few Liberal councillors serving on that Tory-dominated body included William Herapath, though no longer the political union's burning spirit. He lost much of his popularity with the people by participating in municipal government and one erstwhile devotee, criticizing Herapath's abandonment of the union, told him: 'You rose like a rocket, but have fallen like the stick.' Herepath, who later became a J.P., lived to be seventy-one.

How fared others who had been closely associated with the riots? Sir Charles Wetherell, whom many blamed for the disturbances in the first place, finished his parliamentary pursuits when the constituency of Boroughbridge (which he represented) was expunged by the Reform Act. He continued as Recorder of Bristol—a statue of him was erected at Clifton in 1839—until he died on 17 August 1846 from injuries sustained in a carriage accident. He was then in his seventy-seventh year.

Ebenezer Ludlow, the Town Clerk, whose traditional duty of trying cases at Quarter Sessions ended because of revised jurisdiction, sought compensation from the new council for loss of fees. They refused to play ball, so he departed—after settling for a handsome annual pension of £533. Daniel Burges filled the vacant office. The talented Ludlow, an individual of 'habitual garrulity and self-sufficiency', was subsequently appointed Commissioner for Bankruptcy in Liverpool and then to a similar position in Bristol. He sat as chairman of Gloucestershire Quarter Sessions from 1842 until 1849—three years before his death at Almondsbury, aged seventy-five.

Digby Mackworth was sixty-three when he died that same year. In 1838, he had succeeded (on his father's death) to the baronetcy—not long after being promoted to lieutenant-colonel. Mackworth, who was to attain the rank of colonel, became Sheriff of Monmouthshire in 1843 and, also while in his fifties, campaigned unsuccessfully for a seat in the House of Commons.

The other major who figured significantly in the 1831 riots, William Beckwith, rose to be a general and achieved the honour of being Colonel of the 14th Light Dragoons [constituted Hussars in 1861] from 1860 until his death—aged seventy-four—at Silksworth Hall, near Sunderland, in February 1871. He took a considerable interest in local public affairs and was appointed High Sheriff of his home county, Durham, in 1858.

It would be most surprising if the riots had not had some marked effect upon the man who bore the magisterial brunt. After the disorders and their consequences, Charles Pinney deserted the Whigs and 'a morbid mistrust of the popular power led him into the ranks of Toryism'. Despite a verdict favourable to him, the trial was said to have 'broken his spirit' and he never again took a prominent part in public matters.

Towards the end of the 1830s, Pinney also began to lose heart in the family business and his growing wish then was to swap the hectic world of trade for the secluded comfort of retirement at his fine home on Clifton Down. He worked gradually towards that goal and, spending progressively less time at the office, ultimately succeeded around 1850. Thus closed the commercial House of Pinney which sprang from a sugar cane planted on a distant island in the Caribbean sunshine some 160 years previously.

In later life Pinney, well off financially, seems to have settled for a very quiet existence and largely limited his visits into Bristol to an occasional meeting of a benevolent or religious nature. 'He was a man of strict integrity and personally amiable, genial and well-informed', said *The Observer* (Bristol) when he died. Charles Pinney, then in his seventy-fifth year, drifted gently from this life at his home, Camp House, Clifton, during the evening of Wednesday, 17 July 1867.

Only two days earlier, the House of Commons passed another Reform Bill of great importance. 'A leap in the dark', Lord Derby called it.

Appendix

THE TRANSPORTED CONVICTS

WHEN THE EXECUTIONER'S rope abruptly ended the agony of Davis, Gregory, Clarke and Kayes on that cold day at Bristol in January 1832, a different kind of journey into the 'unknown' still awaited nearly thirty of their fellow rioters.

The seemingly endless, and often hazardous, voyage in a creaking ship across vast rolling oceans to the Antipodes was but an introductory ordeal of penal transportation.

Quarters in those floating prisons were cramped and foul-smelling and in rough weather, with the hatches nailed down and air scuttles closed, internees had to endure (sometimes for days) the oppressive atmosphere of the hold. Insanitation, disease and death added to the misery. It sounds frightful enough but by the 1830s, when such transit conditions generally showed a marked improvement on the horrors operating until some two decades earlier, increasing efforts were being made to keep prisoners occupied and on deck as much as possible during the daytime and also in reasonable physical shape.

Responsibility for the welfare, discipline and punishment of the convicts rested with a superintendent-surgeon—subject to the overriding safety and running of the vessel, in which matters, of course, the captain reigned supreme—and attention to their implementation appears to have varied considerably from ship to ship. Even aboard the best, however, it was certainly no pleasure cruise. Rations were reckoned to be adequate and the victuals overall of surprisingly good quality, although regular exercise was necessarily restricted and groups of convicts— some clapped in irons—shuffled about the deck under the gimlet-eyed surveillance of armed military guards.

Upon reaching their far-off destination, prisoners stayed on board for a medical check-up and also to have their personal descriptions entered into bulky registers. These routine procedures might take several days and not until they had been completed were prisoners taken ashore and detailed to work for the colonial government on road and bridge projects, or else 'assigned' to landowners, farmers and other private employers.

Although the attitude generally towards convicts was becoming more humane, they remained virtually slaves and there were still unsympathetic and harsh taskmasters who, on the slightest pretext, would haul the offender before the magistrates for very minor misdemeanours. John West observed in *The History of Tasmania*: 'There were settlers, not a few, to whose care prisoners were entrusted, who were unfit to govern a kennel.'

There existed daunting penalities for the persistent wrongdoer—such as the treadmill, solitary confinement, ruthless chain-gang labour and floggings. Refractory prisoners could be condemned to an incarcerated hell at one of the penitentiaries, where they endured long back-breaking hours of toil on meagre meals as well as frightening chastisements. Some inmates chose suicide rather than suffer a further day at those satanic places, while a few had been known to commit overt murder to guarantee for themselves a blessed release from this world—via the gallows!

The transportation system helped to solve for Britain the problem of overcrowded gaols at home and, simultaneously, to rid her forever of some dangerous and incorrigible criminals. By no means all those dispatched to New South Wales and Van Diemen's Land since the founding of that first penal settlement at Port Jackson in 1788 were fundamentally bad, however, a large number having been judicially banished for trivial offences and a much smaller percentage on political grounds. Some succeeded in doing their time without blemish, many more with only an admonishment or two for small transgressions. Nevertheless, in an environment of deprivation, monotony and rigid discipline, it often required a strong will and not a little luck to avoid being dragged down. Predictably, attempts to abscond were common.

A convict's existence and future frequently depended not only upon his own conduct but, to an extent also, on the kind of employer to whom he was assigned. It became something of a lottery. Some masters were unfeeling and their overseers cruel, others displayed much tolerance and many offered incentives for hard work in the way of extra 'indulgences'—like tobacco, tea and even liquor—to augment the official quota-scale of lodging, food, clothes and bedding prescribed by the authorities. For those convicts prepared to co-operate, particularly if they had experienced abject poverty and despair in Britain, their situation was less than an ordeal and, indeed, some had probably never had it so good. There were numerous pitfalls to temptation and punishment, however, and it should not be overlooked that also among the convicts were some desperate, depraved and intimidating characters.

If a prisoner remained industrious and kept out of serious trouble, he could expect some fairly early reward. Initially, this would usually take the form of a ticket-of-leave [a man transported for seven years could make application after four, a man for fourteen after six and a 'lifer' after eight] and this entitled the holder to work for wages in a specified area; even so, he was still a convict and, among other dictates, had periodically to attend musters. Continued good behaviour would earn him a conditional pardon, which meant he was free provided he stayed in the colony for the remainder of his original sentence. Absolute pardons (full remission of unexpired sentence) were rare.

Nineteen of the Bristol rioters were destined for Van Diemen's Land where, in the main, discipline was then more stringent than that in New South Wales. Lieutenant-Governor George Arthur, a religious and controversial man, seems to have regarded the island as a huge gaol for the punishment and redemption of convicts consigned to his care. This angered free settlers, who resented its use as a permanent dumping ground for Britain's criminals. Arthur doubtless saw his role as an improver of misguided souls (and he is said to have abhorred severity against prisoners), but it is certain those labouring under the system did not appreciate such high-minded philosophy.

Comparatively few ex-convicts, it appears, returned to Britain. Most could not afford the fare or even bother to work their passage home anyway and, sometimes long before discharging their debt to society, many had already planned for themselves a fresh and successful life 'Down Under'. Erstwhile prisoners thus merged with a rising influx of free immigrants arriving in that massive, exciting and potentially rich continent.

News reaching England intimated the lot of the responsive convict in Australasia was equal, if not superior, to that of numerous law-abiding Britons at home who festered amid industrial squalor or bent aching backs to the soil. Some of the rosier reports gave an impression of prisoners leading a leisured existence in a bounteous land which, not unnaturally, prompted an indignant outcry that punishments were insufficiently strict and transportation no longer an effective deterrent to crime.

An article in the *Launceston Advertiser* (Van Diemen's Land) of 22 August 1831, claiming to be 'a true picture intended for the eye of our numerous English readers', hit out at critics who declared the convict was on a soft number. After outlining some of the 'comforts' to be enjoyed—among them flogging, torturous labour and dangers to be encountered in hostile forests—the writer went on:

We have hitherto spoken only of the reception met with by a well-disposed prisoner—one who wishes to reform. If he be in any way refractory, let the good people of England thoroughly understand that he is sure of a most adequate reward. A short answer, when spoken to by his master or overseer, or a common soldier, or even a convict constable, is a crime punishable by flogging; getting tipsy places him in the stocks; missing muster may get him flogged or into the chain gang, where he works in irons on the roads. Should he commit any second offence, Macquarrie-harbour, Port Macquarrie, Norfolk Island or Moreton Bay is his fate, where every rigidity of discipline—nay, sometimes even cruelty—is exercised. The hardest of labour, and but one meal a day of the coarsest food, is the lot of a man who goes to a penal settlement. To these places it does not take a felony to send a prisoner; many have been removed there for very trivial offences.

Nineteen of the rioters were among 222 convicts from all over Britain to be packed aboard the *Katherine Stewart Forbes*, leaving London at the end of February 1832 for Van Diemen's Land, those from Bristol being the 'lifers' (except Henry Green) and James Ives. When eventually Green sailed in the *Parmelia*, which departed from Sheerness to New South Wales on 28 July, he had among his 199 captive shipmates William Christopher and Aaron Martin (seven years each for riot-stealing). Also in that barque were two Bristol rioters committed from Gloucester Assizes to be banished for life: John Wakefield—'a poor stupid-looking boy', one newspaper said—convicted of damaging the gaol at Lawford's Gate and Henry Hurd, guilty of riotous assembly and attacking John Mack's house. Similarly sentenced with Hurd had been William Spokes and Joseph Mills, who went respectively to New South Wales in the *Mary III* (from London, 4 September) and the *Camden* (from Sheerness, 21 September).

Three 'riot' thieves, given a seven-year stretch overseas, got no farther than Woolwich. Under the laconic heading, 'How Disposed Of', relevant registers of the *Justitia* prison hulk reveal that Charles Huish and James Street were pardoned on 28 March 1834; no such joy greeted Richard Neville before he died on 26 September 1835, aged forty-three. The worthless distinction of being the last convict associated with the Bristol disturbances to leave Britain fell to twenty-three-year-old Joseph Keates (seven years' transportation)—in the *Heroine* from Portsmouth on 14 May 1833, reaching New South Wales in 128 days. His crime? Filching a violin.

There was nothing melodic about the progress of the *Katherine Stewart Forbes*, however, and the convicts jammed inside experienced a grisly episode even before they lost sight of home. The 457-ton ship had dropped anchor at Woolwich in the murk of early February, having already taken on at Deptford a military guard composed of a captain, a subaltern, three NCOs and thirty-nine privates (plus four women and a child). On Friday, the 10th, a batch of eighty prisoners was transferred under armed supervision from the *Justitia*, followed by a further seventy the next day, when an additional thirty-two from another source were delivered to the dockyard also for embarkation. Forty more arrived from Chatham on Monday, the 13th, bringing the total to 222; the overall complement of 308 was made up by army personnel and the ship's officers and crew.

All appeared ready for sailing but, with one thing and another, there was a long delay. Rain alternated with dense fog and the convicts found themselves 'a good deal' exposed to the miserable elements as they had to be on deck for spells while the prisons were cleaned. Not until the drab morning of Monday, 27 February, did the Master (John Anderson) issue instructions to get under way and the ship moved slowly down the Thames, soon to pass Northfleet where she had been constructed in 1818.

Among the prisoners was nineteen-year-old Joseph Massam, convicted at the Liverpool Michaelmas Sessions of larceny. He complained of feeling unwell and the ship had barely touched open water before the surgeon, John Stephenson, confirmed the dreaded news that the young man was suffering from cholera. Alarm spread. So did the killer disease. Having continued down the English Channel, the *Katherine Stewart Forbes* hove to in Plymouth Sound during the evening of 2 March, by which time there were five 'very malignant' cases in the sick-bay. The vessel was not permitted to remain, however, the Master being 'peremptorily ordered by the Port Admiral to proceed to sea' the following morning.

Stephenson nevertheless managed to get a small supply of medicine as well as the temporary services of an assistant surgeon of the *San Josef*, at anchor nearby. To comply with quarantine regulations, an 'infected' ship then seeking the sanctuary of a British port was required to go either to Standgate Creek [in the estuary of the River Medway] or to Milford Haven.

During the night of Saturday, 3 March, and the whole of the next day, the weather deteriorated and Stephenson recorded in his medical journal:[1] 'We attempted to reach Milford, but the wind being foul, we were obliged to bear up for Standgate Creek.' Although it was 'tolerably fair' on the 5th, a gale and churning sea on the 6th caused the ship to pitch and roll considerably; every bed was occupied in the 'dark and stinking' hospital just outside of which, on the lower deck, groaned 'upwards of 200 seasick convicts'.

Four cholera cases, one of which proved fatal, were registered in the last three days of February, while during the first fortnight of March seven deaths (all convicts) resulted from twenty-one fresh cases. Ironically young Massam, the initial patient, recovered. In such restricted quarters, where the stench and sight of vomiting prisoners must have been overpoweringly

[1] PRO ADM 101/40.

abominable, it seems incredible there was not a far more serious outbreak. Indeed John Stephenson, who merited praise for his efforts, found the prisons 'disgustingly filthy' at the time of the storm, after which 'we got smooth water and fine weather and we were enabled to open the scuttles, ventilate the prisoners etc., etc.'

The last death from cholera occurred on 5 March, but the *Katherine Stewart Forbes* had to stay in isolation at Standgate Creek until the 25th. Only then was the ship, which had returned almost to her original point of departure, allowed to continue the voyage. Although there were no further cholera victims, a total of thirteen deaths (including the eight in home waters) was logged before the vessel eventually arrived at Hobart Town on 16 July. A thorough medical examination by the colonial surgeon began the next day and, after the convicts disembarked on 23 July, orders were carried out to burn all clothing and bedding on board which might be contaminated.

In *Bristol Past and Present*, Nicholls and Taylor wrote that seven of the rioters died of cholera aboard ship before she sailed from London and also that Matthew Warry was 'shot dead by the sentinel' when he jumped into the Thames in a bid to swim to shore and freedom. Neither story is borne out by official contemporary documentation, however. Warry's name and those of the other Bristol men transported to Van Diemen's Land were duly recorded in the register of incoming prisoners for 1832, signed by Josiah Spode (principal superintendent of convicts).

None of the rioters in the *Katherine Stewart Forbes*, therefore, died of cholera; only one of them, George Andrews (he was nineteen), even received treatment for the disease and his seems to have been a relatively mild attack. James Ives endured lumbago, John Mecay had some hernia trouble, Charles Williams suffered from a bout of constipation and several more of the Bristol prisoners also reported sick with minor ailments during the passage, but all were declared fit for duty when they reached Hobart Town.

One listed 'lifer' was absent, however. Although his name appeared in the convict conduct register James Courtney, it was there noted, 'did not arrive'. On the very day (25 March) the *Katherine Stewart Forbes* sailed after being quarantined in

Standgate Creek, he had been transferred to the prison hulk, *Retribution*, at Sheerness. Eight weeks later—on 18 May—while his fellow Bristolians still rolled on the high seas, Courtney walked from that anchored gaol a free man—the recipient of a pardon. Exactly why remains a tantalizing mystery. What would have happened to him, one also wonders, had the convict ship not been forced back because of cholera?

On arrival at Van Diemen's Land, several rioters went on to 'Public Works' while most found themselves assigned to private employers. Charles Williams and the 'well-behaved' James Ives were soon before the magistrates and convicted for their part in 'conspiring' to take over the ship during transit and 'inducing others' to join them. Ives was sent to labour in the 'interior'; Williams got sentenced to three years at Macquarie Harbour, a penal establishment on the west coast. It was a notoriously mean place, approachable virtually only by water and that year, by very reason of its remoteness from the central administration, a phasing-out programme had already commenced.

Convicts, including Williams, were transferred progressively to a new penitentiary at Port Arthur on the island's east coast and within much easier reach of Hobart Town—and considered 'an almost perfect site for such an institution'. Discipline there was just as rigorous, punishments equally harsh, a shark-infested sea slapped besieging rocks and the prison guards were augmented by a number of 'fierce half-starved dogs'.

George Andrews also served an agonizing term (for housebreaking) at that repressive stronghold. None of the Bristol men avoided trouble altogether; in fact, some frequently ran foul of the law. A few spent part of their time as convict constables, in which capacity chances existed to shorten one's own sentence by securing the conviction of others or to gain monetary rewards (even immediate liberty, perhaps) by apprehending, or giving useful information about, a much-wanted outlaw. 'They were', commented John West, 'objects of fear and detestation.'

What of Richard Vines, reprieved shortly before he was due to hang at Bristol? On 8 March 1832, he had been taken aboard the *Justitia* hulk where his behaviour was regarded as 'orderly'. With 199 other prisoners, he sailed in the *England* on 4 April and arrived at Hobart Town on 18 July—just two days after the *Katherine Stewart Forbes*. Vines went to work for a Dr B. Wilson, staying with him for four years (committing several punishable offences during that time) before absconding. Upon recapture, he was sent to toil in a road party. Things went from bad to worse, however, and further attempts to escape reaped him a spell in a chain-gang, a two-year term of hard labour at Port Arthur and then a flogging of '75 stripes'.

On 22 October 1839, Richard Vines began what was to prove his final penalty—twelve months' road-work in the Hobart Town Surveyor's Gang—but the young man, who had eluded the rope back home, died unsung on the very last day of that year.

The information contained in the following detailed dossiers on the transported Bristol convicts is reproduced by kind permission of the Archives Office of Tasmania, Hobart, and the Archives Authority of New South Wales, Sydney:

VAN DIEMEN'S LAND

Arrived per *Katherine Stewart Forbes*
16 July 1832

GEORGE ANDREWS

Sentence—Life. Gaol Report—Not Known [*ie, no previous convictions*]. Hulk [*ie, 'Justitia'*] Report—Orderly. On Board [*ie, ship during transit*]—Disorderly. Wife (Mary) at native place, Bristol.

Description

Trade: labourer and groom. Height: 5 ft 7 in. Age: 20. Complexion: fair. Head: long. Hair: brown. Visage: small. Forehead: perpedicular. Eyebrows: dark brown. Eyes: blue. Nose: small. Mouth: medium width. Chin: round. Remarks: slightly pock-pitted.

Colonial Offences

29 January 1833	Sharpe [*ie, convict's employer*]: Neglect of duty when in charge of cattle—admonished.
15 October 1833	Sharpe: Neglect of duty in leaving his master's cattle at large by which they were impounded—returned to Public Works, six months Constitution Hill Road Party.

21 October 1833	Public Works: Stealing a white cord waistcoat and a pair of moleskin trousers, the goods of John Hearne—acquitted.
9 November 1833	Road Party: Absconding—imprisonment and hard labour, 12 months Bridgewater Chain Gang.
14 January 1834	Bridgewater Chain Gang: Refusing to work under a plea of not having shoes—40 lashes.
31 January 1834	Bridgewater Chain Gang: Absconding—75 lashes.
17 February 1834	Bridgewater Chain Gang: Breaking and entering the dwelling house of John E. Finch and stealing a waistcoat, value 9d—seven years.
22 November 1838	Griffiths: Disorderly conduct—admonished.
1 August 1840	Griffiths: Misconduct in drawing timber across the public street—admonished.
1 October 1840	Griffiths: Absent without leave—cells 10 nights, doing his work by day.
8 December 1840	Griffiths: Drunk and furiously driving and cruelly using his master's horse—12 months hard labour in chains and assigned to the interior.
5 January 1842	Perth: Absconding—three months hard labour out of chains.
3 July 1843	Rand: Misconduct in absenting himself at night by getting out of the window without leave—six months hard labour and returned to Government service.
28 September 1843	Insolence to his overseer—six days solitary confinement.
7 January 1845	Ticket-of-Leave.

(Tasmanian State Archives: CON 18/10 & 31/2)

PATRICK BARNETT

[*Known in VDL as Barrett*]. Sentence—Life. Gaol Report—Not Known. Hulk Report—Orderly, single. On Board—Quiet and inoffensive.

Description

Trade: ploughman. Height: 5 ft 2½ in. Age: 35. Complexion: dark. Head: round. Hair: black. Whiskers: dark brown. Visage: round. Forehead: medium height. Eyebrows: black. Eyes: grey. Nose: sharp. Mouth: medium width. Chin: small, short. Remarks: stout made.

Colonial Offences

28 December 1837	Connolly: In a public house after hours—admonished.
31 August 1838	Drunk—admonished.
11 February 1839	Connolly: Drunk—admonished.
7 August 1840	Ticket-of-Leave.
5 December 1840	Ticket-of-Leave: Feloniously receiving—fully committed to Willis Comers for assignment in the Campbell Town district.
19 February 1841	Ticket-of-Leave restored by order of the Lieutenant Governor.
20 September 1843	Conditional Pardon.

(CON 18/10 & 31/4)

THOMAS EVANS BENDALL

Sentence—Life. Gaol Report—Not Known. Hulk Report—Orderly, single.

Description

Trade: labourer. Height: 5 ft 5½ in. Age: 20. Complexion: fair. Head: long. Hair: brown. Visage: narrow. Forehead: medium height. Eyebrows: brown, meeting. Eyes: light blue. Nose: long. Mouth: medium width. Chin: small, round.

Colonial Offences

12 December 1832	Mrs Bolger: Neglect of duty and insolence to his mistress—in cell four nights, doing his work by day.
22 January 1833	Bolger: General neglect of duty and insolence—tread wheel for one week.
29 March 1833	Reynolds: Neglect of duty and making use of profane language—tread wheel for 10 days.
20 April 1833	Reynolds: Insolence to his mistress—25 lashes.
3 May 1833	Reynolds: Abusing and assaulting his fellow servant, Margaret Hobbs—six months on the Spring Hill Road Party, recommended not to be permitted to come to Hobart Town.
28 August 1833	Road Gang: Mutinously assembling with 21 others and declaring his resolution to abstain from labour—expressing contrition, reprimanded.
18 November 1833	Road Party: Fighting and wrangling in the Hut at the Road Party—reprimanded.

18 August 1835	Foord: Neglect of duty—25 lashes.
8 July 1837	Public Works: Making use of obscene language to Mrs Ann Saunders—25 lashes.
3 September 1838	G. Davies: Larceny—[case] dismissed.
2 January 1840	Hospital wardsman: Misconduct in making use of improper language in the public streets—severely reprimanded.
10 October 1840	Hospital wardsman: Misconduct in introducing improper food into the hospital—severely reprimanded.
12 October 1840	Loane: Misconduct and insolence—seven days solitary confinement on bread and water.
7 October 1841	Ticket-of-Leave.
22 February 1842	Ticket-of-Leave: Misconduct—seven days hard labour on the tread wheel.
3 November 1842	Ticket-of-Leave: Drunk—fined 5s.
26 July 1844	Ticket-of-Leave: Misconduct—10 days hard labour.
26 August 1845	Recommended for Conditional Pardon for the Australian Colonies.
4 August 1846	Approved.

(CON 18/10 & 31/4)

BENJAMIN BROAD

Sentence—Life. Gaol Report—Convicted before, bad character; has a brother transported. Hulk Report—Orderly, married, one child. On Board—Well conducted. Wife (Alice) at Bristol.

Description

Trade: stonemason-cutter and bricklayer. Height: 5 ft 8½ in. Age: 23. Complexion: sallow. Head: round. Hair: dark brown. Visage: small. Forehead: retreating. Eyebrows: dark, meeting. Eyes: dark hazel. Nose: medium length. Mouth: medium width. Chin: medium small, dimpled.

Colonial Offences

23 August 1834	Public Works: Improper conduct in cock fighting—admonished.
3 January 1835	Public Works: Absent from his work without permission—the privilege of working for his own benefit on a Saturday suspended until his conduct shall be favourably reported upon.

29 July 1835	Public Works: Out after hours and drinking—seven days solitary confinement on bread and water.
4 October 1837	Public Works: Misconduct in having in his possession the certificate of Marmaduke Greenwood—the indulgence of sleeping out of barracks withdrawn.
2 December 1837	To be allowed a Ticket-of-Leave on the Queen's birthday next for his good conduct upon the occasion of the late fires at Government House and the Rev Mr Palmer's.
21 January 1839	Ticket-of-Leave: Being in a public house—four days cells on bread and water.
29 October 1840	Ticket-of-Leave: Being in a public house after hours—48 hours tread wheel.
11 May 1845	Recommended for Conditional Pardon for the Australian Colonies.
15 January 1846	Approved.

(CON 18/10 & 31/5)

TIMOTHY COLLINGS

Sentence—Life. Gaol Report—Not Known. Hulk Report—Orderly, married with three children. On Board—Inoffensive with one exception. Wife (Mary) at Bristol.

Description

Trade: ploughman. Height: 5 ft 10½ in. Age: 30. Complexion: dark. Head: large, round. Hair and whiskers: brown. Visage: round. Forehead: high, retreating. Eyebrows: dark brown, arched. Eyes: light grey. Nose: small. Mouth: medium width. Chin: large.

Colonial Offences

23 March 1839	Cartwright: Absconding—to be kept in hard labour (Green Ponds) for three months and returned to his service.
10 August 1840	Ticket-of-Leave.
20 September 1843	Conditional Pardon.

(CON 18/10 & 31/7)

STEPHEN GAISFORD

Sentence—Life. Gaol Report—Convicted before, bad character. Hulk Report—Orderly, single.

Description

Trade: bread and biscuit baker. Height: 5 ft 6 in. Age: 23. Complexion: fair. Head: round. Hair: light brown. Visage: oval. Forehead: medium height, retreating. Eyebrows: brown. Eyes: dark brown. Nose: long. Mouth: medium width. Chin: long.

Colonial Offences

24 June 1839	Post Office messenger: Disorderly conduct— admonished.
24 August 1839	Post messenger: Misconduct in having been tippling in a public house—14 days hard labour out of chains.
2 July 1840	Ticket-of-Leave.
16 February 1841	Ticket-of-Leave: Larceny—discharged.
16 February 1841	Drunk—14 days on the tread wheel.
6 March 1841	Ticket-of-Leave: Out after hours—seven days hard labour on the tread wheel.
29 March 1842	Ticket-of-Leave: Breach of Quarter Sessions Act—fined £2.
14 July 1842	Conditional Pardon.
24 February 1846	Extended.

(*CON 18/10 & 31/16*)

CORNELIUS HICKEY

Sentence—Life. Gaol Report—Convicted before, bad character. Hulk Report—Orderly, single.

Description

Trade: blacksmith. Height: 5 ft 3¼ in. Age: 23. Complexion: ruddy. Head: round. Hair and whiskers: brown. Visage: oval. Forehead: nearly perpendicular. Eyebrows: brown. Eyes: dark grey. Nose: small. Chin: straight. Remarks: [*tattoos*] man above 'E' on left arm; man, woman, 'M', 'C' and 'H' on right arm; crucifix, anchor and 'H' below left elbow.

Colonial Offences

24 November 1835	Public Works: Feloniously stealing a £1 note, the property of Charles Tavisher—case discharged.
19 February 1836	Messenger: Drunk—three days solitary confinement on bread and water.
8 June 1836	Messenger: Repeated insolence and drunkenness—three months hard labour in chains in the Bridgewater Gang.

3 October 1837	Mr Page: Misconduct in wasting his master's provisions—two months hard labour and conduct to be reported at the expiration of this period with a view to his being assigned, if deserving, Campbell Town; if well conducted under punishment, to be returned to his service.
23 August 1839	Blayton: Insolence and other disorderly conduct—36 lashes.
3 March 1841	Ticket-of-Leave.
18 April 1842	Misconduct—deprived of his Ticket-of-Leave and 12 months hard labour; dismissed from the Police.
29 October 1842	Crown: Misconduct—reprimanded.
10 January 1843	The remainder of this man's punishment sentences to be remitted.
25 April 1844	Ticket-of-Leave: Breach of Police Act—committed to the common Gaol for seven days.
9 September 1845	Recommended for Conditional Pardon for the Australian Colonies.
6 May 1846	Approved.

(CON 18/10 & 31/20)

DANIEL HIGGS

Sentence—Life. Gaol Report—Not Known. Hulk Report—Orderly, single. On Board—Well behaved.

Description

Trade: labourer. Height: 5 ft 3½ in. Age: 20. Complexion: fair. Head: round. Hair: brown. Visage: small. Forehead: high, retreating. Eyebrows: brown. Eyes: dark blue. Nose: small. Mouth: medium width. Chin: small. Remarks: 'H', 'D', anchor, man and flag on left arm; sailor, woman, keg, 'E', 'B', 'D' and 'H' on right arm.

Colonial Offences

9 September 1836	Foord: Repeated neglect of duty and insolence—12 months imprisonment and hard labour in chains at a Road Party and returned to the service of the Crown; Sandy Bay Road Party, conduct to be reported at the end of three months.
31 July 1837	[Police] Constable: Assaulting Mary Ann Crisp and being in liquor—reprimanded.
7 November 1837	Constable: Neglect of duty—10 days solitary confinement.

30 April 1838	Constable: Gross misconduct and drunkenness. It appears that the misconduct of this man in a great manner is owing to the disgraceful conduct of Mr D. L. Marshall. He is fined only 5s and not again to be stationed at Ross.
20 August 1839	Constable: Drunkenness—reprimanded.
12 September 1839	Constable: Neglect of duty—three days solitary confinement on bread and water and deprived of his pay during that period.
1 July 1841	Constable: Gross misconduct as Watch House keeper in permitting Bridget Bateman, a prisoner of the Crown, to go with him to the Township and get drunk, getting drunk himself—fined 20s and, in default of payment, one month at the House of Correction; this charge is not correctly worded, fine remitted.
17 July 1841	Constable: Gross misconduct—case dismissed.
9 February 1842	Constable: Drunkenness—three days solitary confinement.
19 February 1842	Constable: Drunk—one month hard labour on the roads, Picton; Ticket-of-Leave suspended.
25 May 1842	Constable: Drunk—three days solitary confinement; third conviction since June 1841; dismissed from the Police; to Oatlands for assignment.
21 April 1843	Launceston: Drunk and disorderly—one month hard labour.
14 June 1844	Ticket-of-Leave.
31 March 1845	Drunk—fined 5s.
9 November 1846	Using indecent language—fined 5s.

(CON 18/10 & 31/30)

JAMES IVES

Sentence—Fourteen years. Gaol Report—Well behaved, gave useful information to the court whereby property was discovered. Hulk Report—Orderly, married with four children. Wife (Martha) at Bristol.

Description

Trade: labourer. Height: 5 ft 3¾ in. Age: 40. Complexion: fresh. Head: round. Hair: brown. Whiskers: reddish, small. Visage: round. Forehead: medium height, retreating. Eyebrows: light. Eyes: blue. Nose: medium length. Mouth: medium width. Chin: short.

Colonial Offences

23 July 1832 — Public Works: Gross insubordination on board the prison ship, *Katherine Stewart Forbes*, in the month of April last to wit on the 4th, 5th and 6th, and conspiring to take that vessel and inducing others to join in the same—to be [assigned to work] in the interior.

14 November 1835 — Constable: Disobedience of orders—reprimanded.

12 February 1836 — Constable: Disobedience of orders in taking prisoner in charge into a public house—suspended from rank and pay for one month, during which time to be employed keeping the Watch House clean; one month Reibey's Ford Road Jetty.

25 February 1836 — Constable: Gross neglect of duty in allowing a prisoner of the Crown in charge to leave his goods etc. with an innkeeper—six months hard labour with a road party; six months additional hard labour.

24 March 1836 — Late Constable: Neglect of duty in taking a key to Carrick for the purpose of bringing a false charge against John Marshall—six months additional hard labour with a road party at the expiration of existing sentence.

3 September 1838 — Scot: Drinking in a public house—two days cells on bread and water.

24 January 1839 — Ticket-of-Leave: Permitted to remain in the employ of T. & J. Corbett, of Launceston.

19 June 1839 — Ticket-of-Leave: Larceny—fully committed for trial.

13 August 1839 — Quarter Sessions: Existing sentence extended three years; [subsequently] three-year extension passed at Launceston Q.S. 13 August 1839 remitted, but to be sent to Port Arthur for two years on probation.

17 September 1842 — Oats: Gross misconduct in having a quantity of money and other articles in his possession under suspicious circumstances—eight months hard labour.

1 January 1844 — Ticket-of-Leave.

1846 — Certificate of Freedom.

(CON 18/10 & 31/24)

PATRICK KEARNEY

Sentence—Life. Gaol Report—Not Known. Hulk Report—
Orderly, married with two children. On Board—Well conducted, but violent. Wife (Mary Ann) at Bristol.

Description

Trade: linen draper. Height: 5 ft 10½ in. Age: 25. Complexion: fresh.
Head: round. Hair: reddish brown. Whiskers: reddish brown, thin.
Visage: oval, freckled. Forehead: high. Eyebrows: brown. Eyes: dark
blue. Nose: medium length. Mouth: medium width, lips projecting.
Chin: round. Remarks: crucifix, 'J', 'N', 'R' and 'J' inside right arm.

Colonial Offences

16 November 1832	Constable: Drunk—suspended for one month.
24 December 1832	Constable: Illegally impounding cattle and disobedience of orders—dismissed from his office as constable.
28 September 1833	McLeod: Drunkenness—severely reprimanded.
6 June 1834	McLeod: Making false complaints of his rations and neglect of duty—admonished.
26 December 1834	McLeod: Drunk and absent from his master's all night and other misconduct—36 lashes.
2 March 1835	Con: Being at large in the township without a pass and with fighting and disorderly conduct during the time of Divine service—50 lashes.
26 December 1835	McLeod: Absenting himself from his master's premises and getting drunk—cell on bread and water, three days and nights.
4 July 1836	McLeod: Drunkenness, insolence and neglect of duty—reprimanded, having promised to reform.
20 March 1837	McLeod: Getting drunk and procuring a pass under false pretences—admonished.
20 July 1837	McLeod: Drunk and over-staying his pass and being found in John Lee's house—12 days solitary confinement.
7 December 1837	McLeod: Gross misconduct—48 hours solitary confinement and returned to his service.
7 December 1837	McLeod: Suspicion of felony—discharged.
17 December 1838	McLeod: Insubordination—reprimanded.
25 January 1839	McLeod: Drunkenness—to sit two hours in the stocks.

8 April 1839	McLeod: Out after hours—to sit in the stocks three hours and returned to his service.
1 October 1839	McLeod: Out after hours—four hours in the stocks.
5 October 1840	McLeod: Suspicion of felony—dismissed.
21 October 1840	McLeod: Misconduct sending for his master when given in charge by him and saying that, if his master persisted in the charge, he would inform the Police Magistrate that some of McLeod's cattle were stolen property—six months imprisonment and hard labour in chains; recommended that he be removed to the other side of the island; Jerusalem Chain Gang, then Malcom's Huts for assignment.
13 April 1841	The unexpired portion of this man's punishment sentence is remitted.
7 May 1841	Rawlings: Misconduct—admonished.
21 March 1842	Rawlings: Neglect of duty—one month hard labour and to be returned to Government (Glenorchy Road Party, then Hobart for assignment).
22 April 1842	Just received from Glenorchy Party: Drunk— three months hard labour in the Glenorchy Party.
13 July 1842	Misconduct—two months hard labour.
1 November 1842	Being drunk—four months hard labour on the roads; Picton Party, then Oatlands for disposal
1 January 1844	Ticket-of-Leave.
29 January 1844	Drunk, out after hours and absent without leave—six months hard labour and Ticket-of-Leave suspended.
23 June 1844	Remainder of above sentence remitted and Ticket-of-Leave restored.
26 August 1844	Assault—six months hard labour and Ticket-of-Leave suspended.
14 August 1845	Breach of Police Act—fined 30s for balance and 5s for each weight.
24 December 1846	Breach of the Act 2nd Victorian[?]—fined 5s and 7s 6d costs.

(CON 18/10 & 31/26, 32/4)

APPENDIX: THE TRANSPORTED CONVICTS

JOHN MECAY

Sentence—Life. Gaol Report—Not Known. Hulk Report—
Orderly, married, three children.

Description

Trade: blacksmith and chain-cable maker. Height: 5 ft 10 in. Age:
25. Complexion: sallow. Head: round. Hair: brown. Visage: small.
Forehead: low. Eyebrows: brown. Eyes: brown. Nose: straight.
Mouth: medium width. Chin: medium, small. Remarks: scar on left
cheek-bone; 'J.M.' inside right arm.

Colonial Offences

20 August 1832	Labourer, Commissariat: Found at the ship launch during Divine service—tread wheel for six days.
14 May 1839	Oatlands.

(CON 18/10 & 31/30)

WILLIAM REYNOLDS

Sentence—Life. Gaol Report—Not Known. Hulk Report—
Orderly. On Board—Well conducted. Wife (Mary) at native
place, Bristol.

Description

Trade: butcher and stock-keeper. Height: 5 ft 4½ in. Age: 30. Com-
plexion: sallow. Head: round. Hair and whiskers: dark brown.
Visage: narrow. Forehead: high. Eyebrows: dark brown. Eyes: hazel.
Nose: medium width. Chin: round. Remarks: deeply pock-pitted.

Colonial Offences

5 March 1833	Glover: Neglect of duty—dismissed.
24 April 1834	Glover: Neglect of duty and disobedience of orders—reprimanded.
9 March 1838	R. Radcliffe: Neglect of duty, disobedience of orders and insolence—admonished.
3 May 1838	Gross misconduct in wilfully mismanaging a bullock belonging to his master—four months imprisonment with hard labour and then returned to his master.
31 May 1838	Spring Hill: Gross insolence on 25 May and on several other occasions—six months impris-onment and hard labour to commence from the expiration of his previous sentence, after which to be returned to Government.

24 May 1841	Ticket-of-Leave.
10 November 1842	Ticket-of-Leave: Misconduct in aiding and assisting in a fight, violently resisting Constable Sumler and being drunk—three months hard labour and recommended to be deprived of his Ticket-of-Leave; first offence for $4\frac{1}{2}$ years; Ticket-of-Leave suspended.
8 October 1844	Recommended for Conditional Pardon.
9 June 1845	Ticket-of-Leave: Having wood in his possession, the property of the Crown—fined £2.
25 February 1846	Conditional Pardon approved.

(*CON 18/10 & 31/37*)

JAMES SIMS

Sentence—Life. Gaol Report—Not Known. Hulk Report—Orderly, single. On Board—Good.

Description

Trade: farmer's labourer. Height: 5 ft $4\frac{3}{4}$ in. Age: 19. Complexion: dark. Head: round. Hair and whiskers: black. Visage: small. Forehead: low, retreating. Eyebrows: dark. Eyes: brown. Nose: acquiline. Mouth: small. Chin: small. Remarks: slightly pock-pitted.

Colonial Offences

16 July 1833	D. Lord: Disobedience of orders—admonished.
4 February 1834	D. Lord: Disobedience of orders—36 lashes.
19 January 1835	Lord: Found in a public place after hours—reprimanded.
28 August 1835	Lord: Suspicion of stealing flour—discharged on his master promising to remove him to his farm in the interior.
29 February 1840	Lord: Disobedience of orders and insolence—solitary confinement for one week.
2 January 1841	Lord: Absent without leave—seven days solitary, remitted at the intercession of his master.
3 July 1841	Ticket-of-Leave: Resisting a constable in the execution of his duty—fined 5s.
July 1845	Conditional Pardon approved.

(*CON 18/10 & 31/39*)

JAMES SNOOK

Sentence—Life. Gaol Report—Not Known, bad. Hulk Report—Orderly, single. On Board—Disorderly.

Description

Trade: brickmaker. Height: 5 ft 5 in. Age: 20. Complexion: fresh. Hair: brown. Visage: round. Forehead: high. Eyebrows: brown. Eyes' dark brown. Nose: small. Mouth: medium width, lips thick. Chin: short. Remarks: stout made; indecent figure, 'T' inside left arm, man 'M' and 'S' inside right arm.

Colonial Offences

31 October 1833	Rowlands: Out after hours—reprimanded.
25 November 1833	Loan Gang: Out after hours—reprimanded.
28 January 1834	Loan Gang: Neglect of duty—to be placed in the Brickfields Gang.
25 March 1834	Public Works: Neglect of duty—tread wheel for six days.
12 June 1834	Public Works: Absent from his gang without leave—reprimanded.
26 July 1836	Carr: Out after hours—reprimanded.
21 February 1838	Davies: There being a strong suspicion that he had stolen some potatoes from his master's farm, but there not being sufficient proof he is returned to the Government (Picton).
3 May 1841	Ticket-of-Leave: Misconduct in purposely mixing about 50 sheep of Mr Young's with his master's flock and with suspicion of intending to make away with them—to be kept to hard labour out of chains six months; Ticket-of-Leave suspended for that period and not again to reside in this district; Glenorchy, afterwards to reside in Hobart.
26 September 1843	McShern: Misconduct in being in town without a pass—admonished and to leave town.

(CON 18/10 & 31/39)

MICHAEL SULLIVAN

Sentence—Life. Gaol Report—Not Known. Hulk Report—Orderly, single. On Board—Violent, but generally well conducted.

Description

Trade: ploughman. Height: 5 ft 11 in. Age: 25. Complexion: dark. Head: round. Hair and whiskers: black. Visage: oval. Forehead: medium height. Eyebrows: black, meeting. Eyes: hazel. Nose: sharp. Mouth: medium width, habitually open. Chin: small. Remarks: Scar on left cheek, scar on right side of chin.

Colonial Offences

12 June 1834	McDougal: Out of hours and striking Constable Wickendam when being taken into custody by him—tread wheel for four days.
17 October 1834	McDougal: Inciting Samuel Willis, a boy assigned to McDougal, to pilfer leather from his master—imprisonment and hard labour, six months Westbury Road Party.
16 March 1835	Road Party: Fighting on the evening of the Sabbath day—36 lashes.
1 December 1835	McDougal: Drunk and disorderly—cell on bread and water for 14 days.
8 August 1836	Driving his horse and cart on the footpath—cell at night one week, doing his work by day.
19 December 1837	Indecently exposing his person to Mr McDougal's granddaughter, a child of eleven years of age—to be removed to Port Arthur and there to be kept to hard labour in chains for three years.
28 February 1838	Fighting at his work—reprimanded.
19 June 1838	Having a quantity of potatoes privately cooking in the Government garden and having tobacco improperly in his possession—three days solitary on bread and water.
13 March 1839	Negligently performing his work—48 hours solitary on bread and water.
4 July 1839	Having tobacco in his possession and refusing to be searched—three days in cell on bread and water.
16 January 1840	Having leather improperly secreted at his place of work—three days solitary confinement on bread and water.
21 October 1840	Misconduct—three days solitary.
10 February 1843	Ticket-of-Leave.
11 July 1844	Drunk—fined 5s.
23 December 1845	Recommended for Conditional Pardon.
31 October 1846	Approved.

(CON 18/10 & 31/39)

JOHN TOWELL

Sentence—Life. Gaol Report—Not Known. Hulk Report—Orderly, married with one child. Wife (Mary) at native place, Twerton.

Description
Trade: maltster and brewer. Height: 5 ft 11¾ in. Age: 23. Complexion: dark. Head: round. Hair and whiskers: dark brown. Visage: large oval. Forehead: high, retreating. Eyebrows: dark brown. Nose: medium. Mouth: medium width. Chin: small. Remarks: long arms.

Colonial Sentences

5 June 1833	Roberts: Drunk and insolent to his master—in cell on bread and water for five days.
6 July 1833	W. Roberts: Drunk and using abusive language to Mr O'Sullivan—25 lashes.
23 October 1833	Roberts: Assaulting and beating Ann Drain—complaint dismissed.
15 September 1834	Roberts: Insolence and refusing to work—reprimanded.
19 October 1835	Watchman: Gross misconduct in rescuing a prisoner charged with larceny—12 months hard labour in chains (Grass Tree Hill).
26 December 1836	Woodward: Absent without leave, neglect of duty—cells for 10 days on bread and water.
18 January 1837	Woodward: Absconding—hard labour in chains 12 months; not to be re-assigned till favourably reported; 12 months at Campbell Town Road Party.
1 May 1837	Government Gang: Refusing to work—reprimanded.
29 March 1838	Woodward: Disorderly conduct—hard labour out of chains for two months and returned to the Government (Green Ponds, then Picton for assignment).
19 November 1838	Palmer: Absent without leave—reprimanded and returned to Government.
9 March 1840	Thomson: Gross insubordination—to be removed to Port Arthur and there held to hard labour in chains for two years.
19 May 1843	Ticket-of-Leave.
26 August 1845	Recommended for Conditional Pardon for the Australian Colonies.
4 August 1846	Approved.

(*CON 18/10 & 31/43*)

MATTHEW WARRY

Sentence—Life. Gaol Report—Not Known. Hulk Report—Orderly, single.

Description

Trade: baker. Height: 4 ft 7¾ in. Age: 20. Complexion: dark. Head: round. Hair: brown. Visage: oval. Forehead: low, retreating. Eyebrows: dark, meeting. Eyes: dark brown. Nose: long. Mouth: medium width. Chin: long. Remarks: deformed.

Colonial Offences

2 September 1833	Wilson: Suspicion of purloining his master's flour—dismissed.
29 April 1836	Anderson: Making use of bad language—treadmill for six days.
8 May 1837	Anderson: Found in a disorderly house after hours—cells on bread and water for seven days.
4 July 1837	Anderson: Absent all night—cells 14 days on bread and water.
4 January 1838	Anderson: Drunkenness and misconduct—six months hard labour on the roads (Green Ponds).
12 September 1838	Anderson: Neglect of duty—three months hard labour and returned to public works (Sandy Bay and then penitentiary for assignment).
24 December 1838	Prisoners Barracks: Missing muster—hard labour on the roads for three months (Sandy Bay Road Party).
16 March 1840	Ross: Being drunk, out after hours and other misconduct—solitary confinement for 14 days.
3 February 1841	Ticket-of-Leave.
1 December 1843	Recommended for Conditional Pardon.
14 January 1845	Approved.

(CON 18/10 & 31/46)

CHARLES WILLIAMS

Sentence—Life. Gaol Report—Not Known. Hulk Report—Orderly, married. On Board—Generally well conducted. Wife (Mary Ann), and one child, at Bristol.

Description

Trade: cabinet maker and carpenter. Height: 5 ft 7 in. Age: 23. Complexion: fresh. Head: round. Hair: dark brown. Visage: small. Forehead: medium height, retreating. Eyebrows: dark brown. Eyes: brown. Nose: small. Mouth: medium width, lips projecting. Chin: small. Remarks: pock-pitted: small blue mark on left arm.

Colonial Offences

23 July 1832	Public Works: Gross insubordination on board the prison ship, *K. S. Forbes*, in the month of April last, to wit on the 4th, 5th and 6th, conspiring to take that vessel and inducing other to join him in the same—Macquarie Harbour for three years.
6 September 1833	Purloining Government tools for the purpose of aiding him to escape—36 lashes (Port Arthur).
28 August 1834	Hutton: Assaulting and abusing his fellow servant, Elizabeth Cook—three nights in the cells and to do his work by day.
13 September 1834	Hutton: Suspicion of stealing from the person of William Day eight £1 notes—there being no proof, but a very strong suspicion, he is to be imprisoned and kept to hard labour for 12 months in the Bridgewater Chain Gang and not to be returned to the loan gang; removed to Public Works, Oatlands.
4 September 1835	Public Works: Neglect of duty—reprimanded.
16 October 1835	Public Works: Disorderly conduct in fighting when ordered to grind an axe—reprimanded.
13 December 1839	Carpenter, Royal Engineers Dept.: Insolence to his overseer—reprimanded.
8 July 1840	Carpenter, R.E. Dept.: Disorderly conduct in tippling in a public house—reprimanded.
20 July 1840	Ticket-of-Leave.
20 January 1841	Ticket-of-Leave: Misconduct in being absent bagatelle in a public house after hours—cells for 10 nights, doing his work by day.
17 January 1841	Ticket-of-Leave: Midconduct in being absent from church—admonished and ordered to pay for the summons.
27 January 1841	Ticket-of-Leave: Misconduct in making a false statement—discharged and ordered to remove to an interior district.
28 February 1844	Recommended for Conditional Pardon.
March 1845	Approved.
10 February 1846	Extended.

(*CON 18/10 & 31/46*)

Arrived per *England*
18 July 1832

RICHARD VINES

Sentence—Life ('cast for death, but respite'). Goal Report—Not
Known, orderly. Hulk Report—Orderly, married, one child.
Wife (Elizabeth) at native place, Clifton.

Description

Trade: groom and carter. Height: 5 ft 8¼ in. Age: 22. Complexion:
dark. Head: round. Hair and whiskers: dark brown. Visage: oval.
Forehead: high. Eyebrows: dark brown. Eyes: brown, speck in left.
Nose: medium length. Mouth: medium width. Chin: small.

Colonial Offences

15 August 1833	Dr Wilson: Neglect of work, fighting and disobedience of orders—30 lashes.
14 April 1834	Dr Wilson: Neglect of duty, lying and disobedience of orders—two months in Notman's Chain Gang and to be returned to his master.
12 July 1836	Wilson: Insolence—seven days solitary confinement.
6 August 1836	Wilson: Absconding—12 months imprisonment and hard labour and then returned to his master's service.
4 October 1836	Spring Hill Road Party: Absconding—present sentence at Spring Hill Road Party extended six months.
14 October 1836	Absent from his gang without leave, with intent to abscond—imprisonment and hard labour in chains for two years.
2 November 1836	Bridgewater Chain Gang: Absentee/absconding—to be removed to Port Arthur and kept to hard labour for two years.
26 January 1837	Absenting himself from the Public Works, Coal Point, on 16th instant and remaining so till apprehended by Constable James Smith the same day near Weelge Bay—75 stripes.
22 October 1839	Mr Mackay: On suspicion of stealing a quantity of wheat—recommended to be worked on the roads for twelve months on probation and returned to Government; twelve

months probation Town Surveyor's Gang, Hobart, then for assignment.

(CON 18/10 & 31/44)

NEW SOUTH WALES

Arrived per *Parmelia*
16 November 1832

WILLIAM CHRISTOPHER

Sentence—Seven years. Former Convictions—None. Occupation—Farm servant. Religion—Catholic. Education—None. Native Place—County Waterford. Married; two children.

Description

Age: 31. Height: 5 ft 4 in. Complexion: sallow and spotted. Hair: dark brown. Eyes; hazel grey. Remarks: lost one front tooth of upper jaw; scar on back of right-hand.

Christopher obtained a Ticket-of-Leave (recommended, September 1836) for the District of Patrick Plains; he received a Certificate of Freedom dated 3 December 1840 [*a document stating a convict's sentence had been served*].

HENRY GREEN

Sentence—Life. Former Convictions—None. Occupation—Seaman. Religion—Protestant. Education—Reads and writes. Native Place—Dorsetshire. Single.

Description

Age: 31. Height: 5 ft 6½ in. Complexion: brown. Hair: dark brown. Eyes: hazel and speckled. Remarks: anchor, cable, heart and 'H' on lower left-arm.

Green obtained a Ticket-of-Leave in January 1841 and allowed to remain in the District of Braidwood; in February 1847, he was granted a Conditional Pardon 'to take effect in all parts of the World, except the United Kingdom of Great Britain and Ireland'.

HENRY HURD

Sentence—Life. Former Convictions—None. Occupation—brickmaker. Religion—Protestant. Education—None. Native Place—London. Single.

Description

Age: 20. Height: 5 ft 5½ in. Complexion: ruddy and freckled. Hair: dark brown. Eyes: brown. Remarks: small mouth: scar inside right thumb, three warts on back of same; scar back of left thumb; blue ring on left middle finger.

Hurd was granted a Ticket-of-Leave on 15 March 1844 and permitted to stay in the District of Maitland; the concession was 'cancelled, having been tried for an assault with intent to commit a rape upon a child—but was only found guilty of the common assault' [probably in February 1848 when he was sentenced to three months imprisonment for assault; the Ticket-of-Leave was subsequently restored].

AARON MARTIN

Sentence—Seven years. Former Convictions—None. Occupation—Stable boy. Religion—Protestant. Education—Reads. Native Place—Bristol. Single.

Description

Age: 21. Height: 5 ft 3¼ in. Complexion: fair ruddy. Hair: brown. Eyes: grey. Remarks: small anchor on upper left-arm, 'AM' on lower right-arm.

Martin obtained a Certificate of Freedom, dated 1 October 1841.

JOHN WAKEFIELD

Sentence—Life. Former Convictions—None. Occupation—Gardener's labourer. Religion—Protestant. Education—Reads and writes. Native Place—Gloucestershire. Single.

Description

Age: 19. Height: 5 ft 2 in. Complexion: fair ruddy. Hair: dark brown. Eyes: brown. Remarks: small scar on left cheek-bone; broad featured.

Wakefield granted a Conditional Pardon, dated 31 December 1847.

Arrived per *Mary III*
5 January 1833

WILLIAM SPOKES

Sentence—Life. Former Convictions—None. Occupation—Potter and bargeman. Religion—Protestant. Education—Reads and writes. Native Place—Bristol. Married; two children.

Description

Age: 22. Height: 5 ft 5½ in. Complexion: dark sallow. Hair: brown. Eyes: hazel. Remarks: 'WSMS' on upper, 'JS' on lower right-arm; 'MSSS' on upper left-arm.

Spokes obtained a Ticket-of-Leave, dated 11 February 1841, and allowed to remain in the District of Patrick Plains; received a Conditional Pardon, dated 10 July 1848.

Arrived per *Camden*
18 February 1833

JOSEPH MILLS

Sentence—Life. Former Convictions—None. Occupation—Shoemaker. Religion—Protestant. Education—Reads and writes. Native Place—Bristol. Single.

Description

Age: 24. Height: 5 ft 3¼ in. Complexion: ruddy. Hair: light brown. Eyes: greenish. Remarks: nose a little cocked; blue ring on right middle finger; small mole on right cheek.

Mills obtained a Ticket-of-Leave, dated 16 May 1841, and permitted to stay in the District of Maitland; granted a Conditional Pardon, dated 31 December 1847.

Arrived per *Heroine*
19 September 1833

JOSEPH KEATES

Sentence—Seven years. Former Convictions—None. Occupation—Seaman. Religion—Catholic. Education—None. Native Place—Bristol. Single.

Description

Age: 25. Height: 5 ft 6¼ in. Complexion: brown. Hair: sandy brown. Eyes: grey. Remarks: ears pierced for rings; nail of forefinger of right-hand split; blue ring on middle finger of left-hand.

Keates granted a Certificate of Freedom, dated 20 May 1839.

The original records on the above eight men are held in the
Archives Authority of New South Wales, Sydney, the relevant
reference numbers being: AO 4/4017 & 4/4018 (indents for
ships, giving personal details of convicts); AO 4/4109, 4/4147,
4/4148 & 4/4187 (tickets-of-leave); AO 4/4368 & 4/4452 (conditional pardons); AO 4/4348 & 4/4363 (certificates of freedom).

Principal Sources of Information

MANUSCRIPT MATERIAL

PUBLIC RECORD OFFICE, LONDON
Home Office Papers
HO 9/4, 5 & 7 (Convict Registers: *Justitia* prison hulk, Woolwich, and *Retribution* prison hulk, Sheerness); HO 10/29, 30, 48, 49 & 50 (Lists of Convicts in New South Wales and in Van Diemen's Land, 1832–1835); HO 11/8 & 9 (Convict Transportation Registers, 1831–1834); HO 27/43 (Criminal Register for England and Wales, 1832); HO 40/28 (Correspondence: Disturbances, 1831); HO 41/10 (Entry Books: Disturbances, April–December 1831); HO 52/12 (Military Court of Enquiry, Bristol, November 1831).

War Office Papers
WO 3/83 (Correspondence: Bristol Riots and Military Aid); WO 12/210 & 1156 (Regimental Muster Rolls: 3rd Dragoon Guards, 1831–1832, and 14th Light Dragoons, 1831–1832, respectively); WO 25/781 & 784 (Army Officers' Services: 3rd Dragoon Guards and 14th Light Dragoons respectively); WO 71/280 (Courts-Martial, 1832).

Admiralty Papers
ADM 101/40 (Medical Journal of surgeon-superintendent John Stephenson, *Katherine Stewart Forbes*, February–July 1832).

Probate Room
PROB 11/1798 & 1879 (Wills respectively of Lt-Col Thomas Brereton and Lt-Col Andrew Coghlan).

BRISTOL UNIVERSITY LIBRARY
The Pinney Papers

BRISTOL REFERENCE LIBRARY

Troubles in Bristol by Politics, Fire and Pestilence (B 10112), a unique scrapbook of newspaper clippings, pamphlets, posters, illustrations etc.

ARCHIVES OFFICE OF TASMANIA

Convict Department—CON 18 (Descriptions of Convicts); CON 31 & 32 (Conduct Registers).

ARCHIVES AUTHORITY OF NEW SOUTH WALES

Indents for Convict Ships (AO 4/4017 & 4018).

BOOKS

Bateson, Charles: *The Convict Ships 1787–1868.* Brown, Son and Ferguson, 1969.

Brace, Keith: *Portrait of Bristol.* Robert Hale, 1971.

Brock, Michael: *The Great Reform Act.* Hutchinson, 1973.

Clark, C. M. H.: *A History of Australia.* Melbourne University Press, 1968.

Eagles, John ('A Citizen'): *The Bristol Riots, their Causes, Progress and Consequences.* Cadell, London; Blackwood, Edinburgh; 1832.

Gurney, Mr (shorthand transcript): *Trial of Charles Pinney.* Cadell, London; Blackwood, Edinburgh; 1833.

Latimer, John: *The Annals of Bristol in the Nineteenth Century.* W. and F. Morgan, Bristol, 1887.

Little, Bryan: *The City and County of Bristol.* Werner Laurie, 1954; S. R. Publishers, 1967.

Nicholls, J. F. and Taylor, John: *Bristol Past and Present* (volume 3). J. W. Arrowsmith, Bristol, 1881.

Pares, Richard: *A West-India Fortune.* Longmans, Green, 1950.

Rolt, L. T. C.: *Isambard Kingdom Brunel.* Longmans, Green, 1957.

Shaw, A. G. L.: *The Story of Australia.* Faber and Faber, 1955.

Walker, Frank: *The Bristol Region.* Thomas Nelson, 1972.

West, John: *The History of Tasmania.* First published, 1852. New edition (with an introduction and annotations by A. G. L. Shaw), Angus and Robertson, in association with Royal Australian Historical Society, 1971.

Weyman, Stanley J.: *Chippinge.* Smith, Elder, 1906; Pan Books, 1971.

BOOKLETS AND PAMPHLETS

Mackwroth, Digby: *A Personal Narrative of the Late Events in Bristol, Chiefly Within My Own Knowledge.* 1831.

Manchee, Thomas John: *The Origins of the Bristol Riots and the Causes of the Subsequent Outrages.* 1831.

Payne, Herbert: *Bristol Riots 1686–1831*. 1974.

Ralph, Elizabeth: *Government of Bristol 1373–1973*. Bristol Corporation, 1973.

Somerton, William Henry: *A Narrative of the Bristol Riots*. 'The Bristol Mercury' Office, 1831.

Thomas, Susan: *The Bristol Riots*. Bristol Branch of The Historical Association, 1974.

NEWSPAPERS AND PERIODICALS

The Bristol Gazette; The Bristol Liberal; The Bristol Mercury; The Bristol Mirror; Felix Farley's Bristol Journal; A Free Reporter (Bristol); *The Observer* (Bristol); *The Bath Chronicle; Bath Journal; The Gloucester Journal; Albion and Star; Annual Register; Bell's Weekly Messenger; Blackwood's Magazine; The Dublin Evening Post; The Examiner; The Gentleman's Magazine; The Globe; The Limerick Chronicle; Morning Advertiser; Morning Herald; The Morning Post; The News; The Spectator; The Sun; The Times; The True Sun; The United Service Journal.*

REFERENCE WORKS

The Army Lists; Beaven's Bristol Lists; Burke's Landed Gentry; Burke's Peerage, Baronetage and Knightage; Dictionary of National Biography; Mathew's Bristol Directories; Modern English Biography.

Index

by Ann Hugh-Jones

(The figures in *italics* indicate illustrations)

Agricultural riots, 12, 163
Albion and Star, The, 155
Ames, Mrs M., 49, 102, 110
Andrews, G., 131, 188–89, 190–91
Annals of Bristol (Latimer), 45, 91, 124–25
Army: pensioners, 98, 119; Recruiting Office, 34, 71, 73–74, 77, 118, 150; *Regulations*, 73, 148, 151, 164; Units, *see* Military
Arthur, G. (NSW), 184
Assembly Rooms, *10*, 33, 89
Assizes, 20–21, 25–28, 31–33, 37–38, 45, 119
Attorney-General, *see* Denman

Baillie, J., 24, 28, 109
Barnard, F. T., 92
Barnett, P., 131, 191–92
Bath, 23, 25, 49, 70, 75, 80–81, 148; *Chronicle*, 89, 136
Beaufort, Duke of, 31, 121
Beckwith, Maj. W., 96–99, 115, 163, 166–67, 171, 181
Beeston, 14
Bell's Weekly Messenger, 155
Bendall, T. E., 124, 131, 192–93
Bengough, G., 35, 38, 122
Berkeley Square, 62, 75, 80–84
Birmingham, 12–13, 24; Political Union, 12, 30, 71
Bishop of Bath and Wells, 25, 31

Bishop of Bristol, 25, 54, 67–69, 72
Bishop's Palace, *11*, 66–69, 72–74, 97, 107, 123–25
Blethyn, T., 89
Blue Bowl Inn, 34–35
Bosanquet, Sir J. B., 121
Boyse, Taskmaster, 58–59
Brereton, Lt-Col T., *16*, 17, 34, 42–44, 51–56, 61–63, 68, 70–71, 73, 77–81, 85, 92–97, 99–110; letter to Fitzroy Somerset, 114–15; C.-in-C.'s verdict on, 116; Court of Enquiry, 116–17; 118; court-martial, 139–48; death of, 148–50; inquest, 152–53; funeral, 153–54; press comment on, 153–56; *see* also trials of: Warrington, Pinney
Brereton, C. L., 18, 140, 150
Brereton, M. S. C., 18, 140, 150
Brice, W., 81
Bridewell gaol, 58–59, 65, 123
Brimel, T., 125
Bristol Assizes, *see* Assizes
Bristol civic administration: Chamberlain, *see* Garrard; City Council (1836), 180; City Solicitor, *see* Burges; Constabulary, 15, 19, 119, *see* constables and special constables; Magistrates, *see* Magistrates; Mayor, *see* Pinney; Mayor's Clerk, *see* Burges; Town Clerk, *see* Ludlow
Bristol Medical School, 30

Bristol newspapers, *see Gazette, Liberal, Mercury, Mirror, Felix Farley's Bristol Journal, Observer*

Bristol Political Union, 28–30, 55, 61, 64, 95, 110, 119, 176, 180

Bristol, Recorder of, *see* Wetherell

Bristol Sheriffs, *see* Bengough; Hare; Lax

Broad, B., 131, 193–94

Broad, J. S., 92

Brock, M., *The Great Reform Act*, 14

Brunel, Isambard Kingdom, 33, 65, 90, 93

Brussels, 12

Buck, Rev C., 89, 124

Budgett, H. H., 98

Bulgin, H., 63

Bull, C., 124

Burges, D., 19, 27, 41, 49, 72, 81, 172, 180

Bush, J., 70, 76

Bush, S., 48

Byrne, J., 55

Camden (prison ship), 186

Camplin, Ald. T., 72–74, 84–85, 144, 160

Cardiff, 70, 136

Carpenter, Dr L., 33, 59

Case, R. E., 21, 23

Casualties, civilian, 101

Cathedral, 54, 68–69, 122

Cavalry, *see* Military

Chaillou, Professor, 92

Charles (ship), 25

Cholera, in Bristol, 168; on prison ship, 187–88

Christopher, W., trial of, 125; sentence, 131; transportation of, 185–86; NSW dossier, 209

Civil force, *see* constables, special

Clarke, W., 123, 127–29; petition for reprieve of, 132; execution of, 133–36; line drawing, 137

Claxton, Capt. C., 2, 25–27, 93

Clifton Hotel, 83, 102

Clifton Parish Church, 154

Cobbett, W., *Political Register*, 11

Codrington, Capt. C. W., 76–79, 81, 171

Coghlan, Lt-Col A., 148–50

Coleman, J., 89, 131

Collings, T., 131, 194–95

Colston's School, 156

Commercial Rooms, 38, 108

Commissions of Enquiry, *see* Royal Commissions

Committee of Enquiry, into actions of city magistrates, 167–77

Compensation, claims for, 90, 178

Congreve, Capt. A., 96

Constables, parish: no full-time paid constabulary, 19, 119; 36–41, 46–47, 49, 62, 68, 119–21

Constables, special (hired): recruiting of, 3, 19–20, 25, 2, 28–29, 62, 66, 94–95, 117, 119–20, 122; in action: 34, 37, 40, 44, 46, 48, 72, 97, 99–101, 104–05, 107–08, 121, 133

Convict settlements, 131, 183–90

Convict ships, 182–89; *see* also: *Camden, England, Heroine, Justitia, Katherine Stewart Forbes, Mary III, Parmelia, Retribution*

Convicted men, *see* rioters

Cossens, J., 40, 77

Council House, 19, 21, 31, 47–48, 52–53, 63, 66, 71–72, 74–75, 77, 94, 96, 125

Court of King's Bench, London, 168

Court-martials: of Brereton, 118, 139–51, 157; of Warrington, 157–67

Court proceedings, *see* trials

Courtney, J., 123, 131, 188–89

Crook, J., 69

Crook, T. H., 69

Crosby, T., 126

Cross, W., 88

Custom House, 11, 18, 51, 65, 87, 92, 107

Dalbiac, Maj.-Gen. Sir J. C., 116–17, 139, 151–53, 157–67

Daniel, H., 75

Daniel, Ald. T., 61–62, 171

Daniell, Lt-Col J., 18

Davis, C., trial of, 125–31; petition for, 132–33; execution of, 133–36; line drawing, 135

Davis, Martha, 88

Dawson, Lt J., 48, 146

Day, Rev W., 134
Deane, Sgt E., 146
Denman, Sir T., 86, 125, 169–71
Denney, Tpr W., 163
Dineage, Sgt S., 72
Dodington Park, 70, 76
Dodington Yeomanry, see Military
    Units
Dooley, Tpr M., 73
Dragoons, see Military Units
Drinkwater, J. E., 178–79
Dublin Evening Post, 101
Dyer, J., 131

Eagles, Rev J., 101
Earl of Liverpool (ship), 2, 25–27, 105
Edgeworth, Father F., 170
Election, General, 12, 24
Electoral system, 13–14
Ellard, Maj. H., 116–17, 147
Ellis, W. J., 152
England (convict ship), 189
Enquiry, see Commission of; Com-
    mittee of; Military Court of
Erle, W., 141, 147, 150
Evans, T., 58–59
Evans, T. M., 141, 150
Examiner, The, 174
Excise Office, 10, 18, 27
Executions (of rioters), 133–36

Fane, Lt-Gen. Sir H., 139–51, 165
Felix Farley's Bristol Journal, 32, 56,
    100, 112, 134, 136, 175
Fergusson, Lt-Col J. F., 106, 116–17
Field, W., 64–65
Fires: 5, 6, 7, 8
Fisher's Horse Repository, 34, 56, 77
Francis, Lt G., 80
Free Reporter, A., 169
Fripp, D., 75, 80–84
Fripp, Ald. W., 27–28, 75, 172;
    Mayor, 180
Fry, J. S., 90
Furlong, W., 92

Gage, Capt. J. W., 34, 44, 47–48,
    52–53, 56; commendation of, 115;
    court-martial witness, 142–47; 151,
    163, 166

Gaisford, S., 131
Gambier, E. J., 178–89
Gaols, see Bridewell, Gloucestershire
    County Prison, New Gaol,
    Taylor's Court
Gardiner, C., 45
Gardiner, J., 75, 105, 107
Garrard, T., 47
Gawler, Maj. G., 118
Gazette, The Bristol, 32, 48, 55, 65, 87,
    90, 100
George, Ald. J., 49
Gilbert, J., 126
Giroux, C., 92
Globe, The, 174
Gloucester, 30, 65, 96
Gloucestershire County Prison, 5, 37,
    64
Goldney, Ald. G., 49
Goldney, S. O., 83–84, 159–61
Goss, E., 171
Grant, Rt Hon. C., 165–66
Gray, Rt Rev R., 25, 54, 67–69, 72
Gray, Rev R. (nephew of Bishop),
    68–69
Green, B. H., 63
Green, H., 131, 185, 209
Gregory, T., 124–31, 133–36; line
    drawing, 137
Gresley, C., 159
Guildhall (Bristol), 35–37, 52–55, 59,
    62–63, 121–22
Guppy, T. R., 90
Gutch, J. M., 32

Hall, J. W., 26
Ham, J., 110
Hare, W. O., 19–20, 27–28, 37,
    172
Harris, W., 83–84, 159–61
Herapath, W., 30, 55, 61, 63–64, 95,
    180
Heroine (convict ship), 186
Hibernia Tavern, 64–65
Hickey, C., 131, 195–96
Higgs, D., 123, 131, 196–97
Hilhouse, Ald. A., 49, 52, 60, 65, 145,
    153, 159
Hilhouse, Ald. G., 64, 81
Hill, Gen. Sir R., 45–47, 70, 115–18
Hodges, E., 69
Home Secretary, see Melbourne
Hopton, R., 93

Horse Guards (London), 17, 30, 44, 62, 70, 117, 144–45
House of Commons, 20, 24–25, 33, 118
House of Lords, 11, 13, 14, 25
Huggins, P. T., 168
Huish, C., 131, 186
Humphries, W., 60, 134
Hunt, H., 11
Hurd, H., 65, 186, 209–10

Ives, J., 124–25, 131, 185, 188–89, 197–98

Jackson, Maj.-Gen. Sir R. D., 106, 115–16, 118–20
James, Daniel, 48
James, David, 131
Johnson, J., 90
Jones, John, 125
Jones, W., 67–68
Justitia (prison hulk), 131, 186, 189

Katherine Stewart Forbes (prison ship), 185–88
Kayes, J., 124, 127–31, 133–36; line drawing, 137
Kearney, P., 123–31, 199–200
Keates, J., 131, 186, 211–12
Kelson, Cornet C., 61, 68, 73–74, 85; 115; at Brereton's court-martial, 143, 147, 151; 153; at Warrington's court-martial, 158–59, 162–63, 166
Keynsham, 30, 56–57, 70–71, 94, 97
King Street, 33, 90–91, 105, 126; Merchants Hall, 116, 139–48
Kingsley, C., 91
Kingswood miners, 33, 70, 98, 176
Kington, T., 82, 159
Krinks, H., 131

Lamb, Hon. G., 27, 105, 119
Lane, T., 125
Latimer, J., Annals of Bristol, 45, 91, 124–25
Law, Rt Rev G. H., 25, 31
Lax, J., 38, 75, 91
Leary, Lt P., 97

Lee, Rev H., 122
Leigh's Horse Bazaar, 34, 84, 159
Lewis, J., 69
Lewis, Lt J. C., 101–02
Liberal, The Bristol, 32, 102, 136, 175
Little, S. G., 60
Littledale, J., 169–73
Livett, J., 69
Loinsworth, A. L., 147, 152
London, riots in, 14
Londonderry, Marquis of, 14
Loughborough, Lt-Col Lord, 116–17
Love, Lt-Col J. F., 70, 106
Ludlow, E., 32, 37, 40, 44, 53–55, 62, 72–74, 81; at Military Court of Enquiry, 116–17; at Brereton's court-martial, 145–46; 153, 172, 180
Luxton, S., 124

Macclesfield, Lt, 82
Mack, Mrs J., 64–65
Mackworth, Maj. D., 45–47, 50–51, 66; A Personal Narrative, 93–94, 98; 97–100, 104, 107, 115, 151, 163, 166–67, 172–73, 180–81
Magistrates: recruitment of constables, 19–20; attempted recruitment of sailors, 25–27; challenged by Political Union, 29; issue of posters by, 3, 4, 13, 31–32, 54–55, 99, 108; public meeting, 62–63; 69–70; letter to Codrington, 78–79; 96, 110–11; Brereton's condemnation of, 117, 154; condemned by Press, 133; law regarding, 164; Committee of Enquiry on conduct of, 167–77
Manchee, T. J., 30, 98, 110
Manchester, 11, 13, 24
Mansion House, 11, 18, 20; Recorder's arrival at, 38–39; arrival at, 38–39; mobbing of, 38–47, 50–52; Mayor's letter from, 49–50; salvage from, 65–66; 72, 74; burning of, 86–87, 104
Martin, Aaron, 131, 186, 210
Martin, James, 32
Martin, Sgt-Maj. J., 93
Mary III (convict ship), 186
Mason, W., 125
Massam, J., 187

Mayor of Bristol: *see* Pinney, C.; also successors: Stanton, Fripp, W.
Mecay, J., 123–31, 188, 201
Melbourne, Lord, 27–28, 30, 44, 71, 78, 105; citizens' letter to, 108–09; 114, 119–20, 167
Members of Parliament, *see* Baillie; Protheroe
Mercury, The Bristol, 27, 30, 32, 42, 87; condemnation of magistrates, 99–100; 110, 112, 134; praise of Brereton, 155–56; 167
Miles, Col Sir E., 116–17
Military Court of Enquiry, 116–17
Military court-martials: of Brereton, 118, 139–51, 157; of Warrington, 157–67
Military parade, 115
Military Units:
 Cavalry: 3rd Dragoon Guards, 17, 30, 34, 49, 52, 56, 61, 67–68, 71, 74, 82, 92–94, 115; 14th Light Dragoons, 17, 30, 34, 43–44, 46–47, 52–57, 62, 70–71, 94, 96–98, 114–15, 117; Royal Horse Artillery, 115; North Somerset Yeomanry (Bath), 80–81; Bedminster, 81, 97; Dodington and Marshfield, 70, 76–81, 84, 115 *Infantry*: 11th Regiment of Foot, 70, 106; 52nd Light Infantry, 106, 115
Mills, J., 65, 186, 211
Miners (Kingswood), 33, 70, 98, 176
Mirror, The Bristol, 32; Codrington's letter to, 79; 112
Morning Advertiser, The, 154–55
Morning Herald, The, 133, 155
Morning Post, The, 155
Morris, T., 101–02
Municipal Corporations Reform Act, 178
Muniments, city, 63, 65–66
Musters, J., 13

'Nails', the, 19
Newcastle, Duke of, 13–14, 21
Newcomb, J. W., 69
New Gaol, 17, 34, 60–61, 64, 98, 107; executions at, 132–36
Newport, 45, 106

News, The, 174
New South Wales: convict settlements, 131, 190; convicts' dossiers, 209–12
Neville, R., 131, 186
Niblett, I., 62
Nicholls, J. F., and Taylor, J., *Bristol Past and Present*, 188
Norton, J., 69
Nottingham, 13–14, 112

Observer, The (Bristol), 181
Olive, Mrs, 83, 102

Pares, R., *A West India Fortune*, 10, 21–22
Parfitt, Capt. H. T., 87
Paris, 12, 14
Park Street, 22, 75, 77, 106, 122
Parke, J., 169
Parker, Mary, 125
Parmelia (convict ship), 185
Pearson, Maj.-Gen. T., 57, 71, 73; letter to Brereton, 145; 162
Pensioners, military, 98, 119
Perry, W., 126
Petition (for clemency), 15, 132
Phillips, Mrs (school), 92
Phillips, Capt. W. H., 150
Phipps, G., 126
Pile Hill; 7
Pinney, A., 22
Pinney, C., political attitudes and business interests of, 14, 18–24; 25–28, 37–38, 40–42, 44, 46, 49–52, 54, 62–63, 70–75, 78–79; letter from, to Brereton, 81, 84; 94, 96, 99, 102–03; letter from, to Melbourne, 105; 108, 110, 115; at Military Court of Enquiry, 116–17; evidence of at court-martial, 145-46; accused of perjury by Brereton, 153; actions of investigated by Committee of Enquiry, 167–77; trial of, 169–73; elected alderman, 180–81
Pinney, Frances M., wife of Mayor, 47, 49–50, 83
Pinney, Mrs J. F., 102, 111
Pitchforth, Mary A., 140, 148–50, 152

Police: Bristol, *see* constables; London, 12, 14, 27–28
Political Unions: Birmingham, 12–13, 24, 30, 71; Bristol, 28–30, 55, 61, 64, 95, 110, 119, 176, 180
Ponting, R., 65
Posse comitatus, see Constables, special
Posters, issued by magistrates, 31–32, 54–55, 99, 108; *2, 3, 4, 13, 15*
Powell, J. G., 26–27
Powell, J. G. Jnr, 169
Pretor, J., 22
Price, J., 131
Prison governors: Evans, T., 58–59; Humphries, W., 60, 134
Prison ships, *see* convict ships
Prisoners, *see* rioters
Prisons, *see* gaols
Prospect Cottage, 73
Protheroe, E. D., 24, 28, 109
Prowse, J., 59

Queen Square, *9, 10, 11, 12,* 18–19, 38–49, 52–54, 74, 82, 84–85; main damage to, 86–95; 97, 100, 104–05, 115; *see also* Custom House, Excise Office, Mansion House

Raglan, Lord, *see* Somerset, Lord F. J. H.
Ralph, B., 69
Recorder of Bristol, *see* Wetherell
Redfield House, 140, 147–49, 152–54
Reeves Hotel, 74, 82, 147, 159, 162
Reform Bill (1831), national riots provoked by rejection of, 11–13; 20–21, 24–25, 27; ratification of, 168; 177
Retribution (prison hulk), 189
Reynolds, W., 124–31, 201–02
Riot Act, the, 41, 52, 77, 82, 173
Rioters: arrests of, 46, 58; released by mob, 59–61, 64; 106; poster calling for identification of, *13;* trial of, 121–31; execution of, 133–36; line drawings of five condemned to hang, 135, 137; summary of fates of, 138; transportation of, 184–90; penal settlement dossiers on, 190–212
Roberts, Rev. T., 170

Rolt, L. T. C., 65
Room, J., 89
Rose, P., 32
Ross, H., 150
Ross, Olivia E., 18
Royal (Special) Commissions of Enquiry: to try Bristol rioters, 118–19, 121–31, 138; into state of civic authorities, 178–79
Royal Proclamation, 112–13
Russell, J., 92

Sailors: Meeting, 25–27, *2;* 90
Savage, Ald. J., 60, 66, 159
Scarlett, Sir J., 169–73
Selfe, S., 60
Sheffield, 13, 24
Sheppard, T., 46
Sheriffs, 94; *see* Bengough; Hare; Lax
Ships, convict, *see* convict ships
Shute, Capt. H., 81
Sims, J., 124–31
Snook, J., 131, 202–03
Somerset, Maj.-Gen. Lord F. J. H., 30–31, 70–71, 106–08; Brereton's letter to, 114–15; 144–45; 151
Somerton, W. H., 32, 110
Special Commissions, *see* Royal Commissions
Spectator, The, 174
Spokes, W., 65, 186, 210–11
Stanton, D., 169
Stephenson, J., 187–88
Still, Frances, M., 23
Stone, W., 58–59
Stratton, W., 61
Street, J., 131, 186
Strong, W., 92
Sugar interests, 18–23, 90, 169, 181
Sullivan, M., 131, 203–04
Sun, The, 133

Tankerville, Lord, 14
Tasmania, 138, 183–85, 188–90; convicts' dossiers, 190–209
Taunton, Sir W. E., 65, 121, 169
Taylor's Court (gaol), 65
Temple Ward, *4*
Tenterden, Lord, 169
Tetbury, 70, 76

Theatre Royal, 33, 90
Thomas, J., 131
Thomas, Susan, 30
Thompson, Capt. A., 139, 147–48
Times, The, 21, 127, 141, 155–56
Tindal, Sir N. C., *14*; 118, 121–27
Totterdown, 34–35, 121
Towell, J., 123–31, 204–05
Town Clerk, *see* Ludlow
Trevelyan, G. M., 13
Trials: of Lt J. C. Lewis, 101–02; of rioters, 121–31; court-martials: of Brereton, 139–48; of Warrington, 157–67; of city magistrates, 167–77; *see also* Military Court of Enquiry, 116–17
True Sun, The, 174
Tussaud, Mme M., 33, 89

Unions, *see* Political Unions
United Service Journal, The, 106

Van Diemen's Land, *see* Tasmania
Ven, J. P., 29
Vigor, the Misses, 92
Vines, R., 124, 127–31, 133; line drawing, 137; 189–90, 208–09

Wakefield, J., 186, 210
Walcott, Maj. E. Y., 116–17
Walker, J., 131
Waring, S., 63, 90–91
Warrington, Capt. W. H., 34, 55, 61, 73–74, 82, 84–85, 94, 116–18; court-martial of, 157–67
Warry, M., 123, 131, 188, 205—06
Wellington, Duke of, 14
West, J., *The History of Tasmania*, 183, 189
Wetherell, Sir C., *1*, 20–21, 24–29, 31–40, 44, 52, 54, 63, 118–19, 176, 180
Weyman, S. J., *Chippinge*, 47
White Hart Inn, Bath, 80–81
White Horse Inn, Bristol, 89
White Lion Inn, Bristol, 62
Whitmore, Mrs M. A., 18
Whittuck, S., 98
Wilkins, Capt. C., 80–81
William IV, 20, 25, 33, 42, 112–13, 166
Williams, C., 131, 188–89, 206–07
Williams, J., 123
Wilson, Dr B. (Hobart), 190
Wilson, J., 141, 152
Woulds, Mr, 92